David J. Krieger, Andréa Belliger
Interpreting Networks

David J. Krieger is co-director at the Institute for Communication & Leadership, Lucerne, Switzerland. His research focus is on new media, communication, system theory, and network theory.

Andréa Belliger is pro-rector of the Teacher's Training University of Lucerne and co-director of the Institute for Communication & Leadership. Her research focus is on e-society, new media, communication science, and e-health.

David J. Krieger, Andréa Belliger

Interpreting Networks

Hermeneutics, Actor-Network Theory & New Media

[transcript]

Bibliographic information published by the Deutsche Nationalbibliothek
The Deutsche Nationalbibliothek lists this publication in the Deutsche Natio-
nalbibliografie; detailed bibliographic data are available in the Internet at
http://dnb.d-nb.de

© 2014 transcript Verlag, Bielefeld

Cover layout: Kordula Röckenhaus, Bielefeld
Cover illustration: Trudy Obscure / photocase.com
Typeset by Michael Rauscher, Bielefeld
Printed by CPI – Clausen & Bosse, Leck
Print-ISBN 978-3-8376-2811-1
PDF-ISBN 978-3-8394-2811-5

Contents

Introduction

This essay attempts to bring together the seldom associated perspectives and discourses of philosophical hermeneutics, actor-network theory, and new media studies. Can philosophical hermeneutics contribute to understanding the deep changes in society and culture that the rise of global networks and new media have initiated? Does a network society based on digital communication offer new possibilities for constructing meaning and for conducting the conflict of interpretations such that demarcation lines between the empowered and the disempowered become flexible and processes of closure and exclusion are transformed into processes of variability? Does the shift away from a postmodern emphasis on difference, pluralism, and closed systems toward a new paradigm of open networks call for a reinterpretation of the social, of the foundations of knowing and acting, as well as for a new understanding of the real and the rational?

We argue that interpretation can be interpreted as the construction of meaning through *networking*. The concern of hermeneutics has always been to overcome the fragmentation of meaning, whether caused by historical distance to original texts and artifacts, linguistic and cultural differences, or by alienation in the psychological or social construction of identity. Interpretation is called for, when understanding finds itself challenged to put together the fragments of personal, social, cultural, and ontological identity. Postmodern critique has deconstructed, decentered, and displaced identity on all levels. The job is now done and we are faced with the Humpty Dumpty question of how to put the pieces back together again. Postmodern deconstruction has not made hermeneutics obsolete. On the contrary, laying bare the differences, the fragments, the distances, and gaps has made hermeneutics more relevant than ever. A multi-cultural, multi-religious, global society is more than ever dependent on world governance, on communication and consensus across many divisions, boundaries, and diverse interests in order to guide collaborative action. Postmodernism has accentuated this problem, but has offered no solution. Still, postmodernism has not been in vain. It has made it clear that the construction of meaning cannot be a merely a textual exercise, an effort of reading, a semiotic endeavor, a "grand narrative," but must include action and artifacts. This is where networks become important.

Networks are everywhere. A new interdisciplinary science of networks has arisen and has attracted much attention in recent years. Networks are being discovered, described, analyzed, and studied in disciplines as different as physics, biology, chemistry, informatics, communication, economics, mathematics, philosophy, and sociology. This not only makes it timely and relevant to reinterpret traditional discussions on universal forms of order in terms of networks, but it poses the problem of defining what is actually meant by the concept of a network and network science. The concept of network is as broad and as heuristically important as the concept of system. In many respects, it can be observed that where heretofore systems were in the limelight, networks have assumed center stage. This raises the question of the relation of the two concepts. Are networks the same as systems? Are they different? Is network science an extension of systems science or even the legitimate successor to systems theories and models? Are there basic concepts and methods within the broad spectrum of network sciences that do not fit neatly into the systems paradigm, but instead, can constructively contribute to a renewal of the program of philosophical hermeneutics and answer the Humpty Dumpty question of order in a postmodern world?

The concept of network as developed by what has come to be known as "actor-network theory"—ANT for short—describes the basic forms of social as well as epistemological and ontological order. Society consists of actor-networks. And since for ANT everything is social, including nonhumans and nature, the entire world appears as a "collective" of actor-networks. Accordingly, the conditions of the possibility of disclosing a world of meaning can be described by those processes, activities, and forms of communication that construct networks. Recalling Wittgenstein's language games which are neither purely cognitive nor purely embodied action, it can be said that social, epistemological, and ontological order cannot, even analytically, be distinguished into separate domains such as nature, society, and technology, but are integrated into "forms of life." Being, knowing, and action are inextricably bound together in networks. Wittgenstein's forms of life and his concept of language games may be seen as useful metaphors for understanding what actor-networks are all about. Language games are not closed systems, but constructs of communication whose normative rules can be challenged and transformed through communicative action. Indeed, insofar as language is like a game, and a game is action guided by normative rules, then meaning is action guided by norms. Similarly, from the point of view of actor-network theory, it can be claimed that networks arise, are maintained, and are transformed on the basis of certain forms of communicative action that are governed by what we will propose to call *network principles* or *network norms*.

Network norms are the regulating principles of that activity that constructs meaning, an activity that can be called *networking*. Network norms guide communicative action such that social, epistemological, and ontological order emerge. They are not deterministic laws. One doesn't have to follow them. But if one doesn't follow them, the result is disorder. They are norms in the same sense that Habermas' criteria of meaning, truth, correctness, and truthfulness can be said to be normative. They take the place of—and therefore conflict with—many of the fundamental distinctions, such as subject/object, culture/nature, private/public, human/machine, by means of which modern Western society has come to structure its semiotic space. This conflict, and the accompanying challenge to rethink basic concepts, should not be fought out on the terrain of modernity. It is not a matter of discussing how networking blurs the difference between, say, the private and the public or society and nature and what consequences this may have. The challenge is to drop the older categories altogether and draw the map of the world differently than did modernity. Interpreting networks, that is, understanding networking means understanding those normative principles that guide those particular communicative activities that build, maintain, and transform networks. This is where new media studies come in.

Hermeneutics makes it clear that we are dealing with meaning and re-opens the question of unity in a fragmented world. Actor-network theory reinterprets the construction of meaning as networking. New media studies show how networking after the digital media revolution is done. Following the actors is important, but understanding and describing the general norms that guide their networking is a task that demands particular attention to conditions of communication, that is, to media. In the last decades much has been researched and written about so-called "new media." Still there is little consensus on what new media are, what makes them "new," and if they should be considered "media" at all. It is an open question, whether the forces that are obviously transforming society can be traced to new media or if media are not much rather an effect than a cause of social change. Whatever new media may be and whatever their significance at the present juncture of world history may become, one thing seems to be clear to all, they are "digital." There is good reason to speak of a digital communication revolution similar in scope and consequences to the revolution initiated by the invention of writing or of the printing press. It can be said that we are currently witnessing the transition to a digital culture much the same as history has witnessed the transition from an oral to a written culture or to a mass media culture. It is therefore reasonable to assume that new media studies can significantly contribute to understanding what a global network society is all about.

Philosophical hermeneutics brought meaning down to earth and located it in the historical concreteness of language. Actor-network theory showed that language is not purely cognitive, but an activity. Networking is communicative action in the sense of making connections and associations. Communicative action, as Wittgenstein showed, is a ruled-governed activity. Networking therefore can be assumed to be constituted by norms. The norms that govern communicative action can be termed network norms. Furthermore, communication is made possible by and is dependent upon media. New media studies thus become a privileged access to describing network norms. On the basis of new media studies we will identify and describe certain network norms. These are connectivity, flow, communication, participation, transparency, authenticity, and flexibility. This list is provisional and non-exhaustive. Communication technologies, social and cultural practices, as well as the self-understanding of media users are changing almost daily. Nonetheless, there is sufficient consensus on central concepts, issues, and characteristics of digital culture that it is possible to sketch out the lines along which research and controversy will run. In the spirit of heuristic provocation, therefore, we will view philosophical hermeneutics and actor-network theory from the perspective offered by new media studies in order to speak of networking as constituted by network norms that are understood as the basic concepts, structures, and characteristics of a global network society.

Network norms make up what can be thought of as a *social operating system*. The concept of a social operating system is based on new media studies and the digital communication revolution. Nonetheless, it is derived from the foundational insight of philosophical hermeneutics that all knowledge and action is mediated. There is no representation of the world and no construction of networks without media of some kind. For philosophical hermeneutics language was considered the primary form of mediation. If Heidegger had commented upon McLuhan's dictum that the media is the message, perhaps he would have said, "Of course, language speaks." Actor-network theory deepens and enriches the concept of mediation by understanding it in terms of "translation," that is, the construction of hybrid actors and networks. New media studies largely follow McLuhan and focus on the social and cultural effects of digital media which are the form in which knowledge, action, and identity are "mediated" in the global network society. The concept of the social operating system has a complicated family tree. It is derived from philosophical hermeneutics, from the description of actor-networks, and from the affordances of new media. This unlikely parentage puts it in the position to offer an alternative to the imperatives of algorithmic logic, functionality, and systemic closure that dominate present day solutions to the problem of complexity.

Complexity can be seen as one of the most pressing problems facing the global network society. Increasing complexity in all areas from technical infrastructures, to mega-cities, interdependent networks of communication, transportation, energy, information, etc., is emerging as the major challenge in the world today.[1] Complexity means risk. It means that prediction and control become increasingly difficult, if not impossible. Small mistakes lead to large scale disasters. The typical reaction to problems of complexity in all areas is control systems. Cyber-physical systems integration or cyber-physical equivalency is a case in point. These systems use ambient computing, sensor technology, mobile devices, wireless internet, and similar technologies in order to turn complex real-life situations and processes into automated information and communication systems, in short, cybernetic machines. This idea is admittedly nothing new. Already Norbert Wiener (1950) proposed cybernetics as a theory for communication, information, and control in both humans and machines. J. C. R. Licklider (1960), a pioneer of computing and the internet, spoke of a "man-computer symbiosis" that will "involve a very close coupling between the human and the electronic members of the partnership."

---

1 | See Helbing (2013) "Globally Networked Risks and How to Respond."

In the fast-moving, complex environment that characterizes society today the effects of human error become the major source of uncertainty and can take on catastrophic proportions. Reducing human error by integrating human action into automatic information and decision systems is no longer an option, but the inevitable solution. Human action, however, is multi-dimensional, and not merely instrumental. Human action cannot be reduced to pressing the right button at the right time, or failing to do so. Human action takes place in socio-technical networks that cut across all areas of life. Pressing a button is a matter of social struggles, economic choices, political positions, moral and religious values, and world views. These guide the awareness of problems and the allocation of resources. They are finding themselves being reconfigured along the demarcation between the imperatives of security, functionalism, and control on the one side and innovation, freedom, and contingency on the other. How can the risks of complexity and the justified needs for security and control in a global network society not lead to a cybernetic functionalism in which human error, or as Paul Ricoeur would say, "fallibility," are reduced to a minimum and with it human choice, freedom, and creativity?

The critique of techno-instrumentalism, the conflict of the human and the machine, already a theme of the industrial age, is today being discussed in terms of the attempt to integrate human knowledge and action into automated information systems whose strength is predictability and control under conditions of over-complexity. Algorithms are the generalized symbolic media of the network age. Money, power, certification, knowledge, social capital, that is, the mechanisms of social integration are being mediated more and more by algorithms. We are entering a post-human world in which cognition, decision, and action are the results of heterogeneous networks composed of human and non-human actors, where the conceptual work of generations of thinkers within the parameters of modernity no longer can guide us, where long fought and hard won battles must be radically reinterpreted and seen from new perspectives. This situation demands that the question of technology be reopened on a new basis and investigated on a terrain that no longer is demarcated by subjects, objects, societies, a demystified nature, and a desocialized science. Much of the discussion about the emergence of a global network society and about the uses of the new science of networks (Barabási 2004) is dominated by the promise of introducing prediction and control into domains that have heretofore been considered irreducibly contingent. Automated information systems, ubiquitous computing, big data, the internet of things, networks of intelligent agents with instantaneous access to unlimited information will know more and will be able to make better decisions, faster, and above all with less risk than humans in almost all situations, from logistics, production and distribution to transportation, energy, communication, business and finance, and even education, health care, and science. How should we behave and how shall we understand ourselves when, as David Weinberger (2012) asks, the smartest person in the room is the room itself?

We propose the concept of a *social operating system* as a way of thinking about building, maintaining, and transforming networks without subscribing to an algorithmic rationality and becoming dependent on cybernetic models of order. This claim could be misleading, since to speak of an alternative is to imply difference and choice. The idea of a social operating system should not be considered in opposition to cybernetics. It is not an anti-technical concept. It is a socio-technical concept. There is no alternative to the vision of Wiener, Licklider, and others who have prophesied the convergence of humans and technology, a post-human world populated by cyborgs. The traditional opposition between technology and society that characterized much of the discussion about technology at least since Marcuse's vision of the "one dimensional man" in the 60's is obsolete. Whether as master or as slave, technology cannot be opposed to society; it is society. What makes the *social operating system* a viable alternative to the logic of algorithms is not that it is somehow non-technical and purely social or "democratic," but much rather that it points to the chaotic, unpredictable, uncontrollable, and "serendipic" character of the human-computer symbiosis.

The social operating system moves not away from but towards the edge of chaos. It orchestrates communicative action in such a way that freedom, creativity, and responsibility drive self-organization and the emergence of unpredictable—and thus uncontrollable, and therefore risky—events. On both sides of the technology debate, weather socio- or techno-determinism, it has for decades been a commonplace for all to plead for the subjection of technology to the political process. The political process, however, as all social processes, is itself a socio-technical network, which links up, crosses, and entangles itself with economic, cultural, religious, educational, and scientific networks. In the global network society it makes little sense to think of politics as an isolated domain, a closed, functional system governed by its own unique code of exclusion and inclusion. No one must "leave" science in order to "enter" politics, no more than scientists must leave society in order to enter into contact with nature. As we will see, the typically modern division of the world into semi-autonomous domains of knowing and acting can no longer adequately describe the social space of networks or set the parameters for networking. Instead of speaking of politics as something different from science, and the social as something different from nature, and both as different from business, education, religion, or art, we will introduce the concept of the *socio-sphere* as the space of networking. The social operating system operates in such a way that a socio-sphere emerges as the stage upon which social processes, including politics, take place. There is therefore much at stake in a description of the emergence of social order through processes of reducing complexity beyond the imperatives of prediction, control, and security. It may be a good thing for both humans and non-humans, including algorithms, to be able and willing to take risks. The concept of the social operation system and the concept of a socio-sphere created by it attempt to describe the conditions under which this could be true.

On the epistemological level, this essay takes up the program of philosophical hermeneutics to describe the general conditions of knowledge and action and the processes by which meaning is constructed. At least since Kant this task as been associated with the endeavor to discover the transcendental conditions of the possibility of knowing located in "reason." Kant firmly established the ideas of "critique" and "reason" as the foundational forces of order in a world no longer under the control of extra-human powers. In order to fulfill this role, however, reason had to free itself from human weakness, from all prejudice, particularity, and bias. Reason needed to construct itself as "transcendental," that is as purified of the conditions of embodiment and historical contingency. It is upon this basis that modernity has been built. From the perspective of "pure" reason it is possible to obtain objective knowledge untainted by instincts and interests, political and cultural idiosyncrasies, ideological illusions, and historical prejudices.

This position, which goes back at least to Descartes' critique of tradition, has come to be known as "critical rationality" or "critical theory." It is based upon the supposed possibility of locating reason—Descartes's *res cogitans*—outside the conditions of embodiment, time, space, and contingency. Philosophical hermeneutics broke with the tradition of critical rationality by giving up the critical position which somehow placed the construction of meaning outside of or beyond historical and social reality. It brought reason back down to earth without, however, giving up the question of the general conditions of the constitution of meaning. Hermeneutics became the self-explication of that being, whose being is meaning, a being that is a question for itself and therefore necessarily shares the contingency, open-endedness, and uncertainty of meaning.

Actor-network theory admittedly does not see itself in the lineage of philosophical hermeneutics. On the contrary, ANT shares the general disdain of hermeneutics typical of poststructuralism. Nonetheless, the concerns of ANT for constructing instead of deconstructing meaning, for an embodied, historical knowing, and for the inextricable association of knowledge and action are also the concerns of philosophical hermeneutics. The explication of a world of meaning starting from an ancient philosophical fragment, a poem, a work of art, or an industrial power plant corresponds to the program of actor-network theory to follow the actors in their laboratories, in the rain forest, in the factory, and describe how they make associations, connections, relations, and assemblies linking actors together up to the level of global collectives. As Latour (2005: 11) put it: "Dispersion, destruction, and deconstruction are not the goals to be achieved but what needs to be overcome."

Following the lead of philosophical hermeneutics and actor-network theory this essay will portray rationality as consisting of cooperative action that is conditioned, but not limited by differences in criteria of validity, culture, and convictions. This means that the still unresolved debate between hermeneutics and critical theory, which arose in the 1970's and has patiently waited till the storm of deconstruction abated, will be taken up again. It will be argued that Habermas' universal pragmatics of communicative action offers fewer resources to explain the functioning of global networks than the open horizon of hermeneutic understanding as it can be interpreted from the perspective of actor-network theory. Rationality, it will be claimed, can be found within the context of those communicative practices that effectively build and maintain networks. In opposition to postmodernism and poststructuralism we will claim that rationality does not lie in dismantling grand narratives and laying bare differences, but in making associations, linking things together, building collectives, in short, networking.

Networks can be considered the heroes of this story. Networks consist of actors, who, much like fractals, are themselves networks. These networks are hybrid and heterogeneous. They are made up of human and non-human actors. They cut across heretofore strictly separated domains of nature, society, and mind. They are built up of associations that are constantly at issue, operating under the pressure of shifting loyalties and flexible ties, enforced alone by the communicative efforts of all actors involved and by their complexity and scale. If hermeneutics shows that interpretation and understanding can be interpreted as networking, then actor-network theory shows that actors are themselves networks and that it is networks that do the interpreting. "Interpreting networks" therefore has a double meaning, describing both what interpretation does, and also who is doing it. Networks are doing the interpreting, as well as being interpreted. In both cases what is at stake is the construction of meaning. This implies that rationality consists in making associations. From the perspective of new media studies, this view leads to a definition of rationality as the particular kind of networking that results from the social operating system. The norms and principles of the social operating system—connectivity, flow, communication, participation, transparency, authenticity, and flexibility—constitute the no longer transcendental, but nonetheless universal conditions of knowledge and action. They make up what it means to be "rational" in the global network society. They take the place of Kant's transcendental principles of order. They are the rules, so to speak, of the language-game of networking. They set the conditions of exclusion or inclusion, of success or failure in the network society.

Philosophical hermeneutics, actor-network theory, and new media "translate" each other and form thereby a theoretical foundation for understanding the global network society. Foundational claims of this sort can easily be attributed to philosophical hermeneutics and actor-network theory, but are seldom encountered in the discourse of new media. On what basis can it be asserted that new media studies can contribute the theoretical resources we need in order to outline a general theory of order, knowledge, and action? If Luhmann's dictum that society consists not of people, but of communications is true; and if McLuhan's famous slogan that the medium is the message is taken seriously, then it is plausible to argue that major transformations in the technology of communication are accompanied by major transformations in society. The idea of a social operating system must be understood within the context of the digital communication revolution, a revolution which has consequences for epistemology and ontology. Epistemologically this leads to a revision in what modernity has defined as rationality. But understanding rationality as networking also has consequences for how reality is to be understood. For philosophical hermeneutics meaning is being just as for actor-network theory the real is the social. When all there is is networks, what becomes of reality?

Reinterpreting reason and rationality as networking has consequences for our understanding of reality. Ontologically, this leads to a definition of the real as *mixed reality* in which being is a mixture of physical as well as so-called "virtual" reality. Physical space-time and cyber space-time are functionally equivalent and practically interdependent. Indeed, one could speak of cyber-physical equivalence. The world of meaning constructed by the social operating system is a *mixed reality* in which the physical restraints of space and time are no longer privileged ontological parameters of knowing and acting, but are mixed with so-called virtual reality in hybrid, heterogeneous actor-networks. Mixed reality should not be reduced to a kind of overlapping of physical and virtual worlds, which remain analytically as well as practically distinct. The idea of mixed reality emphasizes the irreducibly heterogeneous quality of the real. Mixed reality, therefore, will not be described in terms of a physical part and a virtual part that are somehow combined, but in terms of *filters* and *layers*.

A filter is a like search query. Filters organize information around concerns. Information enables action. A layer is an organized field of knowledge and action, both physical and virtual, for a certain concern. It is the world, both physical and virtual, as it is understood and disclosed from a certain perspective, a certain interest, or program of action. Traditionally, knowledge and action were primarily determined by the filters of space and time. One had access to information and possibilities for action on the basis of physical, spatial, and temporal givens. There was only one filter and only one layer. Within mixed reality the filtering function of space and time has forfeited its dominance. Physical restraints are no longer determinative for knowledge and action. In this context Castells (1996) speaks of a "timeless time" and the "space of flows" characteristic of network society. In opposition to Castells, however, we will argue that there is no natural or even artificial hierarchy of filters and layers, no privileged access to reality, even if certain networks are at any time larger and more powerful than others and even if networks compete for hegemony. To limit one's world to that which can be known and acted out within the physical constraints of space, time, and embodiment is no longer rational, indeed, it is no longer possible. Not to participate in some way in the global information and communication networks is not a viable option. The network society is a construction of network communication. There is no alternative and no escape. Attempts not to participate in networking and not to follow network norms appear increasingly irrational and resemble psycho-social pathology.

The social operating system operates by applying filters and layers and constructs thereby a "socio-sphere," a world of knowledge and action within a mixed reality. The basic units of this world may be said to be actor-networks. From the point of view of new media, actor-networks can be reinterpreted as constructions arising from the application of layers that are accessed by filters. Actor-networks do not simply exist. They are not things, substances, or essences. They are not even systems. They are much more like processes, performances, socio-technical rituals, and en-actments. They are inextricably symbolic, social, technical, and natural at once. They are driven by the dynamics of making connections, of binding things together, of extending associations, of "translating" and "enroll-ing" actors into networks. The ontology of actor-networks is less qualita-tive than quantitative. They can be more or less real. This does not mean, however, that actor-networks are more or less "virtual." The opposition of physical reality to a supposed virtual reality is misleading and from the pragmatic point of view useless. In the global network society reality is always already a mixture of the physical and virtual in much the same way as before the new media revolution reality was always a mixture of words and things. The concepts of the social operating system, the socio-sphere, of mixed reality, and of filters and layers are proposed as alternatives to distinctions such as words and things, nature and society, subject and object, and other modern categories.

What has come to the fore in actor-network theory and new media studies is that it can make sense to speak of reality in terms of more or less.[2] To speak of something being "more or less" real means that reality is inversely proportional to the amount of effort required to transform an actor-network, to open up a functional system, a "black-box," and to re-

---

2 | "The real is not one thing among others but rather gradients of resistance." (Latour 1988: 159)

configure a network. It could be said that "network permanence" replaces "object permanence" as the decisive characteristic of the real. Reality becomes a "quantitative" measure of effort to create, maintain, and transform networks. From the epistemological perspective, rationality may be said to describe the ways in which this can be done. Size does make a difference. The larger, the more complex, the longer lasting a network is, the more real it is and the more rational are those communicative practices that construct, transform, and maintain it. This is so for families, associations, machines, institutions, companies, nations, and cultures. Reality is not a given, but a task, it is a network effect.[3]

Philosophical hermeneutics speaks of "effective historical consciousness" and a "fusion of horizons" (Gadamer 2004) in order to describe how networks are built, maintained, and transformed. These concepts usually describe how past or foreign traditions are integrated into the world horizon of the interpreter. Hermeneutical understanding operates to overcome alienation, fragmentation, and isolation. It is an operation of integration and association. It builds quite unashamed grand narratives, world views, values, and ideologies. But as postmodernism has convincingly shown, there is no longer an interest-free, objective, impartial, and somehow transcendental position from which it could be decided which network is the best, the most civilized, just, and humane. But postmodern cynicism with regard to grand narratives does not mean we can live without them or that they serve no important purpose. The search for meaning must not always be naive. After postmodernism has robbed us of our naiveté what remains is obviously not consensus, but instead a conflict of interpretations upon which one cannot simply turn ones back or burry one's head, like Diogenes, in a barrel. The conflict of interpretations remains. But the struggle now takes place on the terrain of the socio-sphere and with the weapons of the social operating system.

This essay attempts to show that the principle insights of hermeneutics, that is, the primacy of semiotic coding instead of material or genetic coding, the historical, finite, yet open horizon of reality, the communicative, non-subjective construction of meaning, and finally the goals of integration and association may be interpreted as activities of constructing actor-networks. It will furthermore be argued that today and in the future

---

3 | "Each network makes a whole world for itself, a world whose inside is nothing but the internal secretions of those who elaborate it." (Latour 1988: 171)

it is impossible to make associations that are large, stable, and durable without digital media. The collective is through and through digital and therefore a mixed reality made up of filters and layers that are implemented, enacted, and controlled by the social operating system. This means that the construction of meaning is inseparably bound up with new media and digital information technologies. Cognition is distributed. Knowledge shifts away from a psychological or mental exercise that humans do and which is based on reading and interpreting "texts" to the not exclusively human communicative and action-oriented constructing of associations under the conditions of digital information and communication technologies. Associations are constructed between culture and nature, immaterial and material entities, as well as human and non-human actors. Networking cuts across the typically modern boundaries separating signs, things, machines, actors, social systems, organizations, institutions, cultures, and nations. Interpretation is therefore not a cognitive or a psychological act. There is no significant difference between manipulating signs, observing a chemical reaction, designing and building a power plant, driving an automobile, cooking diner, or holding a seminar on Kant. In all these activities what is significant is the network that is constructed, de-constructed, transformed, or reaffirmed by the agency of all the actors involved, and not merely the human beings.

The important point from this perspective is not the primacy of action, performance, and practice. We are not proposing a theory of action instead of a theory of cognition. What is important is that knowledge and action are distributed throughout the network. The distribution, as actor-network theory claims, is "symmetrical." Cognition, action, performance, influence, and causality are not attributes that can be ascribed to human beings alone. This means that the social operating system and the socio-sphere are not merely social, but natural, technical, even super-natural as well. The idea of the social in the concepts of a social operating system and socio-sphere should not be understood in the traditional sense of sociology. The actor is the network and the network is the actor. It is the network that constructs meaning and does the interpreting. It is the network that acts, performs, and does things. Networks are interpreting and not merely interpreted. The individual actors who participate in the network—weather they be human or non-human—are themselves networks that have at any certain time been more or less "black-boxed" into functional roles that are experienced as identities and ascribed to things. They are what they are and can do what they can do, because of the chain of associations in which they are "enrolled" and which constitutes the network. In networks it is not only cognition that is distributed, but also competence, influence, and decision making. As Latour (2005: 245) put it, "Hermeneutics is not a privilege of humans, but, so to speak, a property of the world itself."

The understanding of hermeneutics as networking and networking as guided by the social operating system that is proposed in this essay conceptualizes a constructivist, relational ontology and a vision of society characterized by fundamentally different distinctions and demarcations than those typical of Western modernity. As Bruno Latour has pointed out, there is no longer the need for such binary oppositions as those between mind and matter, things and signs, humans and machines, society and nature, and God and the world which have set the parameters of thinking within Western modernity. Instead, the search for order leads to an examination of the characteristics and dynamics of networks and networking and attempts with the resources of philosophical hermeneutics, actor-network theory, and new media theory to construct a viable position for knowing and acting in a global network society.

1. Hermeneutics

AND WE CAN'T WHISTLE IT EITHER!

As Frank P. Ramsey, challenging Ludwig Wittgenstein, once said, "[...] what we can't say we can't say [...]". Just to make his point clear he added, "[...] and we can't whistle it either" (Ramsey 1931: 238). The point of course is that every attempt to transcend language and thus its supposed limitations, whether it be whistling, pointing, establishing taboos, diagnosing madness, erecting city walls, declaring boundaries such as rivers, oceans, mountain ranges and the like is always already linguistic, that is, semiotically coded and thus a construction of meaning that takes place within meaning itself and nowhere else. Every attempt to get beyond language, signs, and meaning and reach a supposed thing itself, whether it is thought of as somehow beyond the mind, "out there" in the world, or as above the mind, something that can be directly intuited by the mind's inner eye must be mediated by language before it can even get started. This implies that there is no direct, unmediated access to anything and that meaning and whatever boundaries we might construct to delimit that which is named and known from that which is not, or to distinguish between knowing and the known, must themselves be within meaning. In other words, so-called "natural" language is its own metalanguage. Or, when it comes to meaning, the outside is always inside. One can only talk about the limits of language within language. Language is more than mind, for cognition and knowing are within language. As Wittgenstein put it: "The limits of my language are the limits of my world" (Tractatus 5.6).[1] And as Heidegger pointed out: We are always already "in" the world, that is, "thrown" into the world of meaning (Geworfenheit), and it

---

1 | The later work of Wittgenstein can be seen as the consequent thinking through of this claim.

is this world to which we "belong" and which is the starting point of all knowledge and action.

Constructing meaning is interpretation. Constructing the boundaries of meaning is also interpretation. There is no escape from interpretation and no alternative. Even if we try to avoid using language and attempt to whistle what is beyond language this would be another way of *speaking* about *it*, another way of interpreting. The boundaries of meaning and whatever may lie beyond them are within meaning and therefore within language and not outside of it. The early Wittgenstein, who still attempted to hold a transcendental position, thought he had already said too much and consequently declared his own sentences to be meaningless. Heidegger chose instead to make being into the *understanding* of being and universalized the scope of hermeneutics while at the same time eliminating the position of a transcendental knower. Traditionally limited to rules for interpreting texts, or as a methodology for the social sciences (*Geisteswissenschaften*), hermeneutics became in the hands of Heidegger, Gadamer, and Ricoeur *philosophical hermeneutics*. It became a general theory of meaning as well as a theory of being, or ontology. Whatever "is" exists within and on account of the "hermeneutical as" (Heidegger 2010: § 32). Whatever is is not a thing in itself, it is not just what it is, neither more nor less, instead, it is what it appears as. The *is* is an *as*. Being is meaning and meaning is an interpretation, for whatever *is* appears necessarily *as* such-and-such or so-and-so. The tool, for example, appears *as* a hammer, and the hammer *as* a tool. This does not mean that there is a thing in itself out there in the world that someone perceives in a certain way, for example, as a hammer. It means that whatever appears could be seen otherwise. Meaning is contingent, not because it is subjective, perspectival, unfounded, or incomplete, but because it is open ended, unfinished, and ever changing. Any attempt to fix meaning can only be local and temporarily successful. The tool, for example, appears *as* that which is needed to build houses and houses *as* that which is needed to give shelter and enable living in the world. But for whom? And what kind of world are we living in? *Dasein* itself appears "as" always already living in a world of possibilities and therefore a world of questions, including the question of itself. At a certain level the entire world appears *as* "horizon," as the world of the interpreter, as the world *we* live in, as *my* world and *our* world. But it is not the only possible world, not even the best of possible worlds.

Interpretation has to do with world, but the world disclosed in interpretation is a contingent, unfinished, historical world. Finitude and contingency characterize interpretation itself. To be is to be interpreted and interpretation refers beyond any particular thing to the world horizon within which anything can appear "as" this or that, including interpretation itself. Interpretation is self-referential. As every student of logic knows, self-referentiality is the spawning ground of paradoxes. Interpretation interprets itself as interpretation admitting thereby that it could interpret itself in a different way, but if so then only by interpretation. Paradoxes are a sign that we have run up against a boundary of meaning and cannot go beyond. And as Ramsey reminded Wittgenstein, whistling won't help. Instead of whistling or pointing to a realm of Being somehow out there beyond meaning or different from meaning, one is thrown back into meaning with the insight that meaning is also being. Hermeneutics becomes the ontology of that being, whose way of being is the explication of being. This constitutes the universality claim of hermeneutics while at the same time limiting understanding to finitude, that is, to contingency. If something appears in a certain way in a particular situation, it *could* appear differently in a different situation.

The hermeneutical "as" implies that being is contingent, possible, and a question. The "as" is not a pure and absolute "is." It is not identity or immutable presence. It is possibility. Nothing is *necessarily* given, but is always open to different interpretations. There is nothing that is said and done that cannot be said and done differently by someone else in some other time and place, in some other world. The hermeneutical "as" constitutes an infinite horizon of possible meaning while at the same time grounding meaning in finitude and "facticity." At a certain level of generality, understanding closes the circle of world-disclosure and interprets itself and by so doing not only sets its own limits, delimits in a certain way what can and cannot be understood, but also understands itself, allows itself to appear as this or that, in a certain possibility of itself. *Dasein*, as Heidegger says, *exists* as understanding and through understanding a world is disclosed. In his 1923 lectures *Ontology—The Hermeneutics of Facticity* Heidegger (1999) writes: "[...] in hermeneutics what is developed for Dasein is a possibility of its becoming and being for itself in the manner of an understanding of itself" (11). This should be read both epistemologically and ontologically. It positions philosophical hermeneutics against Hegel, structuralism, and systems theory to the extent that they favor totality, actuality, and closure over possibility, contingency, and openness.

Hermeneutics describes the construction of meaning within language. Language in the sense of philosophical hermeneutics is to be understood in the broadest possible sense. It refers to any system of meaning regardless of what it consists of, for example, verbal utterances, gestures, mathematical notations, visual, olfactory or tactile perceptions, music, dance, architecture, clothing, objects, natural entities, mystical experiences etc. The universality claim of hermeneutics demands a universal, indeed, encompassing concept of language. There is nothing that cannot be semiotically coded, and there is nothing that isn't semiotically coded. Even "nothingness" itself, no matter how we experience it, fear it, or embrace it, has inescapably some kind of meaning. Semiotic coding refers on this foundational level not to the grammar or syntax of a language such as English or German, but to a level of emergent order that includes within it physical and biological levels of being as well (Krieger 1996), indeed the "world."

GETTING INTO THE CIRCLE IN THE RIGHT WAY

The fact that hermeneutics has grown out of a long tradition of reflection on the rules of textual interpretation, from Aristotle to Schleiermacher and Dilthey, has created much uncertainty as to the scope and significance of the universality claim of hermeneutics. Traditional hermeneutics is a discipline within the humanities concerned with a field defined by authors, texts, readers, literary genres, historical traditions, exegesis, translation, and so on. What since Heidegger, Gadamer, and Ricoeur, however, has come to be called *philosophical hermeneutics* is neither a discipline within the social sciences nor is it confined to the usual field of language and texts. Heidegger's phenomenological hermeneutics extended the idea of interpretation to the ontological dimension. The world is disclosed, that is, comes to "be" through understanding. This distinguishes philosophical hermeneutics from the theory of textual interpretation and also from a methodology of the social sciences. Understanding is the "explication" of meaning, the unfolding, extending, diversifying, differentiating, and enlarging of meaning. Meaning is not a merely cognitive or linguistic event, but an ontological event. Interpretation in the sense in which philosophical hermeneutics uses the term is therefore not a merely cognitive or even epistemological endeavor, but disclosure of being. This has consequences for the relation of hermeneutics to the social as well as the natural sciences.

In opposition to textual hermeneutics, philosophical hermeneutics is not a method for a particular kind of knowledge, for example, the social or cultural sciences as opposed to the natural sciences. Ever since Dilthey, hermeneutics has found itself caught in the typically modern opposition between society and nature. Hermeneutical understanding of texts and cultural artifacts was seen as the specific method of the human sciences. Whereas the natural sciences explained (*erklären*) a nature in terms of the laws of deterministic causality, hermeneutics understood (*verstehen*) the products of human "causality," that is, texts and cultural artifacts. Although this distinction has long been assimilated to the unshakable conviction of modernity that human society and the world of nature constitute two mutually exclusive ontological and epistemological domains, hermeneutics should not be understood as a methodological alternative to the empirical sciences. The distinction between an empirical, quantitative falsification of hypotheses undertaken by a value-free observer detached from all "prejudices" on the one side, and a qualitative, subjective, perspectival interpretation of the meaning of texts, artifacts, and other cultural entities on the other is not applicable to philosophical hermeneutics. Philosophical hermeneutics is not a particular method aiming at "understanding" instead of "explanation." This is apparent in the claim to universality that is made by philosophical hermeneutics. The claim to universality means that it is through hermeneutical understanding that anything at all appears and becomes meaningful. Interpretation in the sense of philosophical hermeneutics is not defined by the distinction between society and nature. It comes before any distinctions into specific ontological domains.[2]

Hermeneutical understanding is not the result but the presupposition of any specific scientific methodology. Before something can become an object of scientific knowledge it must be understood at least within the scope of a question. It must appear as something that can be investigated. Hermeneutical understanding therefore encompasses any methodologies for specific forms of knowing much as natural language is a precondition

---

2 | This will constitute one of the important similarities between hermeneutics and actor-network theory that will be discussed below.

of all formalized languages. This does not mean, however, that there are not important differences between the social and the natural sciences or that there are not specific methodological rules for the interpretation of texts, works of art, historical artifacts etc. that can be termed hermeneutical. No one wishes to deny that those disciplines that attempt to *understand* social and cultural phenomena are in many ways distinct from those disciplines that attempt to *explain* a natural world governed by deterministic causality. There is little to be gained by confusing literary criticism with physics. There is little to be gained by disallowing different methodologies for different disciplines and refusing to speak of a specifically hermeneutic methodology. But it should not be forgotten that the universality claim of philosophical hermeneutics means that the methodologies of the various sciences make sense on a level below that of a general theory of meaning. What is at stake in interpretation in the philosophical sense is not the methodologies of the sciences, which are constantly changing, merging, and diversifying, but the disclosure of a world of meaning within which society and culture as well as nature appear in a certain, and therefore contingent, way.

If philosophical hermeneutics is not a method for knowing, the famous and much discussed "hermeneutical circle" should not be understood on the level of logic. To say that understanding "exists" (Heidegger) within language implies that interpretation ends at the same place where it begins. This makes interpretation into a circular process. The circle ceases to look like a trap the moment language in this context is not seen as a purely cognitive domain, the psychological or mental manipulation of signs that can be distinguished from and thereby limited by a world of real entities. It may be helpful at this point to view the foundational concept of language in philosophical hermeneutics from the perspective of linguistics and semiotics. According to Saussure, one of the founders of modern semiotics, it is not the things in the world that give meaning to signs, but the relations among signs themselves within a system of differences. For Saussure (1983: 120): "[...] in language there are only differences. Even more important: a difference generally implies positive terms between which the difference is set up; but in language there are only differences without positive terms." Semiotic coding therefore does not assign names to things that were somehow—before language—anonymously present in the world, but introduces differences and "articulates" meaning.

Although Saussure as a linguist distinguished between the structure of language and the actual spoken word and did not draw the conclusion that meaning and being were the same, philosophical hermeneutics did: Meaning is not "in" the world, it is the world. Meaning may be considered an encompassing level of emergent order beyond the physical or the biological levels.[3] Again, the difference between language and what is not language is a distinction within language and not a kind of external limit, border, or boundary of language. Whatever exists within a system of differences has meaning by virtue of these relations alone and can, for that reason, function as a sign. We know what cats are because they are *different* from dogs, birds, fish, and many other things. On the level of meaning, it is difference that constitutes identity. According to Saussure, signs are an indivisible unity of signifier and signified. The signified, that which is usually considered the thing out in the world to which the sign is said to "refer," is not somehow outside of, before, or beyond the sign. It appears *within* the sign. This is so even if things appear "as" distinct from signs. Since there is nothing outside language determining how it makes distinctions and constructs meaning, semiotic coding is necessarily "arbitrary" or contingent. Neither God nor things in themselves determine the world that appears in language. This formulation is paradoxical with good reason, since it is a fundamental characteristic of meaning that it includes its opposite, it boundaries, it's "outside" within itself. When we reach the limits of meaning, paradoxes proliferate. This leads to the paradoxes that troubled the early Wittgenstein about the limits of language and which finally led him to declare his own sentences to be meaningless.

The insight that should be gained from this discussion is that we do not go through the world and stumble upon things and then, much as Adam in the Garden of Eden, decide to give them names. Differences and relations among signs are ontologically indistinguishable from differences and relations among things, indeed so-called things exist "as" these differences and relations. When the hammer exists "as" a tool, then it exists by virtue of its relations to other tools, such as a nail or a saw and by virtue of relations to what is done with tools. Tools exist in relation to materials such as wood or metal that they work upon. Of course all these differences and relations are in language in the broad sense regardless of whether we

---

3 | See the discussion in Krieger (1996: 42ff.) on meaning as an encompassing level of emergent order.

speak, write, think about them, or even just take up the hammer and build a house. Again, meaning and being are the same.[4] The difference between words and things, which in certain contexts may be useful, is at this level of abstraction irrelevant, misleading, and unnecessary. There is no need to attempt to look beyond language to find the world; the world—and its boundaries—are disclosed in language, in so far as we decide to name that which differentiates, relates, associates, and binds together language.

The nearness of hermeneutics to language and texts has lead to much confusion. The concept of language, despite decades of philosophical controversy, is misleading because it almost inevitably suggests a particular form of language, for example, English, German, Chinese, or a formalized language such as algebra or C++. It is furthermore misleading because is suggests the existence of a domain external to language, a world of mute things, somehow outside of language. For this reason it may be helpful to suggest that the philosophical concept of language could be replaced by the concept of "semiotic coding," and as we will argue below by the concept of "networking." Semiotic coding refers to the ordering principle of meaning. Whatever is meaningful is so by virtue of being semiotically coded. Semiotic coding can be located on the level of Heidegger's fundamental ontology, that is, as a process of articulating, of differentiating and relating, of making associations among anything and everything, not merely linguistic signs, which of course are also differentiated and related. The construction of meaning should not be understood as the reaction of the mind to sensory confrontation with a non-linguistic reality. Semiotic coding and the emergence of meaning is not a merely cognitive process, it is not even something humans do, but it is what happens to the world such that it emerges as a world instead of nothing. The famous question of Being, why is there something rather than nothing, should be taken as encouragement and as heuristic advice to direct one's attention to a theory of meaning on the same level and with the same extension as a theory of being. Meaning is necessarily reflexive and universal. We are always already within meaning. Otherwise we could not distinguish self and other. This is why the hermeneutical circle is a circle that one cannot escape from. Understanding begins from previous understanding, just as put-

---

4 | Here again there is an important point of contact between hermeneutics and actor-network theory: "The interpretation of the real cannot be distinguished from the real itself [...]" (Latour 1088: 166).

ting things together and making associations begins not from the things themselves, but from previous connections and associations.[5]

Following Heidegger (1999) we can say that understanding exists as "facticity," as thrown into a historical situation which is always already in some way articulated, that is, interpreted. Understanding comes from previous understanding. And as Wittgenstein (1958: § 199) put it: "to understand a sentence means to understand a language." Reading a text is only possible when one already knows the language and already has a certain pre-understanding of what the text means. The hermeneutic philosophers never tired of pointing out that there is no understanding without previous understanding. Each individual word in a text is understood only in relation to all others in an entire sentence, and each sentence in relation to all others in a book. Reading a word in a sentence presupposes a "horizon" of possible meaning within which the meaning of the sentence is projected. Understanding a sentence presupposes the projection, a pre-understanding, of the possible meaning of the book. Each word is understood with reference to the horizon of meaning within which it appears "as" a word in an English sentence in a book about literature or some other topic. Each word modifies, clarifies, and explicates what the sentence means and what the book as a whole is "really" about, just as every modification of expectations of the meaning of the whole influences how each sentence and each word is interpreted.

Hermeneutical understanding is admittedly a "circular" process. Interpretation begins necessarily from some pre-understanding of what is to be understood. Only a meaningful question is a question, and to understand the meaning of a question is already to pre-understand a possible answer. Pre-understanding, it must be emphasized, is not final understanding. It is contingent, open-ended, and uncertain. It is an expectation that can always be disappointed and revised, corrected, deepened, and refined by moving from the whole to the part and back again. In this circular process neither whole nor part are definitively and finally given. The hermeneutic philosophers distanced themselves emphatically from Hegelian dreams of totality and closure. The hermeneutical circle is much more like a spiral, or as Paul Ricoeur (1981d: 155–159) proposed, an "arc," whereby the actual

---

5 | As we will see below, actor-network theory shows that so-called scientific facts are not results of a direct confrontation with a supposedly pure nature, but with a reality that always already appears within semiotic coding.

use of language brings freedom, contingency, and change into pre-given linguistic structures. This means that the hermeneutical circle never becomes a closed circle. Nonetheless, the hermeneutic method of moving from part to whole and from whole to part in a circular fashion has often been criticized as a "vicious circle." If understanding begins from pre-understanding, critics ask, then how can one ever come to know anything new and unforeseen? Hermeneutics has been criticized for binding knowledge to the past and to what is already known. If we always already know what counts as an answer to a question, we can never be surprised, discover truly new knowledge, and free ourselves of false views and prejudice. Perhaps the evolution of knowledge would be possible, but not a revolution. How could one explain the transition from a Ptolemaic to a heliocentric world view? How could a natural world once filled with spirits and demons suddenly be demythologized and subjected to the rule of determinate causality and mathematical description? And what about a political order based for centuries on the undisputed rights of clergy and nobility? How could there even arise the idea that that the people should be governed by the people? Does not the history of knowledge present us with discontinuity, radical upheavals, and revolutionary transformations that do not fit neatly within the hermeneutical circle?

The hermeneutic circle can escape the accusation of dooming us to redundancy only if understanding is viewed not as a slavish repetition of the past. If understanding is an activity that does something, changes something, transforms meaning, then it is not a slave to the past. As has often been remarked, *traditore – traduttore*, to translate is to betray. If understanding makes its own associations, adds to what is already known, rearranges the associations that are already there, then it is not trapped within a vicious circle. As every writer, every artist, and every performer knows, repetition is creation. Understanding is dynamic and creative. As Heidegger (2010: § 32) puts it: "What is decisive is not to get out of the [hermeneutical] circle but to get into it in the right way." Although pre-understanding is a necessary condition of knowing and acting, this in no way implies closure. On the contrary, being always already within meaning opens up a horizon of endless possibilities. Even on the level of textual hermeneutics the hermeneutic circle is not a closed circle. It does not begin and stop at the covers of the book. An individual text can only be understood within the context of other writings by a particular author, of a particular genre, within a particular social and historical context, a particular culture, a particular political or religious view, an epoch, a particular hope for the future, and so on. The necessary and inescapable horizon of any textual exegesis is, whatever the individual intentions of any interpreter might be, the infinite world horizon of possible meaning. The openness of the hermeneutical circle to a world horizon of meaning, far from precluding new knowledge and the revision of old knowledge, grounds what may be called the "autonomy" or "distance" of the text.[6]

THE AUTONOMY OF THE TEXT

A written work can be said to be autonomous in different ways. Based on Gadamer's concept of historical distance, Ricoeur (1991) lists at least five different forms of distanciation of a written work. First, in the act of writing the ephemeral spontaneity of an intention is articulated into discourse, which subjects it to the structures of a specific language. Second, the discourse then becomes a work, a composition that is subjected to structures of style and genre. Third, the written text becomes an object, an artifact that sits on bookshelves for centuries and is transported all over the world. It distances itself both spatially and temporally from its creator and the original audience. The text can be read and interpreted by anyone, anywhere, at any time, often centuries later and often translated into foreign languages. This leads to the forth form of distanciation, namely, that the meaning of the text is no longer bound to the horizon of its origin, but is conditioned by the horizon of the interpreter. Interpretation becomes not only understanding of the other, but self-understanding, for whatever a text has to say, it says it to the world of the reader and what this world finds relevant and interesting. Finally, the open horizon of the text makes it autonomous with regard to any fixed or absolute meaning. In this pro-

---

6 | See Gadamer's (2004: 263ff.) discussion of "distance:" "The real meaning of a text, as it speaks to the interpreter, does not depend on the contingencies of the author and whom he originally wrote for. It certainly is not identical with them, for it is always partly determined also by the historical situation of the interpreter and hence by the totality of the objective course of history." Paul Ricoeur (1976: 30) prefers to speak of the "semantic autonomy" of the text by which the "text's career escapes the finite horizon lived by its author."

cess, the text becomes "semantically autonomous" (Ricoeur 1976: 30) with regard to both author and reader.

As a historical work, the text opens up a potentially infinite horizon of possible meaning. A potentially infinite surplus of meaning is enfolded in the text, a surplus of meaning that no author, except perhaps God, could consciously intend and no reader, except God could possibly discover. No author of a text or creator of an artifact can say definitively what the text or the object will mean to someone reading it, translating it, or looking at it many years or even centuries later. Any attempt to do so is doomed to failure. The same is true of the reader. The world horizon distances the text from the equally limited and subjective intentions of the reader. No interpreter or literary critic can say what Moby Dick, Macbeth, or Faust will mean to future generations. The possible associations, relations, and implications that any particular reader at any particular time and place may be able to discover in a text or an artifact are much smaller than the infinite possibilities of meaning that can and will be discovered throughout history.[7] Meaning, in other words, belongs to no one. No one can set its limits. No one determines how associations, differences, relations, and distinctions unfold, branch out, cross, grow, and transform. It is much rather the case that the interpreter and the author are caught up in the dynamic of unfolding meaning. As the hermeneutic philosophers contend, readers and authors "belong" to the text and not the other way round.[8]

The discourse of belonging, which is characteristic of philosophical hermeneutics, has caused much misunderstanding and been an aggravating thorn in the flesh of all who find the world to which they belong inhuman, oppressive, and unjust. To ascribe a kind of agency, if not dominance, to artifacts and thus tradition seems to negate human freedom and to imply a kind of slavery to the past. The hermeneutic concept of the autonomy of the text, however, does not mean that authors and readers are mere puppets in the hands of an omnipotent tradition. Authors and readers are just as autonomous as the text and together with it—through

---

7 | "But the discovery of the true meaning of a text or a work or art is never finished; it is in fact an infinite process" Gadamer (2004: 265).

8 | "History does not belong to us; we belong to it. Long before we understand ourselves through the process of self-examination, we understand ourselves in a self-evident way in the family, society, and state in which we live." Gadamer (2004: 28).

what could be described as a process of negotiation—they create the vast
and always changing array of associations that make up the presently experienced world of meaning. Living tradition is not an oppressive past
which somehow attempts to violently and illegitimately reproduce itself
in the present. History is open-ended, dynamic, incalculable, and cannot
be reduced to traditionalism. When meaning is constructed, a sentence is
written, an artifact created, it distances itself from its author and becomes
autonomous in much the same sense as the author and reader are autonomous agents. The text, the sign, the object is a "work" in the double sense
of being worked (passive object) and working (active source of meaning).
The work in this sense is "original" and "originating" and therefore potentially subversive. It is a source of meaning insofar as it carries an endless
horizon of different interpretations within itself. The text, the artifact, any
object whatever, becomes itself an actor, who is also "interpreting" the
author and the reader as much as they interpret it.

For actor-network theory, as will be discussed below in Part 2, entities
are "irreducible" (Latour 1988: 158). The principle of "irreduction" means
that nothing can be reduced to something else, as a mere copy or redundancy, and also that nothing can be absolutely distinct from anything else,
in the sense of not being able to be associated in some way with it. Just as
the autonomy of the text in hermeneutics cannot be defined apart from
the equally autonomous interpretations of author and reader, all entities
for actor-network theory exist by virtue of their activities of forming networks. This makes entities into "quasi-objects," "factisches," and "non-human actors" which exist by means of a process of "translation," of mutual
mediation and conditioning. In much the same way as for hermeneutics
a text or an artifact projects an infinite horizon of meaning, Latour (1988:
192) speaks of every entity as an "actant" that makes associations with
other actants such that "every actant makes a whole world for itself." These
associations do not appear out of nothing. There is no creation *ex nihlo*,
whether of texts or of scientific facts. They build on associations already
given, transforming and extending them into networks. Networks are not
exclusive, closed systems, but are open to each other in the same way that
for hermeneutics the meaning of any text or artifact is open to infinite
interpretations. The principle of "irreduction" in actor-network theory is

similar to the principle of the autonomy of the text in hermeneutics.[9] The irreducibility of the entity grounds a "circle" of meaning similar to the hermeneutic circle. "Between one network and another, as between one force and another, nothing is by itself either commensurable or incommensurable. Thus we never emerge from a network no matter how far it extends." (Latour 1988: 171)

Just as interpretation changes the text as well as the reader, so does "translation" in actor-network theory result in a new kind of association between human agent and technological artefact such that neither is mere passive instrument of the other, but together they build a hybrid entity. For both philosophical hermeneutics and actor-network theory it can be said that when interpretation occurs, it is "history" itself that is doing the work, provided that history is open to the future as well as to the past. Whereas actor-network theory speaks of the dynamics of networking, Gadamer (1975: 267ff) speaks of the principle of "effective history" and "fusion of horizons." Philosophical hermeneutics and actor-network theory both place the event of understanding on the ontological and not the epistemological level. Indeed, as Latour (1988: 159) puts it "nothing is known—only realized." One of the important achievements of philosophical hermeneutics that paves the way for actor-network theory is that it brings ontology out of transcendence into the concrete dynamic and contingency of time and place. Interpretation is not the exclusive privilege of a God-like—or value-free—knower, but is epistemologically pluralistic—all can participate—and ontologically indeterminate—nothing is impossible. Philosophical hermeneutics can therefore not be described either as political conservatism or as a subjectivist epistemology lost in a logical fallacy. As Heidegger (1971) succinctly put it, "language speaks."

If it is language that speaks, what has become of those human subjects who have struggled for centuries to attain the right to speak for themselves? The achievements of critical rationality in the wake of the Enlightenment seem to be placed into question. The impossibility of getting outside language and the condition of being thrown into a historical world formed by the past (as well as the future) predisposes hermeneutics

---

9 | Latour summarizes the "autonomy" of the artifact so: "None of the actants mobilized to secure an alliance stops acting on its own behalf. They each carry on fomenting their own plots, forming their own groups, and serving other masters, wills, and functions."

to see the construction of meaning not as an achievement of autonomous rational subjects who act upon a passive reality. Meaning is less something that humans do than something that happens in the world, indeed "as" the world. This view is controversial and open to misunderstanding. On the one hand, finitude, temporality, and history seem to ascend the thrown of transcendence, while on the other hand, it turns out that human beings alone are not the masters their own destiny. Both Heidegger and Gadamer have been criticized for locating the construction of meaning beyond the initiative and competency of human individuals, or of the human collective as in the Marxist tradition.[10] Paul Ricoeur has attempted to modify this impression by pointing to the critical function of interpretation as manifested in such "masters of suspicion" as Marx, Nietzsche, and Freud.[11] Ricoeur proposes a "hermeneutics of suspicion" which attempts to reformulate philosophical hermeneutics in terms more compatible with human agency and with the typically modern concern for subjecting all traditional authorities to the criticism of autonomous reason and explanatory models. Despite these efforts, it is incontestable that philosophical hermeneutics uses a vocabulary that avoids subjectivism and the primacy of human agency to the point of provocation. It would seem that hermeneutics has sacrificed human freedom to a new God, the omnipotence of history and tradition. The universality claim of hermeneutics appears almost inescapably to mask an ideology of conservatism.

The emphasis on tradition, as already pointed out, need not imply a commitment to the past and a denial of possibilities for innovation, transformation, and even revolution. Rather than robbing humans of agency, hermeneutics should be understood as a plea for including other actors in the process of constructing meaning. No one and no thing need be deprived of agency. On the contrary, heretofore passive objects, a text or a work of art for example, may be seen on the basis of the hermeneutic concept of autonomy as actors in their own right. The result is that there are not less actors involved in the task of interpretation, each contributing their individual points of view, but more. A text, a work of art, an ancient artifact, the symbolism of a dream, a chemical reaction, a microorganism, the traces in the detector of a particle accelerator, indeed, everything, de-

---

10 | For Habermas' critique of Gadamer see Habermas (1971, 1988).

11 | For Ricoeur's intervention in the Habermas-Gadamer debate, see Ricoeur (1970, 1981a).

mands to be understood "on its own terms." In so far as it exists, any entity projects its own horizon of possible meaning. It does not passively allow anything at all to be said about it or anything at all to be done with it. Every entity, no matter what it is, has its own "affordances" which condition the kinds of interactions and associations it can enter into.[12] No matter how a text, a work of art, or anything at all for that matter is understood, there can be other readings, different interpretations, unexpected associations. In this way, any entity at all can be said to "influence" the construction of meaning. The construction of meaning, therefore, should not be seen as a kind of *creatio ex nihilo* on the part of the author or of the reader, but as Gadamer put it, a "fusion of horizons" (*Horizontverschmelzung*) in which the possibilities of meaning that all participants carry with them play an active role. Interpretation produces new meaning and the product of interpretation, whether it is a text, a work of art, a scientific paper, a machine, an event, a blueprint for a house, etc., is an "emergent" entity that is different from the individual influences of author, reader, and other already present artifacts.

Hermeneutical interpretation is a process in which all are actively involved in a conflictual and contingent movement from whole to part and from part to whole in a never ending spiral. At each point supposed meanings are introduced, challenged, revised, explicated, and elaborated, new information emerges, new interpretations are tested against each other, interdependencies discovered, new beings enter the world, old ones are transformed, and the world horizon is extended. Philosophical hermeneutics maintains that the construction of meaning is not the privilege of autonomous rational subjects. Interpretation is non-subjectivist, communicative, and distributed. Interpretation is not to be understood psychologically or epistemologically, but rather ontologically. Despite the focus on reading and on language, hermeneutics is not concerned with mental or psychological activities. In the words of Gadamer (1985: 288) "Effective historical consciousness is inescapably more existence than it is consciousness." And once we no longer limit the dignity of existence to humans alone we might say with Bruno Latour (2005: 245): "Hermeneutics is not a privilege of humans, but, so to speak, a property of the world itself."

---

12 | The term "affordance" was introduced by James J. Gibson (1977) and has gained wide acceptance as a term for the various influences of objects and technologies on human action.

KNOWING IS DOING

The lofty heights of philosophical speculation that seem typical of Heidegger and Gadamer might suggest that hermeneutics has little to do with so-called "praxis." On the contrary, interpretation in the sense of philosophical hermeneutics is not merely an academic issue, for example, an issue between university professors and anxious students, wherein what is at stake is whether the student receives a good or a bad grade in a seminar on Kant. Beyond the academic question whether or not the student has interpreted Kant correctly, interpretation is serious business and has consequences. In the case of interpreting the law or the Holy Scriptures, for example, much depends on what is considered the correct and therefore binding meaning of the text. Interpreting the law or Holy Scriptures is not a matter of simply knowing in a theoretical way the meaning of the legal or religious text; it is a matter of "applying" this meaning in concrete situations that require decision and action. Without decision and action interpretation has not achieved meaning. As Latour would say "Nothing is known—only realized" (1988: 159). This means that hermeneutics is not a merely theoretical matter, it is "application" and therefore a "practical knowledge" (*phronesis*) as opposed to purely theoretical knowledge (*sophia*).[13] Interpretation is not merely cognitive, it is the concrete action taken, for example, by the courts and by religious institutions and their followers. The moment of "application" in hermeneutic understanding should not be seen as something only to be found in legal or religious hermeneutics. To understand anything at all in the sense of philosophical hermeneutics is to apply knowledge in action, whereby knowledge is not something one has outside of or before action, like knowing the recipe before actually baking the cake or studying the blueprint of a house before actually building it.

Already Fichte had placed Kant's transcendental ego on the level of an act by which the subject constitutes itself. The transcendental subject constitutes itself as *Tathandlung*. For Marx it was labor of the human species and the transformation of nature that took the place of Kant's transcendental conditions of the possibility of knowing. Heidegger located the

---

13 | The distinction between theoretical knowledge, moral or practical knowledge, and technical knowledge is derived from Aristotle and discussed in Gadamer (2004: 278ff).

foundations of understanding in *Dasein*'s facticity and existence. Wittgenstein based his later philosophy on a concept of language as an activity, a "form of life." Within this powerful praxis-oriented tradition, to know is to act. It is only through applying the law, the Word of God, moral values, political convictions, expectations, internalized social roles, etc. in concrete situations that their meaning is "understood." Hermeneutical understanding cannot be abstracted from the concrete practices in which it is enacted. Can someone know what it means to be a teacher, for example, without ever having taught? Can someone be an engineer, without ever designing and developing a technical device? Can someone be a professor of philosophy without instructing students, collaborating with colleagues, writing peer-reviewed articles, attending conferences, participating in faculty politics, and much more? Is there even such a thing as a "teacher," an "engineer," or a "professor" without these practices? Even academics, as we all know, is not a purely academic issue, just as science is not pure, value-free, disinterested, and disembodied knowing, but a struggle for a certain interpretation of the world bound up with many interdependent concrete practices in politics, economics, science, art, religion, including even coercion and deceit. Interpretation and the construction of meaning is inextricably bound up with action.

What does this obvious fact of human life have to do with the primacy of language which is so evident in the writings of Heidegger, Gadamer, and Ricoeur? One way to answer this question is with reference to linguistics. Linguistics traditionally divides the study of language into three domains, syntax, semantics, and pragmatics.[14] Syntax consists of the rules, the grammar of a system of signs. Semantics deals with the meaning of the signs. Pragmatics refers to the actual use of language, "doing things with words" (Austin 1962). Insofar as hermeneutics is not a merely cognitive knowledge, but a practical knowledge, it falls, from the linguistic point of view, within the purview of pragmatics. One could say that hermeneutics is the pragmatics of communicative action even if, as is well known, this term has played an important role in the critique of philosophical hermeneutics. Jürgen Habermas' critique of Heidegger and Gadamer under the banner of a universal pragmatics of communication is a topic that will be discussed below. For the moment it suffices to point out that interpretation in the broad and foundational sense of a philosophical

---

14 | Charles W. Morris (1938) made this categorization popular.

hermeneutics is not merely a matter of reading texts and not a matter of whether a certain interpretation "corresponds" to the intention of the author, or even to the text itself. Hermeneutics is an existential issue of what world we are living in and how we are to live in it properly. If meaning is not what we have, but what we are and what we do, then the pragmatic approach to language is a helpful reminder of what is at stake in understanding.

RELATIVISM AND CRITIQUE

We have portrayed philosophical hermeneutics up to this point as the construction of meaning under the conditions of history, open to the future as well as the past, granting autonomy and agency equally to all participants, and praxis-oriented. What more could we want? Why does hermeneutics have such a bad reputation among champions of Enlightenment? One answer to this question lies in the association of hermeneutics with relativism. It should be apparent from what has been said that different interpretations are actually names for different strategies of reality construction. The conflict of interpretations is a conflict of traditions, cultures, and ways of life. For Habermas (1984) different interpretations are "rational" discourse, only insofar as they make claims to validity against commonly accepted criteria of truth, meaning, and value. But as history and the ever present conflicts of a global, multicultural society show, criteria of value, meaning, and truth need not be commonly shared. The presupposition of a common horizon of meaning, a common language or common worldview is merely that, a presupposition, which in a multicultural, global society is not even plausible, let alone a reasonable assumption. The fact that different interpretations appeal to different fundamental criteria implies that communities of interpretation can argue rationally within the confines of their respective horizons, but they cannot argue rationally with each other. Argumentative discourse, as Habermas describes it, is only possible within the boundaries of commonly accepted criteria of validity. For only then can it be decided if a claim to validity is indeed valid. In order for rational argumentation to be possible, it must be possible to settle an argument, to verify/falsify claims to validity. Only when all participants to the discussion share the same criteria of validity can the non-violent force of the better argument win the day. Only then can discourse lead to consensus and consensus to cooperative action. If however the criteria themselves are at stake in communication, the conditions of the possibility of "rational discourse," at least as Habermas defines the term, are not given and all the arguments in the world won't help.

When Galileo asked the theologians to look through his telescope, they replied that a weak and corrupt human perception cannot be measured against the word of God. Then as now, when criteria are at stake, communication moves to a higher level wherein each party attempts to "convert" the other to their beliefs (Krieger 2009). Hermeneutics describes a form of rationality that does not stop at fixed criteria of meaning, value, and truth, but begins from the awareness that criteria are themselves in question and are to be adapted, changed, revised, and extended in the process of explicating meaning. Moving from the whole to the part implies moving from the part back to the whole. In this process both whole and part are transformed. The whole is seen from the perspective of the part and the part from the whole. In fact, it would be possible to describe the hermeneutical circle in such a way that part and whole are interchangeable. The world can be disclosed through a work of art, as Heidegger (2002) points out. The whole is "in" the part as much as the part "in" the whole. This does not preclude change, but describes how knowing and acting are explicated, articulated, developed within meaning. This is what makes certain works, texts, and symbols into what Gadamer calls "classics." They enjoy a privileged position in a cultural tradition. This may also be claimed for religious symbols. They have the ability to disclose a world horizon.

Hermeneutic understanding begins with the concrete artifact and constructs associations, references, draws out lines of meaning, makes comparisons, explicates and unfolds the myriad connections folded up in the text or the artifact. In opposition to Habermas' description of rational discourse, hermeneutic understanding does not appeal to any standard beyond the work. Instead of Habermas' concept of shared criteria, the world horizon within which hermeneutical understanding operates and to which it appeals is not necessarily shared, not given in the same way for all, not something that can be abstracted from historical facticity and held above claims to validity as judge and referee. For hermeneutics, it is not merely claims to validity that can be contested by rational communication, but also criteria of meaning, truth, and value. It is for this reason that the discourse of philosophical hermeneutics is especially interesting in a global, multicultural society, where tradition is up for grabs and the conflict of different strategies for constructing reality is daily business. It is also for this reason that hermeneutics seems to cut itself lose from any ties to solid, objective truth from which alone irrationality, ideology, and injustice could be criticized. Hermeneutics appears to endorse a radical relativism in which no values, truths, and certainties can claim to be able to judge between right and wrong.

The conflict of interpretations at the level of systems of meaning and world horizons is not a discussion *within* epistemology, ontology, or methodology, but a defense of a strategic decision on what epistemology, ontology, and methodology are all about. At this point it is helpful to pause and ask: What does it mean to "defend" a strategic decision? At the least, it is the attempt to convince others to "convert" to certain criteria of truth, meaning, and value. The concept of "conversion" in this context refers to a theory of communication in which the acceptance of criteria and basic values cannot be based upon arguments (Krieger 1996, 2006). Habermas has convincingly shown that communication which cannot appeal to criteria of validity in order to settle claims to truth, rightness, truthfulness, and meaning cannot be considered argumentation, or even—according to his strict definition of the term—"rational." If trying to convert others to certain beliefs is not rational, then what is it? The usual answer to this question has appealed to the discourse of critical theory and the distinction between reason and ideology. Critical theory has described opposing beliefs as "false consciousness" and, as the history of the modern critique of religion demonstrates, attempted to show how these beliefs are reducible to other causes, whether psychological or social (Krieger 2006).

The opposition of critical rationality to ideology, indeed the entire program of a critique of ideology from Feuerbach and Marx to Habermas, is based on the ideal construction of an objective knowing, a disinterested, value-free, and therefore impartial form of knowing which alone is believed to guarantee truth. Habermas' pragmatics of argumentative discourse amounts to an attempt to defend the strategy of the modern interpretation of science and thereby reserve a domain of knowledge from the prejudices and limitations of facticity, a domain of knowledge from which ideology may be exposed and criticized. If there is no position somehow outside of or beyond the conditions of social communication then there is no "critical" position. There are only different interpretations. So-called critical theory can claim no neutral position, no special authority, and no advantage over any other strategy for constructing reality. We are afloat upon a sea of relativism with no compass to guide us.

The natural sciences have played the role of a kind of compass in the self-understanding of modernity. They have assumed the role of the counterpart to ideology, false consciousness, distorted communication and the social and political effects of these in forms of oppression and injustice. They represent a form of knowing that grounds the possibility of a "free floating *intelligentia*" (Mannheim's *freischwebende Intelligenz*), that is, a position in society that can be taken by those who have little vested interests beyond the search for truth and truth alone. The natural sciences have furthermore legitimated the differentiation of a semi-autonomous functional subsystem of society coded by the binary opposition of true/false (Luhmann's *Wissenschaftssystem*) thus establishing a position for knowledge and action outside of interests, religious convictions, personal gain, or political power. Even if the price that must be paid for this knowledge is high in the sense that the object of investigation is submitted to a regime of deterministic causality, and even if it becomes apparent that scientific knowledge aims at prediction and control—goals hardly compatible with freedom and moral autonomy—, still scientific knowledge in the specifically modern Western sense is the basis for the claims of critical theory.

Modern epistemology is based on the specific constellation of a knowing subject free of any personal, social, political, or economic interests on the one side and a demythologized nature free of angels, demons, and spirits on the other. Scientific knowledge represents a form of knowing free of the arbitrariness, subjectivity, and illusions of personal interests, society, culture, and politics. The natural sciences offer therefore a model for a social science that is able to discover the mechanisms of false consciousness and distorted communication in society. Truth, it is assumed, can only result from a knowing that is objective, disinterested, and free of ideological distortion. Latour (1993: 13ff) speaks of a typically modern constitution in which reality is divided into four distinct and opposing domains: nature out there, knowing inside the human subject, God up there, transcendent, and beyond the world, and finally, society as an imminent God, a realm that transcends the individual, but is nonetheless characterized by the weaknesses and shortcomings of human nature. Modernity according to Latour's analysis is structured by a series of dichotomies; subject versus object, humans versus nature, nature versus society, and God versus the world. The realm of knowledge is divided into objective, value free knowledge on one side and subjective opinions, prejudices, and ideologies—including religious beliefs to the extent they enter the public sphere—on the other. Within this typically modern constellation the critique of ideology, as well as the critique of religion, must be based on the ideal of an objective, value-free science. The so-called human sciences can therefore only claim the name of science to the extent that they somehow adopt and conform to the methods and presuppositions of the natural sciences. Furthermore, it is only upon this basis that a social science could claim for itself the legitimacy for critique. It is within this constellation and the options it allows that the modern programs of "enlightenment" and "critical rationality" attempt to legitimate their claims to universality and truth.

Hermeneutics has never been comfortable with the dichotomy between critical rationality on the one hand and ideology on the other. A central theme of philosophical hermeneutics has been the so-called "critique of technology." Reducing the human and social realm to an object of natural science carries with it the danger of turning the subject of knowing and acting into an object of prediction and control. Basing the social sciences on the methodology of the natural sciences would seem to throw the baby out with the bathwater, since freedom and self-determination are lost in the process of gaining objective knowledge of society. Making human beings and society into an object of a form of knowing that is based upon prediction and control tends to turn politics into technology and to celebrate instrumental, that is, technical rationality as the only legitimate basis for social and political action. It is precisely the tradition of the enlightenment, above all, Kant's moral imperative that humans should never be instrumentalized as means, but must always be considered the end of action, that inspired the critique of technology. It was not only the hermeneutical philosophers, but above all thinkers in the tradition of Marxist social criticism such as Herbert Marcuse, Max Horkheimer, Theodor Adorno, and also Habermas, who were well aware of the dangers of instrumental reason and the power of domination and manipulation that it creates. If critical theory is to avoid a one dimensional society ruled by the imperatives of prediction and control, then it is difficult to ground the critical position directly—or indirectly—in the methodology of the natural sciences.

Habermas grounds the possibility of critical theory on the distinction between communicative action and instrumental action. Instrumental action is directed toward prediction and control. It is informed by the instrumental rationality of the natural sciences and guided by technological interests. Communicative action on the contrary is directed toward mutual understanding and is guided by an interest in finding consensus upon which cooperative action free from coercion and ideology is based. Habermas acknowledges the danger of misusing language and communication for instrumental purposes; this is indeed what ideology does. The solution for Habermas lies in cultivating a value-free, disinterested and therefore objective form of communication that is not and cannot be instrumentalized. In his "Theory of Communicative Action" (1984: 18) Habermas speaks of "argumentative" communication; "We use the term argumentation for that type of speech in which participants thematize contested validity claims and attempt to vindicate or criticize them through argumentation." The ideal speech situation of communicative action is a face-to-face dialogue in which principally anyone can participate, whereby all who do participate have equal chance to offer their arguments for or against any claim. They do so in an attitude of hypothetical distance to decision and action, awaiting, as it were, the outcome of the discussion and the achievement of consensus. No statement is more than an opinion. There are no absolute truths, revelations, or proclamations in argumentative discourse. No profit, no king, and no God ever spoke in this way. Every statement is no more than a claim to validity and not the truth itself. Participants are aware that all claims must be proven valid, before they can be accepted. Proof of validity or acceptance is based on commonly accepted criteria of what counts as a valid argument and what counts as true. In this situation it is the non-violent force of the better argument and not prejudices, unreflected world views, and uncritically accepted values that legitimates and guides cooperative action.

Habermas finds the pragmatics of argumentative communication at the basis of democratic ideals and of any legitimate political process. Not surprisingly, it is argumentative communication that also lies at the basis of the scientific method. Indeed, testing hypotheses under reproducible conditions against accepted criteria of verification or falsification in an attitude of disinterested concern for the truth alone lies at the heart of the methodology of the natural sciences. What Habermas describes as a universal pragmatics of communication—and thus as the definition of rationality—turns out to be an abstraction from the methodology of the natural sciences and remains therefore bound to the epistemology and ontology of modern science. In order to avoid the consequence that this kind of rationality plays into the hands of techno-determinism Habermas takes recourse to Freudian psychoanalysis, Chomsky's structural linguistics, and Kohlberg's developmental psychology. The detour through these theories can only succeed if they clearly demonstrate an objective, explanatory form of knowing that is not guided by instrumental reason and by interest in prediction and control. None of these examples, despite whatever their own claims might be, yield knowledge whose objectivity is in any way comparable to the natural sciences. Even if it could be convincingly argued that psychoanalysis is an objective and explanatory science and not an interpretive or hermeneutic science, it would be difficult to claim that such a science is free of any intention or ability to predict and control human behavior. As Habermas (1970: 375) puts it, critical theory must be able to explain (*erklären*) the "mechanisms of systematically distorted communication." Without introducing mechanistic causality, if even through the back door of depth psychology, there is no objective, value-free, disinterested, and thus ideology free position for critical theory to base its claim to legitimation upon.

The hermeneutic philosophers have always attempted to describe a form of rationality beyond the pragmatics of what Habermas has termed "argumentative" discourse, which is a systematic reconstruction of scientific methodology in the guise of a universal pragmatics of communication. Both Gadamer and Ricoeur have pointed out that Habermas' program of value-free, undistorted communication is itself not free of tradition and presupposed values, specifically, those of the Enlightenment. Habermas' program is derived from a world view based on Western European traditions and is by no means free of prejudices, pre-understandings, and cultural commitments, for example, the commitment to a "utopian" (Ricoeur) view of justice as equality, the primacy of individual freedom in the face of demands of family, clan, and nation, and a certain view of legal and political legitimacy by means of Western democratic processes.[15] Indeed, the program of ideology critique is itself a cultural product—how could it be otherwise—one interpretation among others in today's multicultural and pluralistic world. This returns us to the question: What

---

15 | Ricoeur (1986: 237) sums up his position as follows: "Hermeneutics without a project of liberation is blind, but a project of emancipation without historical experience is empty."

is interpretation? What is going on, when horizons of meaning and the boundaries of communication are being constructed? In the following, the attempt is made to answer these questions by linking the discourse of philosophical hermeneutics with actor-network theory and new media theory. We will argue that interpretation can be a viable way to construct meaning in a pluralistic and multicultural world when understood in terms of what may be called "networking."

Every meaningful communicative action, following Habermas, is constructed with regard to criteria of validity. Regardless of which criteria are appealed to, every interpretation not only appeals to certain criteria of validity, but more importantly, attempts at the same time to *make* these criteria valid. How is this done? Grading a paper involves *much more* than deciding if the student has, for example, *correctly* understood Kant, or if both the student and Kant have deepened and differentiated our understanding of certain philosophical issues. Although it is certainly true that texts and arguments are involved when a professor grades a paper, in fact much more is involved. This is apparent when we are not talking about reading texts in educational institutions, but in legal or religious contexts. To interpret the law or the Holy Scriptures means putting them into practice, and by so doing, to establish their truth and validity. A religious faith that is not lived is meaningless. Values that have no influence on action are not values at all. Even within the educational system, grading a paper in a seminar is not a purely cognitive activity, but a complex action that takes place within a *network* of persons, artifacts, activities, materials, technologies, institutions, regulations, values, historical events, traditions and much more. All these things have over time and with much effort and cost been brought into a constellation of relations, associations, and interdependencies such that a now seemingly invisible web of ties holds everything in place and makes it quite natural, even irresistible, to give the student a grade. Heidegger speaks of a "referential context" (*Verweisungszusammenhang*) characteristic of *Dasein's* "Being-in-the-world" (2010: §§ 14–24). Gadamer speaks of a "horizon."

In the phenomenological tradition originating with Husserl the term "lifeworld" (*Lebenswelt*) defined this historically given universal context of knowing and acting.[16] Let us call this constellation of relations, which

---

16 | Edmund Husserl (1936/1970: 108–109) introduced the concept of the "lifeworld", *Lebenswelt*: "In whatever way we may be conscious of the world as univer-

goes far beyond linguistic signs and written texts to include objects, artifacts, technologies, institutions, organizations, in short, everything that
belongs to a tradition or a culture, a "network" and let us call the society
that consists of such constellations a "network society." Interpreting a text,
grading a paper, writing an article, speaking at a conference, conducting
and experiment, filing a tax return, voting, building a house, indeed, doing anything at all, is a matter of net-working. It depends on a constant
and uncertain activity of constructing a variety of associations between
heterogeneous elements. It is the work of putting them all together in
a particular way. Instead of asserting that meaning is constructed with
regard to criteria of validity, we propose that meaning is constructed with
regard to making associations, putting things together in a network; the
more associations, the larger the network, the more the meaning.

At a certain level the networks we construct are our world. It is all we
have. It includes not only texts and ideas, but also people, technologies, institutions, territories, and everything else that can possibly be associated
with each other. The networks we build extend through time and space,
through symbolic and material domains, and they include impartially
human and non-human actors. They are constructed by making associations, ties, connections, and by interactions and transactions, in short, by
"communication." This is however a different concept of communication
than that upon which Habermas, as well as the hermeneutic philosophers
base their theories. To speak of networking as a pragmatics of communicative action is to affirm the idea of Habermas' project of locating the
conditions of knowing and acting within language while rejecting the
conclusion that these conditions ground a privileged position for critique
or that critical theory is anything other than hermeneutic understanding.

Communication is to be understood in this context as a general term
for the construction of meaning. The concept of communication proposed

---

sal horizon, as coherent universe of existing objects, we, each 'I-the-man' and all
of us together, belong to the world as living with one another in the world; and the
world is our world, valid for our consciousness as existing precisely through this
'living together.' We, as living in wakeful world-consciousness, are constantly active on the basis of our passive having of the world [...] Obviously this is true not
only for me, the individual ego; rather we, in living together, have the world pre-
given in this together, belong, the world as world for all, pre-given with this ontic
meaning [...] The we-subjectivity [...] [is] constantly functioning."

here although rooted in language and linguistic practice, goes far beyond language to refer to all activities that build networks. To the extent that communication is what constructs meaning, then it can also be said to refer to that which philosophical hermeneutics has called "interpretation." Defining communication in this broad sense as the construction of meaning by making associations deviates considerably from Habermas' theory of communicative action as well as traditional hermeneutics as primarily reflective, linguistic, and text-based. Philosophical hermeneutics has long recognized the need to extend understanding beyond textual interpretation to include action and communication. For Ricoeur (1991; 1984–1988) actions are carriers of meaning and can be "read" just as much as texts and the construction of identity through narrative includes the construction of collective identity through communication. It might be useful in this context to recall Gregory Bateson's (2000: 457–459) definition of information as a "difference that makes a difference." Constructing meaning is work in the material world and not merely the mental manipulation of signs. Every activity, agency, and effect that introduces differences, relations, and associations can be seen as constructing information. Information however, can only make a difference in communication.

Neither information nor communication is restricted to the mental manipulation of signs. Everything that is addressed, picked up, positioned, stumbled upon, distinguished and related becomes by this very process meaningful. Recalling Saussure, meaning is based on differences and relations. It is the differences and relations that are important for the construction of meaning regardless of whether we are dealing with signs, things, plants, animals, or people. George Spencer-Brown's Laws of Form (1969) begins with the simple, but decisive injunction: "Draw a distinction!" Distinctions do not keep things apart, but bring them together. What is important is how many things are brought together and to what end. When it comes to networks, the important distinctions are not those between the material and the immaterial, signs and what is signified, humans and non-humans; all are associated with each other in such a way that a *world* emerges. Since the world is ideal and material, animate and inanimate, factual and imaginary, etc., the activity of constructing the world falls neither within idealism or materialism. The activity of constructing meaning is neither to be located in a materialist or idealist world view. Building a world of meaning is building networks. *Interpretation—and this is the claim we wish to make—can be interpreted as net-working.* When different world-networks are at stake, then the conflict of interpretations is a "war of the worlds" (Latour 2002). In this conflict what counts are the number of actors, the strength of their associations and their resources, and the ability of key actors to enroll whatever opposes them into their programs of action.

If interpretation is not merely reading and writing texts, but network-ing, what does this mean for the understanding of understanding, and for the self-understanding of the philosophical enterprise as well as for the methodological foundations of the social sciences? What does this mean for the relationship between texts and readers, and between university pro-fessors and their students? What does it mean for the relations between faculties, between universities, and between the educational system and other social systems such as business, politics, art, health care, etc.? And finally, what does this mean for a "postmodern" world society (Lyotard 1984) in which communication is internally divided and fragmented by different cultural rules and at best locally valid criteria of truth, value, and meaning?

The network of communication that constructs today's "world society" (*Weltgesellschaft*, Luhmann 1975) is a more or less fragile product of count-less interpretations on various scales by hybrid actors who themselves are products of heterogeneous networks held together by contingent and constantly contested associations (Latour 2005). If this problematization of the present day situation is not enough to daunt even the most ambi-tious interpreters and networkers, consider that the trump of an objective measure of truth which Western culture long believed to hold in its hand has also disappeared. Nature itself no longer stands outside the game of culture in the position of an unbiased referee able to impartially judge the conflict of interpretations and the validity of world views (Latour 2002). The laboratory studies (Latour/Woolgar 1979; Knorr Cetina 1981) have shown that so-called scientific facts and the objective reality they are supposed to represent do not lie beyond the limits of interpretation and society. As Ramsey might say, if you can't whistle what lies beyond in-terpretation, you can't *experiment* with it either. The Western conviction that science, technology, economics, and therefore democracy are based upon an objective order of nature beyond the idiosyncrasies of culture and tradition is merely one interpretation among others and nothing justifies the hope that a "fusion of horizons" (Gadamer) will lead to mutual un-derstanding or that semiosis (C. S. Peirce) will asymptotically approach

consensus. It should therefore not be surprising that we are witnessing today the rise of prosperous liberal economies, future oriented foundational
research, and innovative technologies within one-party dictatorships and
religious-fundamentalist monarchies devoid of any concept of self-deter-
mined individuals and democratic politics. Returning to Wittgenstein and
Heidegger; beyond interpretation there is nothing, and within interpretation there is everything, but alas, it is only an interpretation.

2. Actor-Networks

The question of interpretation can itself be interpreted as the question about net-working. With regard to the task of science in general, Latour (2005: 104) asserts "[...] to explain is not a mysterious cognitive feat, but a very practical world-building enterprise that consists in connecting entities with other entities, that is, in tracing a network." If grading a paper on Kant, or anything else for that matter, is a task of extending chains of associations and connections in all directions, and again, it doesn't matter if what we are dealing with is material or immaterial, whether it is symbols, objects, people, technologies, or institutions, then interpretation has something to do with *networks*. This remark would add little to the conceptual equipment that philosophical hermeneutics and contemporary social theory have already developed, were it not for the perspectives opened up by the inclusion of nature, technology, and brute things into a newly defined realm of social which has come to be known under the name of "actor-network theory." The concept of "network" has a theoretical potential that is being enriched and differentiated not only by actor-network theory, but also by recent developments in so-called "Network Science."[1] Granted the commonplace that everything is somehow connected with everything, what advantages are there to interpreting this from the point of view of networks, specifically, actor-network theory?

The literature on networks in all fields has grown exponentially in recent years.[2] In the human sciences networks are coming to be seen as the

---

1 | See for example Brandes et al. (2013) for a programmatic statement on what is network science. See also the website http://www.network-science.org/ for an introduction to the area.

2 | See Barabási (2002), Castells (1996), Watts (2003), Latour (2005), Newman/Barabási/Watts (2006), White (2008), Wassermann & Faust (1994), Rainie/Wellman (2012), and Buchanan (2002), to mention only a few.

fundamental ordering principle of society. Ideas and concepts such as "six degrees of separation," "small worlds," "hubs," "power-law distributions," "gatekeepers," and "links" have come to be accepted terminology in the social sciences. Barabási (2002) applied the mathematics of graph theory to social phenomena such as the Internet. Manuel Castells (1996, 1997, 1998) has carefully documented the emergence of a "network society" in which information and communication technologies and the possibilities they have created of overcoming spatio-temporal limitations on knowledge and action are transforming the structure of society and every area of life. Harrison White has developed a theory of social structure on the basis of social network analysis in which actors struggle for identity and control. Network theory and network analysis has been seen by some to constitute a new paradigm for the social and the natural sciences.[3] One important strand in this broad and variegated trend is the so-called actor-network theory. Actor-network theory—ANT for short—is principally represented by Bruno Latour (1987, 1988, 1999, 2005) but founded and influenced also among others by Michel Callon (1980, 1986, 1987, 1991) and John Law (1992, 1999). Actor-network theory was developed within the sociology of science and technology in the 1970's and 80's and is related—albeit critically—to the program of the sociology of knowledge (Scheler, Mannheim, Foucault). Important sources of ANT are also ethnomethodology (Garfinkel), poststructuralism, and semiotics (Deleuze, Greimas, Serres).[4]

ANT shares with poststructuralism the program of a critical stance toward the epistemological and ontological presuppositions of modern science. The typically modern understanding of science as objective, value-free knowledge is questioned by ANT not only on account of the embeddedness of the actual practice of science in social contexts, but also with regard to its methodological foundations and epistemological presuppositions. ANT rejects the dualism of nature and society, object and subject and pleads for a completely different approach to what makes up the social. Latour (2005) is very clear about the relation of ANT to traditional sociology, including the sociology of science. For Latour "the social has vanished [...] there is no society, no social realm and no social ties, *but there exist translations between mediators that may generate traceable associations*"

---

3 | See the programmatic title "Netzwerkanalyse und Netzwerktheorie. Ein neues Paradigma in den Sozialwissenschaften" Stegbauer (2008).

4 | See the discussion of the historical roots of ANT in Wieser (2012).

(Latour 2005: 107–108). On the basis of this radical position ANT cannot see itself as sociology of science in the sense of merely adding the social activities of scientists to the repertoire of topics investigated by traditional sociological methods and theories. It is not a matter of showing how scientists are also human and indulge in power struggles, small talk, have institutional, moral, and political commitments and so forth. It is a matter of showing how science cannot be understood within the categories and methods of modern thought at all, whether it be theory of science or theory of society.

ANT rejects the assumption of a demystified nature under the regime of deterministic causality that can only be known by methodically purifying knowledge of all involvement with its object. ANT rejects the "strange idea" of modern epistemology that "*either* something was real and not constructed, *or* it was constructed and artificial, contrived and invented, made up and false" (Latour 2005: 90). What science studies has shown is that so-called scientific facts are facts "because they were fabricated," whereas to be fabricated means that they "emerged out of artificial situations" (90) in laboratories, field work, and by means of using instruments of all kinds. It is the discovery of this inevitable and inextricable collaboration of humans and non-humans in the construction of knowledge that founds ANT's program of reconstructing social theory from the ground up. If the object of scientific knowledge is the mythical "pure fact" of modern epistemology, then the subject of scientific knowing must be without personal interests, unconditioned by particular historical and cultural situations, uninvolved in the construction of knowledge, a passive observer. The purified subject of scientific knowledge looks much like Descartes *res cogitans*, a purely thinking thing fundamentally distinct from the conditions of space, time, and embodiment. ANT pleads for a view of science not as established knowledge, but as a process of constructing knowledge. Viewing science as a "practice" and not as disembodied cognition reveals a form of knowing that looks a lot like Wittgenstein's "forms of life." Signs, entities, and social interactions are inseparably intertwined. This opens up the possibility of interpreting the construction of knowledge—and rationality itself—as a form of networking.[5] This insight makes it possible to understand science on the basis of the conditions of social communication and

---

5 | "We neither think nor reason. Rather, we work on fragile materials—texts, inscriptions, traces, or paints—with other people. These materials are associated or

thus to construct a theory of knowledge and action outside the traditional categories of modern epistemology and ontology. For Latour networking is what actors do and action is at the same time the construction of meaning:

"[...] existence and meaning are synonymous. *As long as they act, agents have meaning.* This is why such a meaning may be continued, pursued, captured, translated, morphed into speech. Which does not mean that 'every *thing* in the world is a matter of discourse', but rather that any possibility for discourse is due to the presence of agents in search of their existence." (2013b: 16)

Understanding science as a social practice, that is, as a practice of building and maintaining networks sheds an entirely different light on many of the foundational assumptions of modernity and opens up the possibility to rethink not only knowledge and action, but also society, nature, and finally existence itself. So radical is Latour's claim for a new foundation of the social sciences that he challenges his colleagues to choose; "it is either a society or a network" (2005: 131). The traditional object of the social sciences is no longer society in the usual sense of the word, but a "collective" that can only be understood in terms of the structure and dynamics of networks. The claim that ANT makes is that the understanding of actor-networks leads to a very different set of assumptions and basic categories than those canonized within the traditional self-understanding of modernity. How does modernity understand itself? Typically modern, according to Latour is the conviction that science is a specialized functional sub-system of society concerned exclusively with the discovery of objective truth. This view presupposes a desocialization of the subject of scientific knowledge, that is, the ideal of a bloodless, purely cognitive, a-historical knowing, devoid of prejudice, preconceptions, and presuppositions. And on the side of the object there is pure nature, the realm of deterministic causality and nothing but brute facts.

The objects of technology, which were paradoxically at the same time human artifacts and natural objects were seen either as determining forces in society or as neutral tools in the hands of autonomous rational subjects. Within the parameters of modernity the question of technology has ranged between a technological determinism on the one end of the

---

dissociated by courage and effort; they have no meaning, value, or coherence outside the narrow network that holds them together for a time." (Latour 1988: 186)

spectrum and social determinism on the other end. These assumptions had the detrimental effect of blinding out the actual practice of science. There was no place within the modern world view for that which Latour calls "quasi-objects," "hybrids," or "factishes" that are both subject and object, both fabricated and autonomous, both social and natural, both word and thing, both human and non-human. The major discoveries of ANT that place the modern world view in question arose from looking closely at the actual practice of science. The guiding question behind ANT is: How are meaning, knowledge, truth, and the facts that make up the enterprise of science actually "made"?

At least at its beginnings, ANT was much more a program of empirical research than a theory. The empirical investigation of the practice of science revealed a quite different picture than what science thought of itself, including what social scientists thought of science as well as their own enterprise.[6] Instead of pure science, there appeared messy networks of associations that do not respect the distinctions of modern epistemology. The boundaries between the supposedly independent domains of science, economics, politics, art, law, and religion could not be maintained. In the face of this discovery, it became necessary to reconceptualize fundamental assumptions of sociology, epistemology, anthropology, and finally ontology as well. This program of reconceptualization of science, above all the social sciences, but also of their epistemological, methodological, and ontological foundations has become a major influence in the broad area of what can be called network science.

According to ANT, networks have a fractal structure. They are made up of actors who themselves are networks. Networks are constructed by a few simple communicative rules and operations that are applied self-referentially in potentially infinite progressions and regressions resulting in forms of order that can be repeated, stabilized, and identified as actors and their associations. These rules and operations may be summarized in the following way: Actors "translate" and "enroll" or "inscribe" other actors into "programs of action" which "mobilize" and align actors into heterogeneous, hybrid, and scalable associations that can be termed networks. Actors are in principle "mediators" that can be turned into "black boxes" or "intermediaries" by means of functionalizing them into fix input/output schemas. The concept of network in ANT is admittedly problematic and

---

6 | See for example Latour/Woolgar (1979), Latour (1987).

often criticized for having multiple meanings including such aspects as process and structure, concept and entity.

As much as Latour struggles to define the concept of network in distinction to the usual understanding of networks as made up of nodes and links, he retains from traditional definitions the fact that in actor-networks 1) "a point-to-point connection is being established [...]," 2) "a connection leaves empty most of what is not connected [...]," and 3) "this connection is not made for free, it requires effort" (2005: 132). The concept of network in ANT has both methodological and ontological connotations. Methodologically Latour can say: "Network is a concept, not a thing out there. It is a tool to help describe something and not what is being described." (2005: 131) This should not be taken to imply that there are no such things as networks, rather, that when speaking of networks everything depends on how they are known and on the way they are described. When the sociologist of associations follows the actors and meticulously registers their efforts to translate, enroll, and inscribe other actors into programs of action, then networks do seem to exist in the world: "[...] an actor-network is what is made to act by a large star-shaped web of mediators flowing in and out of it. It is made to exist by its main ties: attachments are first, actors are second" (2005: 217). To say that the world consists of actor-networks is to say that careful observation brings to light multifarious activities of making associations which can then be ascribed to actors. In a certain sense, it is the description of traces left by actors that makes a network appear; "[...] a network is not made of nylon thread, words or any durable substance but is the trace left behind by some moving agent" (2005: 132).

At the heart of ANT's unique and somewhat eccentric understanding of the concept of network there lies the concern to distinguished what Latour calls the "sociology of associations" (Latour 2005: 9) from traditional sociology and its commitments to the modern world view.[7] Whatever networks are, they are not typical social structures or macro-entities whose attributes cannot be derived from the individual actors they are made up of. ANT breaks with the assumption that has more or less legitimated a

---

7 | "Even though most social scientists would prefer to call 'social' a homogeneous thing, it's perfectly acceptable to designate by the same word a trail of *associations* between heterogeneous elements. [...] it is possible to remain faithful to the original intuitions of the social sciences by redefining sociology not as the 'science of the social', but as the *tracing of associations*." (Latour 2005: 5)

science of society at least since Durkheim; the distinction between micro-actors and macro-structures. From the perspective of ANT, society is seen to consist of actor-networks, small and large, durable and less durable, and therefore not as made up of micro-individuals on the one side and macro-structures on the other. We will return to this distinction below. For the moment it is important to note that to speak of a "network society" from the point of view of ANT is not to make the claim that society consists of actor-networks in the same sense in which traditional sociology claimed that society consists of interactions, organizations, structures, and systems. The concept of network in ANT is difficult to define and difficult to understand, because it proposes to describe something for which modern science, including its epistemological and ontological presuppositions, has no name. This becomes clear as soon as one takes seriously Latour's claim that the social does not exclude nature and the non-human, but is a web, or rather "collective" of associations that extends from the smallest to the largest and includes anything that can claim for itself a place in the world. Indeed, it is misleading to speak of "society" at all as something that could be distinguished from nature or from human individuals.

On the basis of views such as these, it is not surprising that ANT understands itself as a critique of modernity. This holds true even if Latour, for example, rejects the concept of critique and critical rationality and avoids using these terms, which he explicitly sees as typically modern concepts. The imperative of ANT is simply to "follow the actors" and not attempt to look behind, above, or beneath them in order to discover some kind of conditioning factors operating, so to speak, behind their backs and making them do what they do. The focus is on the "description" of heterogeneous networks consisting of human and non-human actors and not on the "explanation" of social order on the basis of structures or forces hidden from the actors themselves. ANT distances itself explicitly from the concern of traditional sociology as well as those tendencies within network science that are based on the search for mathematically describable regularities in networks. Where traditional sociology, including social network analysis, sees chaos, contingency, and meaninglessness, ANT discovers the "collective" of actors busily making associations and translating and enrolling other actors into programs of action.

Although ANT clearly stands within the tradition of poststructuralism (Hostaker 2005, Wieser 2012), Latour insists that the world not be reduced to texts and signs. The semiotic coding of reality, which is a fundamental assumption of both hermeneutics and poststructuralism, should not be interpreted as an attempt to dematerialize reality, or as a principle ordering systems of signs alone. Signs, human beings, institutions, norms, theories, things, machines and so on build a "circulating reference" (Latour 1999: 24ff.) of mixed beings, that is, techno-socio-semiotic hybrids which "articulate" themselves into a "collective" of constantly changing actor-networks. According to Latour, modernity took this always already mixed reality and distilled out of it a series of artificial constructions in the form of an idealistic realm of signs and rational structures, a demythologized nature under the regime of deterministic causality, and a society subject to passions, power struggles, and ideology. These artificial constructions have led us to believe that nature consists of brute facts whereas society and culture make up a purely symbolic realm subject to the uncontrollable forces of passion and illusion and at best to be regulated by a social contract among free individuals, and of course, the police.

When actors—human and non-human—organize themselves into networks, there emerge connections, associations, relations, and attributes which are entered into, set up, dismantled, and transformed through communicative processes. As an empirical research program in the tradition of ethnology and cultural anthropology ANT describes as closely as possible who the actors are, what they say and do, how they build, dismantle, and transform associations with each other, and what networks emerge from these activities. But ANT is far more than an empirical method. The name "actor-network theory" underlines a concerned with questions of epistemology, ontology, and the foundations of the social sciences, as well as a basic understanding of what society is and how it functions. The attempt to describe order outside the modern world view with its characteristic assumptions about knowing, being, and action is challenging not only for the authors, but also for readers, who are confronted with unexpected and unfamiliar ideas, concepts, and methods.

Is ANT a Network Science?

The first obstacle in understanding actor-network theory is the name itself. Although ANT has devoted much attention to making clear how it is different from traditional sociology, including sociology of science little has been said about its relation to the newly forming network science.

The name suggests that ANT may be seen as one strand in the broad and variegated preoccupation of social scientists with network phenomena. But it is often difficult to understand what ANT has in common with all the other forms of network theory and network research that are currently receiving much attention. Is the concept of network in ANT a mere equivocation that actually has nothing to do with what has come to be recognized as network science? The concept of network theory and network science is itself fuzzy. What exactly is a network? There are a wide range of models and methodologies in many different disciplines that rely on the concept of network. Theories based on the idea of networks range from graph theory in mathematics, complexity theories in physics, studies of molecular and biological networks, neural networks in cognitive science, semantic networks in linguistics, computer networks in informatics, big data networks, and social networks in sociology. Many different disciplines contribute to the language drawn upon by network theories. In an effort to find a common denominator, the National Research Council (2006: 2) summarizes the interdisciplinary nature of network science as "the study of network representations of physical, biological, and social phenomena leading to predictive models of these phenomena."[8] From this definition it is clear that networks are transdisciplinary phenomena that can and should be understood with a view to the possibility of prediction and control. Throughout the literature concerned in one way or another with networks it is common to speak of networks as consisting of what is often termed "nodes" and "links."[9] The internet, for example, consists

---

8 | See also the summary statement (1): "Society depends on a diversity of complex networks for its very existence. In the physical sphere, these include the air transportation network, highways, railroads, the global shipping network, power grids, water distribution networks, supply networks, global financial networks, telephone systems, and the Internet. In the biological arena, they include genetic expression networks, metabolic networks, our bodies, ant colonies, herds, food webs, river basins, and the global ecological web of Earth itself. In the social domain, they include governments, businesses, universities, social clubs, churches, public and private school systems, and military organizations."

9 | See for example the standard definition in Barabasi/Newman/Watts (2006: 2): "In its simplest form, a network is nothing more than a set of discrete elements (the vertices), and a set of connections (the edges) that link the elements, typically in a pairwise fashion."

of computers as nodes and the data transfer channels, whether wired or wireless, as links connecting the nodes. A social network consists of social actors and their communicative or other relations; a biological network consists of molecules and their interactions. The National Research Council concluded that

"[...] the common core of network science is the study of complex systems whose behavior and responses are determined by exchanges and interactions between subsystems across a well-defined (possibly dynamic) set of pathways. The central point is that the behavior of a network is determined both by the pathways (structure) and by the exchanges and interactions (dynamics). Moreover the structure itself may be (and usually is) dynamic." (30)

This definition highlights an ambiguity in network theory that is of decisive importance when it comes to understanding the place of ANT within—or without—network science. The definition assumes a similarity, if not identity, between systems and networks.[10] Network theory, according to the above definition, could be understood to be a branch of systems theory. In many discussions of network science one finds ideas and concepts familiar from systems theory and cybernetics. There seems to be at least two different approaches to networks, the approach from mathematics, physics, informatics, and biology one the one side, and the approach from sociology and the human sciences on the other. Although there are crossovers, for example, social network analysis, which relies on mathematical models and methods, Castells and ANT, for example, do not see networks as systems describable in terms of structure and function and displaying mathematically describable regularities such as a scale-free architecture and power-law distributions. Latour (1988: 198) assumes that

---

10 | In the editors' statement on "What is network science?" in Brandes et al. (2013). The term "system" is used interchangeably with the term "network." Newman (2003: 2) speaks of systems having the form of networks, or "networked systems." Barabási (2012: 7) sees networks at the heart of systems and claims that "we will never understand complex systems unless we gain a deep understanding of the networks behind them." And he makes it clear that the science of networks aims at prediction and control, "the emergence and evolution of different networks is driven by a common set of fundamental laws and reproducible mechanisms" (8).

entities are irreducibly actors and for that reason cannot be successfully integrated into functional systems: "For a system to exist, entities must be clearly defined, whereas in practice this is never the case; functions must be clear, whereas most actors are uncertain whether they want to command or obey; the exchange of equivalents between entities or subsystems must be agreed, whereas everywhere there are disputes about the rate and direction of exchange."

The conceptual relation between networks and systems is uncertain and controversial. The one line of what is coming to be known as network science, including social network analysis, approaches network phenomena as a set of elements and their relations that can and must be described by functionalism and mathematical regularities. On the other hand concepts such as "self-organization," "emergence," "adaptability," and "evolution" are characteristics that can also be found in the networks described not only in physics and biology, but also by ANT, even though Latour, for example, does not use this terminology regularly. In general, it can be said, that the various theories and models of networks make use of a terminology that to a certain extent depend on systemic models of order, whether coming from the social or the natural sciences.

It is furthermore striking that both systems theory and network science claim to describe fundamental forms of order in the physical, biological, and social domains. This more or less explicit claim to universality makes it difficult to assign each to its own domain. It appears that the world is either ordered as a system or as a network, or the two concepts are synonymous, merely different ways of describing the same reality. The latter view is supported by the fact that both networks and systems are often described in terms of complexity.[11] Faced with these ambiguities it is reasonable, indeed necessary, to pose the question of whether network theory is merely a new edition of general systems theory? Can and should networks be modeled as complex adaptive systems? Are networks the same as systems? Does network theory, especially in the line coming out of the social and human sciences, offer a different view of reality and rely upon fundamentally different basic concepts and methods than those network sciences that are closer to the natural sciences and to systems theory? If ANT is to be mentioned in the same context with what has come to be known as network science, then clarification of basic definitions of what a

---

11 | See for example Taylor (2001).

network is and how networks should be investigated is necessary. What is a network if it is not a system? What is a system and how do systems differ from networks? Do ANT and the disciplines that have come to be known as network science have anything in common? Can ANT be considered a network science at all? Before looking more closely at actor-network theory it could be useful to attempt to define as clearly as possible what is being talked about when concepts such as system and network are often used almost interchangeably. This is not an academic issue, since much depends on whether social reality can be successfully modeled as a cybernetic machine. If ANT is to offer a plausible alternative to the logic of algorithms it should be clear what basic concepts and methodological principles stand behind the systems model and the actor-network model.

On Systems, Complexity, Cybernetic Machines, and Networks

What may be referred to as the paradigm of self-organizing systems is not a single theory, but a framework of theories and basic concepts from a variety of disciplines.[12] The components of this framework consist of systems theory, information theory, cybernetics, the theory of autopoietic systems in biology, synergetics, the theory of dissipative structures, theories of biochemical evolution, deterministic chaos, and related disciplines. All these different theories make use of a common stock of concepts such as "system," "complexity," "control," "emergence," "discontinuity," "code," "information," and "self-organization," to mention only a few. These theories also have a common goal, to discover general rules governing the emergence and maintenance of order. This is, of course, not a new goal for the sciences. Ever since the beginning, science in all its variations has asked questions about order and regularity in nature, human existence, and society. Nature manifests order, for example, in galaxies, planetary systems, geological formations, meteorological phenomena, chemical compounds, organisms, tissues, cells, molecules and atoms, and the subatomic realm. Order is not unique to the realm of nature. Human society

---

12 | For orientation on the paradigm of self-organizing systems see Maturana/ Varela (1987), Heylighen (2001), Bak (1996), and the various writings of Heinz von Foerster.

and culture also manifest order. The very idea of the human and social sciences presupposes knowable order in these domains. In the last decades Niklas Luhmann (1984) following Parsons, Heinz von Foerster, Maturana and Varela and others has formulated an encompassing theory of social systems based on the models and terminology of cybernetics and systems theory.

Luhmann's theory of the functional differentiation of advanced societies into semi-autonomous subsystems such as politics, law, science, religion, art, and health care, each of which self-organizes into a self-referential, autopoietic, informationally and operationally closed system by means of its own code of communication is a powerful example of how systems theory can be applied in the social sciences, as well as perhaps the most influential theoretical explication of what Latour considers to be the modern world view. Latour does not speak of systems, but of "domains" (2013: 28ff.) and he is careful to distinguish ANT from what he terms modern social theory. For Latour modern sociology is a product of the epistemological and ontological assumptions of modernity. ANT rejects a world divided up into separate domains. In order to understand what is at stake in the discussion of systems and networks it is helpful to (mis)use Luhmann's theory of social systems as a kind of backdrop for clarifying the concept of networks as used by ANT.

Luhmann's theory of social systems represents one of most powerful conceptualizations of modernity in social theory.[13] In distinction to pre-modern societies, in which the relatively non-complex social activities of economic production and distribution, establishing and maintaining political order, regulating conflicts by legal decisions, acquiring knowledge in the sciences, artistic expression and so on are integrated under the unifying force of religion, modern society is characterized by the differentiation of functions into semi-autonomous systems.[14] In modern "secularized" societies, politics is defined by the explicit exclusion of economic, artistic, educational, and religious activities. In many constitutional democracies it is illegal to strive for economic gain by means of political

---

13 | Luhmann's theory is also important for the reason that it bases society on communication. This aspect will become important for the discussion of new media below.
14 | See Luhmann (1995) and the concise statement of functional differentiation in Luhmann (1989).

office. Art and science should not serve the interests of the state. Religion for its part is excluded from politics, business, education, science, and the other social functions. Each functional sub-system organizes itself by excluding all activities that do not directly serve its purpose, its function within society. Social functions and communicative action are structured according to binary oppositions that operate as a system specific code of inclusion and exclusion. In economics, for example, activities that are not concerned in some way with buying and selling are excluded from the system. A business man may collect art, but it is business and not art, when he does so as an investment. He may donate large amounts to the Church, but if this is done with an eye to tax-deductibility it is business and not belief. In politics on the other hand only those communicative actions that are directed toward attaining and maintaining political power and office are included in the system. A politician who supports economic legislation does so not to make a profit, but to gain votes. If he supports certain legislation in order to make a personal profit, then it is business and not politics. Misuse of political office for personal gain, that is, mixing business and politics is often illegal or at least disdained.

The legal system for its part consists exclusively of communicative actions concerning what is legal and what illegal. Until the question of legality is raised and the courts must decide, nothing happens in the legal system. There is no crime and no legal judgment unless there is an accusation and thus a call for a binding decision on what is legal or not. The educational system is concerned solely with certifying acquired knowledge and skills. Learning goes on everywhere and all the time, but only when it happens in a formal course of study ending with an exam and a certification of skills is it part of the educational system and is acknowledged as such by society and by employers who have no other means to decide if a prospective employee is able to do the job or not. The media system makes the self-observation of society possible, but only in the mode of news, the improbable, the sensational, and the interesting. Redundancy is excluded from the media. Religion concerns itself with transcendence and excludes all worldly activities that are not directed toward God. Only when an event is interpreted as utterly contingent and beyond any means of worldly control does it become included in the religious system. The function of the transcendent in society is to deal with contingency. And art, as is well known, is for art alone. This is a veritable cannon of modernity. Art is for art's sake alone and not for economic gain, political influence, or anything else except art itself—whatever that may be. And no one can say what art is, except art itself. Neither religion nor politics nor business nor education nor law can say what art is. For art is by definition not foreseeable and from the perspective of politics, law, religion or anything else for that matter completely contingent. Science finally is also a semi-autonomous subsystem of society. Science is concerned only with reliable knowledge, with truth or falsity. Science therefore has nothing to do with economics, law, aesthetics, education, politics, or religion.[15]

Within the model of functional differentiation, every subsystem excludes everything in the environment which is not regulated by its particular code and expressed in its own generalized symbolic medium.[16] At the same time each functional subsystem paradoxically includes the whole world from its unique perspective. There is nothing that cannot be scientifically investigated, nothing that cannot be bought and sold, nothing that cannot be regulated by law, nothing that cannot or has not in some way been worshipped, nothing that cannot be considered art, and nothing that cannot serve political interests. The operations of the functionally autonomous subsystems are closed and self-referential, while at the same time and for this very reason being universal in scope. As self-organizing, self-referential, autopoietic systems, they operate only to continue their own operation. They do not function for the sake of any other system or with a view to achieving goals that other systems are concerned with. For this reason, the operations of one system do not constitute "information" for another system, but rather perturbations, noise, or complexity that arises in the environment and must be reduced according to the internal organization of each system. What happens in the economy may well be politically important, but only to the extent that it is not a matter of buying and selling, but of getting votes and holding on to office. If unemployment

---

15 | Latour's critique of modernity begins precisely with the rejection of this thesis. The central discovery of ANT's empirical and ethnological study of science in action is that real science has everything to do with the other social functions and cannot be distinguished from them, indeed, there is only one social function; building networks.

16 | We will return to the generalized symbolic media of the social system below in our discussion of networks from the point of view of new media studies and the social operating system.

leads to social unrest the political system will process this disturbance as information about how to gain votes and maintain power. If the courts decide that industrial waste must be recycled this will have an impact on business, but only insofar as managers now have to calculate profit and loss on a different basis. Natural catastrophes can be dealt with by the religious system as the will of God or by offering hope in a better future. They are dealt with differently by the political system, economic system, science, and the other systems. The press makes an issue out of the potential dangers of climate change, but for science it is a question of verification or falsification alone, and not a question of sensational news, of international treaties, of the costs of renewable energy and so on.

The functional differentiation of modern society enables specialization of communicative action by reducing the complexity of the environment. Only those perturbations in the environment, that can be coded by a system and coordinated by a generalized symbolic medium become information for the system and can be taken up into its operations. In order to be as flexible and viable as possible the system has to be able to encode as many perturbations from the environment as possible.[17] This is achieved by means of increasing internal complexity, becoming more differentiated, including more possible states and processes. In this way modern society has attained an unprecedented differentiation and complexity in the domains of material reproduction, regulation and conflict resolution, scientific knowledge, and the professionalization of labor, to mention only the a few of the social systems. On the other hand, there is no overarching, unifying, integrating form of communication bringing all the different functions under a single "roof" of meaning and value as is typical of so-called pre-modern societies. Instead there is pluralism. There is a proliferation of system codes, jargons, subcultures, ideologies, disciplines, professions, life-styles, and world views. One may indeed speak of a world society or of a global village, but in fact there is no one all-encompassing social system, but much rather a plurality of semi-autonomous subsystems constantly bumping into each other in an awkward and precarious dance of mutual adaptation, technically termed "structural coupling." (Maturana/Varela 1987: 75)

---

17 | See Ashby's Law of Requisite Variety, "only variety can destroy variety" in Ashby (1956).

At the basis of this view of society is Luhmann's reception not only of Parsons, Weber, Durkheim, Habermas and other central figures of modern social theory, but also what can be termed the theory of self-referential, autopoietic, operationally and informationally closed systems.[18] What follows is a rather abstract and summary reconstruction of the systems model which will serve the purpose of allowing a fruitful comparison with actor-network theory and a clarification of the place that ANT could take within network science.

What is a System?

A system can be defined as a functional set of structural relations among selected elements.[19] From the point of view of systems theory, whatever kind of order we may be speaking of, whether in nature or society, we are talking about elements integrated into a whole according to certain rules. A galaxy is made up of stars, planets, gases, molecules, water is made up of hydrogen and oxygen, an organism is made up of cells. All of these are combinations of elements in relatively stable relations, that is to say, they are systems. The same may be said of social and cultural phenomena. Social institutions and cultural phenomena are made up of actors, artifacts, and signs that are related according to rules. The theory of systemic order opens up a unifying perspective from which reality, whether natural or social, may be seen as a systemic phenomenon. The general theory of self-organizing systems attempts to describe the basic characteristics of systemic order. It proposes to show what all complex systems have in common. In the following we will briefly look at some the major characteristics that can be ascribed to complex adaptive systems as such and pose the question, if networks can be described similarly, or if the network model does not differ from the systems model in important ways.

To begin with it can be said that systems typically have a principle of organization that fulfills at least three functions: *selection, relationing,* and *steering*. One of the basic assumptions of general systems theory is that almost everything may be viewed as a system. A system (from Greek *to*

---

18 | There are many contributors to what may be called general systems theory. Especially important for Luhmann are Humberto Maturana, Francisco Varela, Heinz von Foerster, W. R. Ashby, and George Spencer-Brown.

19 | The following description of the system model follows Krieger (1996).

systema) is by definition an ordered composition of elements.[20] A table, for example, consists of a top and of legs. In order to have a table one has first to select the top and the legs out of all possible things in the world. Secondly, one has to put these elements into certain relations with each other. The top has to sit on the legs and not the other way round. This may be termed "relationing." Finally, the relationing of the elements can be considered to "control" or "steer" the function or "operation" of the system. Every system can be said to fulfill a specific function. The table has the function of, let us say, providing a working space at middle body height. Systems are functional as well as dynamic entities insofar as they typically perform some kind of operation for some kind of purpose or end. This accounts for the typical reliance of systems thinking on final causes and not merely efficient causes. This also means that systems do not merely exist, they "act." There is a system, therefore, only when elements are selected, related, and controlled or steered in such a way that a function is fulfilled. The principle of organization that selects, relates, and steers a system may be called a "code." From the point of view of a general theory of systemic order, every system can be understood to be organized by a code that fulfills the three functions of selection, relationing, and steering.

A second common characteristic of complex systems is that they are based upon a *difference* between the system and its environment. This difference is not accidental, but is constitutive for the system. When a system comes into being, there is much in the world that is excluded from it. The very notion of selection implies not only inclusion, but also exclusion. To select is to choose certain possibilities out of a variety of options and thus not to choose others. This means that a system is always made up of less than all possible elements and combinations thereof. Selection necessarily implies exclusion. Exclusion is therefore constitutive of systemic order. Everything that is excluded from a system is called the "environment." Since a system is constituted by selection, every system will have an environment made up of everything that is not selected by the system's code. This implies that a system can be a system only *because* it is distinguished from the environment. If a system is not different from the environment, there

---

20 | See the typical definition offered by Laszlo/Krippner (1998: 47): "In its broadest conception, a 'system' may be described as a complex of interacting components together with the relationships among them that permit the identification of a boundary-maintaining entity or process."

is no system. If the difference between the system and the environment becomes blurred and cannot be maintained, the system disintegrates and disappears. A system, therefore, is based upon a difference. Not identity is constitutive for systemic order, but difference. For example, a company that makes tables hires workers and sets up a factory whose functionality is so organized such that tables are produced. Not just anybody can walk into the factory and start doing things. Only employees are permitted to enter. Not just anybody can be an employee, only those who build tables. Not just anything can be done in the factory, only tables can be produced; not chairs, automobiles, clothes etc. Without clear boundaries there would be chaos and the company wouldn't be able to organize its operations in such a way that it could survive in a highly competitive market.

There is a further important corollary to the difference between system and environment. Obviously, no matter how large and complex a system may be, it is necessarily less complex than the environment. Even if the company were very large and also made chairs and many other kinds of furniture, it would still produce only a small segment of everything that can be produced. No organization can organize everything. Systemic order, based upon selection, relationing, and steering and the construction of a difference between system and environment must therefore be seen as a *reduction of complexity*. Systems always come into being because of the need to reduce complexity. They are viable and survive only if they successfully exclude most of the world. If there could be said to be a "cause" for systemic order, then it could be found in the "problem" of complexity. In short, it could be claimed that order is an attempt to solve the problem of chaos. This is the reason why systems solutions present themselves as soon as complexity is perceived as a problem. As we will see later, networks are not primarily defined by the attempt to reduce complexity. Although it is common to speak of networks as complex, complexity is not a "problem" for networks in the same way it can be considered a problem for systems. It is not because complexity needs to be reduced that networks arise, but because complexity needs to be built in the right way. Networks do not arise from the need to reduce complexity. A network therefore is not constituted by a sharp difference to an environment. As we will see, this does not mean networks have no borders. They have their own forms of inclusion and exclusion.

It is helpful to note in this context that the concept of "difference" in systems theory, just as the concept of "code," is also—and not accidentally—a central concept in semiotics. When Saussure describes language as a system of differences and when Bateson defines information as a difference that makes a difference, they are pointing to an aspect of meaning that can very well be understood from the perspective of systems theory. The concept of "difference" plays a similar role in systems theory to the role it plays in semiotics and in much poststructuralist thought as well. In all these theoretical positions identity is fundamentally dependent on and secondary to difference. In a certain sense, the same can be said of ANT. Latour (1988: 153ff) prefers to speak of the principle of "irreduction" instead of difference.[21] Nonetheless, there is a significant tension in the concept of difference as it is used in the systems model and in the network model. Systems, as well as networks, can be understood from the perspective of a relational ontology, that is to say, reality consists primarily of relations. The world does not consist of entities, but of relations, differences, associations much as Saussure would say that language consists of relations and not *relata*. Entities of all kinds are constituted primarily by their relations. There are important differences, however, in the meaning of difference.

According to the systems model, as noted above, difference is a constitutive principle of systemic closure. The system/environment difference is established by the selection, relationing, and steering of elements. The system/environment difference insures the operational and also informational closure of the system. Without a clear boundary, without a difference between self and other, self-reference would be impossible. The system would not be able to direct its operations toward its own maintenance, since it would not "know" what the system is and what the environment is. In the network model, the difference between a network and what may be considered "outside" or "beyond" the network is not of another quality than the differences and relations making up the network. Difference does not constitute the network, but serves as interface for network operations. We will return to this important distinction between systems and networks below.

The third major characteristic of complex systems is that they *construct their own elements*. Just as a system is always made up of less than what is possible, it is also always more than a mere a collection of parts. A system

---

21 | "Nothing is, by itself, either reducible or irreducible to anything else [...] There are only trials of strength, of weakness. Or more simply, there are only trials." (Latour 1988: 158).

is not a disordered pile of things that previously were lying around in the environment. A table, for example, consists of a top and of legs. Before there were tables, there were no such things as "tops" and "legs" lying about in the world. There were pieces of wood, slabs of stone, etc., but there were no "tops" and no "legs," that is, not until the code that organizes the table selected and related certain wooden, stone, or whatever things for the purpose of providing, let us say, a working space at middle body height. The code, therefore, can be said to have constructed the elements of the system out of things that were lying around in the environment. The elements of the system are not the things that were lying around in the environment. Elements are not things at all. They are functions. This principle has very important and far-reaching consequences. It means, for example, that the elements of a system are not substances in the traditional philosophical sense, namely a given carrier of qualities. Instead, they are functions. A system does not consist of things at all, but of elements that are related in such a way that they fulfill a certain function. A top and legs exist only in tables and only so far as they fulfill certain functions. If there were no tables, there would be no tops and legs in the world. And as soon as tops and legs come into existence, there are also tables. The table system can therefore be said to construct its own elements.

It is from this important characteristic of systems that the idea of "functional equivalence" arises. Just about anything and everything can function as a tabletop or as the legs of a table. If a human being, for example, goes down on hands and knees and holds this uncomfortable position long enough, he or she can serve as a table. Even water, as the Eskimos well know, can serve the function of a table. A tabletop and legs are therefore not substances—it doesn't matter what sort of things they are made of—but functions. And anything that fulfills the function adequately can serve as element of the system. The building, the machines, and the workers in a furniture factory all have functions, and all can be replaced by something, or someone, else that performs the function better, cheaper, quicker, etc.

What matters for a system is how something functions and that the functions of an element arise from the internal relations among the elements.[22] A tabletop, not a substance, is whatever functions as a tabletop,

---

22 | This is reflected in Ackoff's (1981: 15–16) definition of a system as necessarily having the following properties: "1. Each element has an effect on the function-

whether it be wood, metal, glass, water or whatever. Although the environment puts constraints on functionality, elements are constructed by the
code of a system and not by the environment. If general systems theory
claims that everything can be viewed as a system, then it is proposing
a view of reality as a functional totality and not as the sum of all entities. If, as Luhmann says, there are systems, then it follows that there are
no things. In the world of systems there is no-thing at all, but functions
instead. This principle also accounts for the typical holism of systems
theory, which sees system functions and operations as emergent properties that cannot be derived from the parts. Holism is one of the major
characteristics of the systems model and one of important arguments for
its theoretical advantages with regard to the typical analytic model of science. According to the analytic model order is the manifestation of parts
and their interactions and in order to understand order all one needs to
do is analyze something into its parts, describe the properties of the parts
and deduce from these properties the characteristics of the whole. For the
analytic model the whole is not greater than the sum of the parts. There
are no qualities in the whole that are not in the parts and for this reason
there is no final causality as well. For the systems model on the contrary,
the whole is always greater than the sum of the parts and systemic qualities cannot be deduced from the qualities of the parts. One cannot derive
the function of a table top from any piece of wood, stone, or metal that
happens to be lying around in the world. The table is perhaps a poor example, since it is not a natural entity. If we are talking about a system that
is not constructed by a carpenter, God, or anybody else for that matter,
then the properties of the system may be called "emergent" on the basis of
self-organization. This becomes clear the moment biological systems are
taken as examples.[23]

---

ing of the whole. 2. Each element is affected by at least one other element in the
system. 3. All possible subgroups of elements also have the first two properties."
23 | For non-biological systems see for example the hydrogen atom: "the hydrogen
atom, [...] has a typical valence as an integral system made up of a proton and a
neutron in the nucleus and an electron in the lowest energy shell around it, together
with short-lived exchange particles and forces. The chemical valence of the entire
structure is not present in the proton, the neutron, the electron, or any exchange
particle taken in isolation; it is an emergent property of the whole ensemble and a
result of the synergistic relationship among its parts." Laszlo/Krippner (1998: 57).

In the case of organic systems, functionality can clearly be illustrated. A living being, an animal for example, consists of cells, organs, tissue, skin, bones, stomach, liver, heart, etc. These are the elements of the living system. Cells and organs obviously do not lie about in the environment until someone like Dr. Frankenstein comes along and puts them together in order to make a living being. The organic system, that is, the genetic code that organizes the biological system constructs its own elements. The way in which the genetic code programs the development of cells, tissue, and organs is extremely complex and not at all comparable to the way in which an idea or a drawing might be said to "program" the building of a table. Nonetheless, from the point of view of a general theory of systemic order, it may be said that both physical and biological systems consist of elements that have been selected and related into a functional totality. In both cases the processes of selection, relationing, and steering may be said to construct the elements of the system.

The principle that a system constructs its own elements also clearly applies to semiotic systems, for example, a language. The human voice can produce an almost infinite number of sounds, but only very few are selected as words in a specific language. The typical "th" sound of the English language plays no significant role in German. The code of the German language has selected only certain possible sounds that the human voice can utter to become elements of the German language. Just as a table does not need to be made of wood or metal, but can consist of almost anything, a language can select any sound the voice can produce and even more does not need acoustic material at all. Gestures, written signs, and objects of all sorts can serve the same function as verbal signs. A word in a language, therefore, is not a thing or a substance, but—as Saussure noted—a function within a differential system of signs. It is the system, that is, the semiotic code that constructs the significant elements of which a language consists. The principle that every system constructs its own elements provides the theoretical foundation for concepts such as self-organization, emergence, and autopoiesis and also for the school of thought that has come to known as "constructivism."[24]

---

24 | On constructivism see the works of Heinz von Foerster, Ernst von Glasersfeld, and Humberto Maturana and Francisco Varela. For the current discussion see the various issues of Foundations of Science The official Journal of the Association for Foundations of Science, Language and Cognition, Kluwer; as well as the wealth

The fourth and final defining characteristic of systemic order is that every complex system in one way or another is *self-referential,* that is, it refers its operations to itself. If it can be said that every complex system constructs its own elements, then it can also be said that systems have a tendency to maintain their own organization and structure, that is, to resist change. Even such a simple system as a table, for example, tends to resist attempts to use it for some other purpose than that for which it was intended. If someone attempts to use a table as a chair or as a bathtub, they won't have much success. The table selects the state of being a table, rather than the state of being a chair, a bathtub, or whatever. A table, it can be said, operates in order to maintain its own organization, that is, its own structure and function. Once the table system has appeared, that is, once a certain form of order comes into being, disorder is less probable than order. It is not likely that the table will turn into a chair or a cat. It will be the same table when I come back home in the evening as it was at break-fast. It repeats itself and produces redundancy. There arises an asymmetry between order and disorder. Ashby (1956) refers to this aspect of systemic order as the "principle of self-organization."

In order to organize itself something has to operate upon itself. Self-maintenance implies that a system operates in some way upon itself. This asymmetry may also be seen to be a consequence of the system/environment difference. For how can a system refer its operations to itself, if there is no difference between the system and the environment? The system/environment difference is the foundation for any distinction between self and other. From this point of view, it can be said that self-referential operations are a prerequisite for systemic order. Mere boundary maintenance

of material at the Radical Constructivism website: http://www.univie.ac.at/constructivism/; and at the Principia Cybernetica website: http://pespmc1.vub.ac.be/DEFAULT.html. A. Riegler defines constructivism as follows: "Constructivism is the idea that we construct our own world rather than it being determined by an outside reality. In its most consistent form, Radical Constructivism (RC) claims that we cannot transcend our experiences. Thus it doesn't make sense to say that our constructions gradually approach the structure of an external reality. The mind is necessarily an epistemological solipsist, in contrast to being an ontological solipsist who maintains that this is all there is, namely a single mind within which the only world exists. RC recognizes the impossibility of the claim that the world does not exist." (Riegler 2001: 1)

expressed as resistance to change or redundancy may be termed the "minimal" form of self-reference. In terms of classical Western philosophy the code may be said to be the *eidos* or essence of the system, that is, it is that which makes a thing to be what it is. At least in this very minimal sense of structure maintenance, the operations of any system can be termed self-referential.

The idea of self-reference derives not only from the system/environment difference, but also from the controlling or steering function of the code. The code selects certain elements and relates them in certain ways so that the system operates to fulfill a certain function. Selection and relationing are "steered" by the code such that a function is fulfilled. The analysis and description of the steering function in systemic organization is usually the task of *cybernetics*.[25] Cybernetics is concerned with feedback

---

25 | Cybernetics was introduced by Norbert Wiener in Cybernetics: or Control and Communication in the Animal and the Machine. Current discussion can be found at the Principia Cybernetica website: http://pespmc1.vub.ac.be/DEFAULT.html, where "cybernetics" is defined as follows: "Norbert Wiener, a mathematician, engineer and social philosopher, coined the word 'cybernetics' from the Greek word meaning steersman. He defined it as the science of communication and control in the animal and the machine. Ampere, before him, wanted cybernetics to be the science of government. For philosopher Warren McCulloch, cybernetics was an experimental epistemology concerned with the communication within an observer and between the observer and his environment. Stafford Beer, a management consultant, defined cybernetics as the science of effective organization. Anthropologist Gregory Bateson noted that whereas previous sciences dealt with matter and energy, the new science of cybernetics focuses on form and pattern. [...] [Cybernetics can also be defined as (DK)] an interdisciplinary approach to organization, irrespective of a system's material realization. Whereas general systems theory is committed to holism on the one side and to an effort to generalize structural, behavioral developmental features of living organisms on the other side, cybernetics is committed to an epistemological perspective that views material wholes as analyzable without loss, in terms of a set of components plus their organization. Organization accounts for how the components of such a system interact with one another, and how this interaction determines and changes its structure. It explains the difference between parts and wholes and is described without reference to their material forms. The disinterest of cybernetics in material implications separates it from all sciences that designate their empirical

loops by means of which the outputs, or system operations, become inputs into the system allowing for further operations. Insofar as every system is organized by a code that selects, relates, and steers operations, every system can be described from the point of view of cybernetics. A general theory of systemic order is therefore also a general cybernetics. Historically, system theory and cybernetics arose together and complemented each other. The moment that reality as a whole is viewed in terms of systemic order, everything whatever can also be viewed from the point of view of cybernetics. Although we don't usually think of a table as a cybernetic system, it can be said to steer its operations in the minimal sense of maintaining its own structure and resisting change.

The theory of cybernetic or self-steering systems usually describes systems that are dynamic in a much more obvious way than a table. The dynamics of a cybernetic system can be defined as the way in which the operations, the outputs of the system become inputs back into the system, thus creating a circular causality. The circular causality of a cybernetic system has the effect of maintaining the system in a certain state or "reference value." Cybernetic systems are self-steering systems, since the operations of the system function as information for the system. Information is not anything at all that happens in the environment, but only those events that the code of the system has previously selected as "relevant." This circularity can also be termed operational closure. The operations of the system are directed toward the system itself and not toward something else. The system reacts to its own operations such that it can maintain its reference value. A typical cybernetic system is a thermostat. Indeed, the thermostat is one of the most often cited examples of a cybernetic machine. When the temperature in a room falls below a certain point, the thermostat registers this event in the environment as relevant information and turns on the heating unit. When the temperature rises because of the output of the heater, the thermostat registers this event in the environment as information, which information initiates an operation within the system, it turns the heater off. The output of the system thus becomes an

domain by subject matters such as physics, biology, sociology, engineering and general systems theory. Its epistemological focus on organization, pattern and communication has generated methodologies, a logic, laws, theories and insights that are unique to cybernetics and have wide-ranging implications in other fields of inquiry."

input back into the system in a causal circle of operations. Such feedback loops can be positive or negative. They can be so complex that their effects are non-linear and irreversible. To the extent that these effects do not lead to dissolution of the system, they can be described as adaptive. In the case of the heating system, we see that it operates in order to maintain a certain state that is defined by the code as a reference value, for example, normal room temperature. In the case of a table, it can hardly be said to be self-steering in this sense of the word, nonetheless even a table can manifest a minimal self-reference, for it operates to maintain itself as a table.

Organic systems have their own form of self-reference and accordingly their own cybernetics. The kind of self-reference peculiar to living systems is called "autopoiesis."[26] Autopoiesis (from Greek *"auto"* = self and *"poiein"* = produce) literally means "self-producing." Organic systems are self-producing systems, that is, they operate not in order to change some state in the environment, for example, the temperature in a room, but in order to continue their own operations. If the self-steering of a mechanical system such as a table or an air-conditioning unit are termed a 1st order cybernetics, the cybernetics of living systems may be termed 2nd order cybernetics.[27] Organic systems have a circular causality in a way that mechanical systems do not. It is not accidental or irrelevant that the output of a thermostatically controlled heating system raises the temperature of a room, but it is accidental and irrelevant for a cow that the heat it and

---

26 | The theory of "autopoiesis" was proposed by Maturana and Varela (1973: 78) "An autopoietic machine is a machine organized (defined as a unity) as a network of processes of production (transformation and destruction) of components which: (i) through their interactions and transformations continuously regenerate and realize the network of processes (relations) that produced them; and (ii) constitute it (the machine) as a concrete unity in space in which they (the components) exist by specifying the topological domain of its realization as such a network."

27 | Although the term 2nd order cybernetics was introduced by Heinz von Foerster in order to describe reflexive processes, it is being used here in a different sense, namely, to describe the form of self-reference typical to living systems. The form of self-reference typical to physical systems such a table or a hydrogen atom can be termed 1st order cybernetics and the typical self-reference of a semiotic system can be called 3rd order cybernetics. See Krieger (1996) for a discussion of the three levels of systems order.

other cows discharge in the stall raises the temperature in the barn. The cows eat, breath, and so on in order to continue their own rumination and breathing, not in order to heat the stall so that the farmer can milk them more comfortably. Organic systems operate exclusively in order to continue their own operations. They are autopoietic systems. The system itself is what counts and not any changes that might occur in the environment as a result of what the system does. Evolution, within the systems model, may be explained as the adaptive dynamic of autopoietic, operationally and informationally closed systems on the basis of internal variation within the constraints of an over-complex environment.

Finally, with regard to semiotic systems, the kind of self-reference and the kind of cybernetics typical of these systems are of an altogether different sort. For a system of meaning self-reference takes the form of self-identification by means of communication. Meaning systems operate in order to produce meaning. The production of meaning implies the construction of signs, for it is signs that carry meaning. Signs, however, carry meaning only in and through "language," that is, communication. Meaning systems operate, therefore, as communication systems. The way in which communication steers meaning processes can be described by "3rd order cybernetics." 3rd order cybernetics describes the specific operational and informational closure of semiotic systems. The application of systems theory in the social sciences can be seen as various descriptions of how self-referential communicative operations lead to the emergence of what is usually called social structure. For Luhmann's theory of functional differentiation, this means that the political system is coded by the binary distinction of power/not-power such that all communicative actions that are concerned with gaining political office and holding on to it fall within the political system and all communicative actions concerned with making money, getting an education, creating art, making legal decisions, worshiping God and so on are excluded from the political system. All these other forms of communicative action make up the environment of the political system. Since they are in the environment of the political system they can be "perceived" only as perturbations and not as information by the political system. They can only become issues for the political system to the extent they can be subsumed under the imperative of gaining and maintaining power. Everything that happens in the environment of the political system consists of perturbations and complexity for the political system, to which politics reacts according to its own code. The same may be said, mutatis mutandis, for all other functional sub-systems.

In summary, we may say that complex systems have certain common characteristics that constitute them as systems. All such systems are organized by a code that selects, relates, and steers the elements of the system such that it differentiates itself from an environment and fulfills a certain function. This implies the autopoietic construction of system-specific elements, which although constrained by material characteristics, are not substances, but functions. This is a task that can only be accomplished when the system in some way refers its operations back to itself, which means it can be said to be operationally closed and self-referential.

If complex systems have at least the above mentioned four characteristics in common, what makes the many different kinds of systems different from each other? This question is not unimportant, since much confusion has resulted from the tendency to apply concepts, models, and methods, which were developed for the analysis and description of one kind of system, to systems of an altogether different kind. The concept of "information" is a case in point. Information means one thing in the theory of signal transmission (Shannon/Weaver 1963), something completely different in the theory of living systems (Maturana/Varela 1987) and something different again when used in theories of language and culture (Bateson 1988).

If we wish to distinguish different kinds of systems, it is useful to distinguish between different levels of emergent order. "Emergence" may be defined as the non-predictable and non-derivable appearance of structures that are capable of "integrating" previously existing structures. Life appeared non-predictably as an integration of physical and mechanical systems, that is, atomic, molecular, and chemical systems. Life cannot be reduced to mechanical or physical systems or derived from them. Even the simplest biological entity is organized by a code that is sufficiently complex to harness physical processes for the construction of living matter. No physical code can do this. The jump to a higher level of emergent order occurs when a new kind of code, in this case, the genetic code, comes into being. The genetic code has the capacity to use and manipulate systemic order on the physical and chemical level in ways that physical systems cannot. In the same way, human cultural systems appeared non-predictably as integrations of living systems, above all large central nervous systems, and cannot be reduced to these systems or derived from them. No amount of physics or biology will explain a Mozart symphony or even adequately describe a picnic as a cultural event. Much time and energy has been spent trying to explain meaning, thought, self-consciousness, and cultural phenomena on the basis of the operations of the brain. The brain, however, is a biological system. The operations of the brain are those of a genetically coded organism. The brain is not semiotically coded, even if semiotic coding uses the complexity of a large central nervous system in order to emerge as a form of order in its own right.

No description of recursive structuring of nerve impulses, no matter how complex, will adequately account for the meaning of a word or explain a language. Meaning cannot be reduced to biology any more than life can be reduced to chemical processes. The elements of a meaning system are signs and neither nerve cells nor electronic impulses. With regard for the principle that a system constructs its own elements, it becomes conceivable that a sufficiently complex machine, a computer for example, could perform the same function as the brain and form the basis for intelligence. It is an accident that semiotic order emerged from an organic basis. Meaning, as almost all religions and many philosophical systems have claimed, is not dependent on life. No system of meaning, no culture, people, or nation has stepped back from sacrificing biological life for the sake of meaning, without which, as often proclaimed, life is not worth living. Meaning may therefore be seen as a unique level of emergent order that cannot be reduced to organic or inorganic systems. As such, it has its own specific coding, semiotic coding, which is distinct from the coding of natural systems or the genetic coding of living systems.

The emergence of higher levels of order on the basis of lower levels makes it tempting to think of "emergence" as synonymous to "self-organization" and to speak of the evolution of the universe as a self-organizing process (Kaufmann 1993). Of course, it can also be claimed that God, or the transcendental ego, or some other omnipotent agency created the universe and everything within it. In all these cases it has been decided to name the "self" that self-organizes in a certain way. The act of naming is very important for it decides who we are and which of many possible worlds we live in. When a meaning system organizes itself around a certain self-designation, a world of possibilities and impossibilities comes into being. On the level of the system as a whole self-reference is always in some way a "religious" decision. The function of religion in the sense of opening up of a world horizon of meaning arises from the necessary self-reference of any system of meaning. A general systems theory would not attempt to dictate what religious communication talks about. We may believe in whatever we choose or in whatever chooses us. The theory of self-organizing systems has no prejudice with regard to whom or what we say we are, to whom or what created us, but attempts to describe the way in which self-reference on the level of meaning arises. For systems that construct meaning, self-reference amounts to making the system itself into something meaningful. The meaning that a system gives itself can be said to be its "identity." The identity of the system as a whole can be termed "ontological" identity. Within the parameters set by such fundamental distinctions as being/non-being, meaning/meaningless, real/unreal, good/evil, etc. sub-systemic identities on the cultural, social, and personal levels emerge. Throughout history the answer to the question of self-identity has been given (or found) in many different ways, indeed, it can be said that the history of cultures and religions is nothing other than the temporal series of meaningful self-references.

If one can speak of a unified theory of complex systems, then the basic model of such a system is self-organizing (autopoietic), self-referential, operationally and informationally closed. Systems are constituted by a difference between the system and its environment such that information cannot flow into the system from the environment, but must be internally constructed on the basis of the organization or "structures" of the system. The organizing principle of the system constructs its elements such that they fulfill specific, interdependent functions, from which emerges an order that cannot be explained on the basis of the parts alone (holism). The driving force behind the self-organization of systemic order is the "problem" of complexity. According to Ashby's (1956: 206ff) law of requisite variety only variety can destroy variety, which implies that systems attempt to adapt to an always more complex environment by means of building up internal complexity. Complexity refers to the quantity of elements and quantity as well as quality of possible relations that they can enter into. A measure of complexity is the amount of states a system can have or pass through. The more elements and the more relations the organization of a system allows, the more complex the system becomes, the more possible states it can have. The more possible states a system can have, the greater the chances the system can remain viable in the face of unexpected events in the environment. Of course, the more internal complexity a system builds up, the greater the chances of at least the appearance of randomness or even chaos in the operations of the system. The more complex a system becomes the more mistakes it can make, with unforeseeable consequences. This situation has come to be called "edge of chaos," or the "onset of chaos" which can stimulate autocatalytic process and self-organization (Kaufmann 1993). This means that there is no absolute, all-encompassing reduction of complexity to order. On the basis of selection, the system/environment difference, and self-reference, it can be said that the environment will always be more complex than the system, no matter how complex the system becomes, and if it becomes so complex that it can no longer control its own operations and states, then it is no longer viable and dissolves into the environment.

Ecology: System or Network?

The systems model, indeed, what has been called systems thinking entered into general public awareness with the first Club of Rome Report "The Limits of Growth" published in 1972 under the leadership of Dennis and Donella Meadows. The World Model used for the analysis of factors affecting the limits to growth was based on holism and the interdependence of elements leading to emergent properties that could not be derived from the elements individually. The basic concepts, the methodology, as well as the focus on the interaction of society with the natural environment that came to the fore in The Limits to Growth did much to brand the new science of ecology as a systems science. As much as the systems model is associated with ecology—the very term "ecosystem" expresses this connection—it is interesting to note that the object of ecological investigation, what is described in ecology, that is, the interaction of organisms with the environment cannot itself be considered a system. One of the fundamental tenets of the systems model is the constitutive difference between a system and the environment. For example, a frog may be conceptualized as an organic system whose environment is the pond in which it lives. If the interactions of the frog with the environment are considered as a system, then what distinguishes this system from its environment? What is the environment of the pond? If we suppose it is the farm, in which the pond exists, then the ecological principle of interaction of organism and environment demands that the effects of agriculture on the pond and the interactions between pond and farm be taken account of. The entire farm then becomes the system. Again the question arises, what is the environment of the farm? If the farm is near a city, then the ecological impact of the city on the farm must be taken account of. The farm-city complex becomes the ecosystem. Here again the question of what then constitutes the environment arises.

Whenever there is a system, there is an environment that must be conceptualized as different from the system. How could the system select, relate, and steer elements, refer its operations to itself, establish and maintain autopoiesis, if there were no difference between system and environment? As soon as ecology begins to include parts of the environment in the system, the system/environment border is pushed outward and re-established on a higher level. The ecological principle requires that the interactions between the system and the environment form the object of investigation. This immediately includes the environment within the system and establishes a new system that requires a new environment. Ecology therefore leads directly to the Gaia hypothesis. The entire world, indeed, the universe must, in principle at least, be included within the ecosystem. According to the systems model, however, there can be no total system that includes everything. Systemic order is based upon selection, exclusion, and the reduction of complexity. The ecological model, on the contrary, is based on inclusion of all factors and increase of complexity. It would seem that ecology forms a kind of proof-case for systems theory. Can the complex interdependencies typical of ecology be modeled as a form of systemic order and if not how can they be modeled in a different way?

The importance of ecology for the discussion of systems and networks is not to be underestimated. Latour (2004) has proposed to explain the political relevance of actor-network theory as well as the concept of network itself in terms of ecology. Ecology is usually understood to be the science of the interactions between organisms and their environment. An ecosystem is defined as a "community of living organisms (plants, animals and microbes) in conjunction with the nonliving components of their environment (things like air, water and mineral soil), interacting as a system."[28] Indeed, for many, the idea of an ecosystem is the prime example of what a system is. In addition to this, ecosystems are often also described as networks. A few lines further down the same Wikipedia article cited above goes on to say that "ecosystems are defined by the network of interactions

28 | http://en.wikipedia.org/wiki/Ecosystems (accessed January 2014).

among organisms, and between organisms and their environment." To speak simultaneously of systems and networks, as noted above, is typical of many approaches in both systems science and network science. The point is not to repeat what has already been said about the dangers of confusing basic concepts, but to explain why ecology might be an important test case for the comparison of systems and networks. It is no accident, as we shall see, that Latour (2011, 2013a, 2013b) calls for a decision to take sides with ecology as the appropriate vision for a future beyond modernism.

It is furthermore no accident that one of the most concise statements Luhmann made of functional differentiation is in a small book entitled "Ecological Communication" (1989). Luhmann defines the social system as an autopoietic, self-referential and therefore operationally as well as informationally closed system. The operations of the social system are for Luhmann communications. Communication, the flow of information, takes place only within social systems and not between social systems and their environments. This is what self-reference and informational closure means. There is no exchange of information and no communication between system and environment. Ecology, however, proposes to investigate and understand exactly these relations. Ecological communication is therefore not only one of the most pressing problems for today's society, but, from the perspective of the systems model, almost a contradiction in itself. At the outset Luhmann (1989: 5–6) states quite clearly that the ecological question contains a fundamental paradox, namely, "[...] it has to treat all facts in terms of unity *and difference*, i.e., in terms of the unity of the ecological interconnection and the difference of system and environment that breaks this interconnection down." Functional differentiation breaks society down into semi-autonomous subsystems, each of which bans the others into the environment and encodes all communication according to its constitutive binary principle of inclusion and exclusion. Social communication understood as communication within society as a whole outside the functional sub-systems does not exist; rather, society is made up of economic, political, religious, artistic, educational etc. communication, whereby each system excludes all others and banns them into the environment. Communicative actions aiming at making a profit are part of the economic system, but not part of the political system. As soon as political office is used to make a personal profit this may become a sensation and a scandal for the media system, or an issue for the legal system, but it is not politics, and the political system will undertake everything it can to see that it is banned into the environment.

Functional differentiation reorganizes and reconstructs communicative action on the basis of the selection, relationing, and steering activities of different systemic codes. Not only is it impossible for society to communicate with the natural environment, but even the subsystems of society cannot communicate with each other. Society as a whole can only be structured by the difference communication/no-communication. But as soon as communication begins, at least in the modern world, it differentiates itself into the various functional subsystems. The codes of the functional subsystems constitute different kinds of "rationality," an economic rationality, a political rationality, a scientific rationality, a religious rationality, but society as whole has no specific form of rationality. Luhmann admits that "a centerless society cannot assert a rationality of its own but has to rely on the subsystem rationalities of its function systems (1989: 134)." Each functional system sees the world from its unique perspective and interprets events in the environment—whether natural or social—according to its own code. This means that the central concern of ecology, the interaction of the system with its environment, cannot be understood as a system.

The relations of the system to the environment can become a theme of systems science in evolutionary terms as an adaptive interdependence of system and environment. Luhmann follows Maturana/Varela (1987) who define the adaptive relations of a system to the environment as "structural coupling," that is, as a "[...] history or recurrent interactions leading to the structural congruence between two (or more) systems" (75). Regular and recurring perturbations in the environment can "select" certain system states such that these become relatively stable. There emerges what can be observed as adaptive interdependencies between systems and their environments. The relations of system to environment purely external and are left to the mechanisms of natural selection, that is, random variety and accidental selection. Over long periods of time an under conditions of recurring constraints in the environment accidental variations in system states can become "selected" such that the organization of the system changes and thus "adapts" to the environment. On the level of social systems, Luhmann (1989: 15ff) speaks of "resonance." Relations between systems and their environments are left to the "resonance" of the system to disturbances in the environment.

Resonance can be defined as the tendency of any system to enhance its ability to adapt to changes in the environment by means of building up internal complexity. The more internal complexity a system has the more disturbances in the environment become relevant for the system. Systems with a high degree of internal complexity can react to more changes in the environment more quickly and in a greater variety of ways than systems of lesser complexity. Recalling Ashby's Law of Requisite Variety, that variety alone destroys variety; the concept of resonance can be used to explain how systems can be viable, adaptable, and competitive over against an always more complex environment and thus give at least the appearance of communication with the environment. But this is only an appearance. Elements of a system are functions and not actors or mediators. The principle of functional equivalence implies that apart from material constraints anything at all that can be made to serve a particular function and can become an element of a system. The tabletop can be anything that serves this purpose and anything that does, wood, metal, glass, or whatever, is subsumed under the system code and reduced to its function. Everything that isn't selected by the system as an element is excluded, banned into the environment, and can no longer build an association with the system, but only disturb it.[29]

If ecology is understood as the concern for whole encompassing systems and everything in the environment and if these relations are to be more than mere coincidences of natural selection, then it would seem that the systems model has little to do with ecology. An "eco-system," if this term is not a contradiction in itself, attempts to describe the unity of the system and its environment and is not concerned with the separate system-specific rationalities of the many individual organisms that live structurally coupled to each other. On the basis of the systems model, Luhmann (1989: 138) is forced to admit that "system rationality increasingly loses its claim to be world rationality." What "world rationality" would be remains unanswered within the systems model for the simple reason that there can be no all-encompassing world system. The system/environment difference is constitutive for systemic order. There is no systemic order, only accidentally stabilized external dependencies, to be found when the

---

29 | Contrary to Latour's principle of "irreducibility," the system model is based on reduction and exclusion. Everything is either reduced to something else, or excluded from everything else. There are no hybrid actors, no mediators.

environment is somehow included in the system. But it is precisely the totality that concerns ecology. Could it be that what ecology has brought to the forefront of social theory cannot be adequately described in terms of the systems model, but demands a different model, perhaps a network model? Does network theory allow the conceptualization of relations that cannot be explained in terms of selection, rationing, and steering?

These questions serve as basis for posing further questions about the difference between systems and networks. Do networks share the same constitutive characteristics as systems? Can networks be analyzed and understood in the same way as systems? In order to answer this question, at least with regard to actor-network theory, it is helpful to begin with methodology. How are networks known? Perhaps what we are looking at depends on how we look at it.

OBSERVING NETWORKS

On the level of the observer ANT is in some respects similar to Luhmann's theory of social systems. Luhmann (1984) proceeds equally from an ontological and an epistemological assumption. Ontologically, it is assumed that there are systems, that is, reality is ordered systemically. Nature and Society consist of systems. Epistemologically, systems appear only to an observer. Systems are constructions of observation. In a similar way, ANT assumes that the "collective"—Latour prefers this term instead of speaking of world or society—consists of actor-networks. There *are* actor-networks. On the other hand, actor-networks appear only to the observer. For the theory of social systems as well as for ANT—and we might add hermeneutics as well—being and meaning are the same, the real is semiotically coded. Let us recall at this point our opening remarks on language and meaning. There is no unmediated access to a reality somehow outside of distinctions and differences, that is, outside semiotic coding. Meaning constructs its own boundaries within itself by constructing distinctions, for example, the difference between being and non-being, meaning and the meaningless, society and nature, subject and object. The boundaries of meaning are not brut matter, the physical body, or a pure nature, a "thing in itself." If material entities and nature were not semiotically coded, we couldn't speak of them, let alone study them or experiment on them. Scientists do not confront pure nature and somehow rest its secrets from it. They make associations between heterogeneous actors within a realm of meaning that is neither exclusively social nor natural.

Observation therefore is not a merely cognitive act, but an ontological event. To observe a social system is to construct this system in the same way that describing an actor-network amounts to participating in the construction of an actor-network. "For the sociologists of associations, any study of any group by any social scientist is part and parcel of what makes the group exist, last, decay, or disappear." (Latour 2005: 33) The coupling of epistemology and ontology makes ANT and the theory of social systems self-referential theories. They claim not only to be able to explain everything in the world, but also to explain the explaining that they themselves do. For this reason, both understand themselves to be universal theories.

What distinguishes ANT from systems theory, as well as other sociological theories, is the insistence upon a "general symmetry" (Callon 1986b; Latour 1987) in the description of human and non-human actors. ANT draws different distinctions then does systems theory and many of the basic distinctions that modern social theory does draw, ANT does not. Perhaps the most significant distinction that ANT does not draw is that between society and nature, between action and non-action or speaking with Luhmann, between communication and non-communication. The point of the methodological principle of generalized symmetry therefore does not mean that the traditional concepts of society and nature should be brought together or considered as somehow mixed together, but much rather, they should be avoided altogether.[30] For ANT observation is based upon the exclusion of any asymmetry in the use of descriptive language when it comes to what is human and what is non-human. There is no a priori difference between what belongs to society and what does not. This is to say that the social is a concept that is not opposed to anything. A concept without opposite becomes a placeholder open to anything and everything that the actors say they are. There is nothing a priori in society and nothing a priori outside of society. There is no fundamental system/environment difference lying at the basis of networks. The collective cannot be understood according to traditional categories of what makes up the social, whether it be communications, humans, structures, rules, roles,

---

30 | See Latour (2005: 76) "To be symmetric, for us, simply means not to impose a priori some spurious asymmetry among human intentional action and a material world of causal relations."

social forces, etc. Neither humans, nor natural entities, nor machines are to be considered a priori as either social or natural. These terms should be left behind. Observation does not a priori exclude anything from the network of associations that makes up the collective. Instead of beginning with some definition of what makes up society, of what is part of the social and what is not, ANT looks at what activities are constructing a network.

This perspective leads to a fundamental definition of networks as processes, that is, as open-ended. Unlike systems, networks have no environment, and they are not constructed by operations of selection, relationing and steering. Stability, identity, duration, and resistance to change are not constitutive characteristics of networks, but much rather possible products of networking, effects of the relatively successful attempts of actors to translate and enroll other actors into their programs of action. From the methodological point of view, this implies that the same concepts, methods of analysis, and vocabulary of description are to be applied equally to both human and non-human actors. The focus is equally upon who or what is constructing the network without first dividing the world into domains of subjectivity and intentionality on the one side and passive natural entities on the other, or social structures and forces on the one side and asocial individuals on the other. The very idea of a non-human actor is already a result of the principle of general symmetry, for it prohibits speaking of humans alone as social actors and defining action with regard to psychological intentionality. What the ANT observer sees is not social structures, social facts, or social forces, not even a finished network, but *activities of networking.* What the systems observer sees are self-referential, closed systems, busily selecting, relating, steering, constructing their own elements, and excluding all the rest. For ANT there is no given social object to be described. The investigator has only one option, to "follow the actors." What results from observation is therefore not a description of an entity. The consequence of this is that the object of science and technology studies is not science, but, as the title of one of Latour's early publications makes evident, "science in action."[31]

Observation in ANT becomes a "symmetrical anthropology" (Latour 2008) whose terminology is used without distinction for describing technical artifacts, social practices, natural entities, animals, and whatever

---

31 | See the title of Latour's early book (1987) "Science in Action: How to Follow Scientists and Engineers Through Society."

else might play a significant role in constructing and maintaining an actor-network. The intention of this methodological principle is to avoid the assumptions of modernity with its exclusive distinctions between society and nature, human and machine, sign and thing and thus allow reality to appear, bottom up as it were, without the distortion of modernistic categories. The meaning of this methodological principle has been succinctly stated by Callon & Law:

"Often in practice we bracket off non-human materials, assuming they have a status which differs from that of a human. So materials become resources or constraints; they are said to be passive; to be active only when they are mobilized by flesh and blood actors. But if the social is really materially heterogeneous then this asymmetry doesn't work very well. Yes, there are differences between conversations, texts, techniques and bodies. Of course. But why should we start out by assuming that some of these have no active role to play in social dynamics?" (Callon/Law 1997: 168)

Distributed Agency—Mediators and Intermediaries

This does not mean that ANT pretends to be free of all assumptions. Observation for ANT is based on the assumption that networks are made up of "actants," a term derived from the semiotics of Greimas (1983). Greimas was concerned with the structure of narratives, such as fairy tales. The structural analysis of narratives identifies roles that are played in a story. These roles are played by what Greimas called "actants." An actant can be anything, a gun, a sword, a crown, a treasure, a house, a city, the wind, a human being, an animal, etc. Whatever influences the turn of events in a story is an actant. Playing a role means doing something or making a performance. A performance is not a mere event, something that happens, but must fit into the logic of the narrative, that is, it must be an answer to a challenge, a response to events that proceeded and thus a factor influencing events that follow. A performance is not just anything that can be done. In a narrative not just anything can happen. A performance demonstrates certain competencies or characteristics of the actant, for example, intentionality, resistance, impulse, cowardice, heroism, bravery, or effectiveness. If a performance is an integral part of a narrative, without which the narrative would not be the same, or perhaps, make no sense at all, then it can be said to follow a script. Just as a role that an actor plays on stage follows a script, so must actants do that which "fits" in the narrative. In order to fit in the narrative a particular role cannot stand alone. The role of the hero cannot fit into a narrative if there is no villain or no one to be saved. Roles are always played in relation to other roles.

Actants do not merely act; they also react to other roles played by other actants. Roles in a narrative are interdependent and influence each other. When an actant does something others have to somehow take account of this and react accordingly, otherwise there is no story, but only a meaningless collection of unrelated episodes. In the semiotics of narratology an actant is neither a subject nor an object in the sense of traditional epistemology. It is something—anything at all—that in some way influences, conditions, and changes the course of events in the narrative. Furthermore actants are not necessarily individuals in the usual sense of the term. Latour, following Michel Serres speaks of quasi-objects or hybrid actors. The performance of the actant can often not be reduced to pure intentionality, but instead depends upon a constellation of heterogeneous elements that come together and are associated in unexpected ways. The knight is a brave and heroic knight not only because of his courage and will, but also because of his horse, his shield, and his sword. Without horse, shield, sword, and many other things, he would be a mere man and not a "knight" at all. He could not perform the heroic role that the story calls for. The knight is not the individual man defined by his psychological intentions, but the hybrid actor consisting of horse, shield, sword, etc. The actants and the influences that actants have upon one another arise from processes of association that are described by ANT as "translation."[32] Through translation an actor, that is, not just any knight, but a particular knight, for example, Sir Lancelot, is "enrolled," or "inscribed" in the narrative and plays a certain role (which is the generalized actor or actant). The actor can be said to pursue a "program of action" that is prescribed by his script.

---

32 | Latour traces his understanding of translation to Michel Serres via Michel Callon. "My use of the word translation comes from Michel Serres through Michel Callon's sociological usage: Some Elements of a Sociology of Translation: Domestication of the Scallops and the Fishermen of St. Brieuc Bay." It is surely no coincidence that Serres' Text is entitled *Hermes* (1974) and that translation is a central concept of hermeneutics. Translation in hermeneutics is never a mere duplication of meaning, but always a "fusion of horizons," a creation of new meaning even though, and because of, the constraints imposed by both text and reader.

Latour (1994: 29–64) offers an illustration of what is meant by trans-lation, enrollment, programs of action, and the hybrid actors that arise from these activities in the case of a man with a gun. Usually when a man with a gun plays a role in a narrative someone gets hurt. Those who claim that human agents alone are actors will say that the shooting is done by the man alone. The gun had nothing to do with the crime, other than be-ing accidentally used by someone with a criminal intention. The gun, the technical artifact is thereby seen as a neutral instrument that can be used for good or bad. Those on the other hand who see guns as dangerous in themselves will say that putting a gun into someone's hands makes them a criminal and it is the influence of the gun that is to blame. Both views consider only the one or the other. Either the man or the gun is the actor and the other as a mere "intermediary," a neutral instrument. ANT on the contrary considers both together as a hybrid network.[33] Latour is arguing against a socio-determinism that sees technical artefacts as neutral in-struments without agency as well as a techno-determinism which claims that technology is a force in itself determining human action. He claims that both the man and the gun form a hybrid network which performs according to its own program of action. The man and gun "mediate" each other such that neither is a mere intermediary, but both are mediators. Both translate each other. By means of mutual mediation, a new actor ap-pears with its own program of action.

"Translation does not mean a shift from one vocabulary to another, from one French word to one English word, for instance, as if the two languages existed independently. Like Michel Serres, I use *translation* to mean displacement, drift,

---

33 | For the distinction between "intermediaries" and "mediators" see Latour (2005: 37ff.). "An intermediary, in my vocabulary, is what transports meaning or force without transformation: defining its inputs is enough to define its outputs. For all practical purposes, an intermediary can be taken not only as a black box, but also as a black box counting for one, even if it is internally made of many parts. Mediators, on the other hand, cannot be counted as just one; they might count for one, for nothing, for several, or for infinity. Their input is never a good predictor of their output; their specificity has to be taken into account every time. Mediators transform, translate, distort, and modify the meaning of the elements they are supposed to carry." (39)

invention, mediation, the creation of a link that did not exist before and that to some degree modifies two elements or agents." (Latour 1994: 32)

The man is a different person with the gun in his hand. He has been modified by the "affordances" of the gun just as the gun is modified by finding itself in the hands of a criminal. The transformation of both man and gun through their interaction is "mediation," that is, a mutual translation of man and gun. The concept of mediation in ANT is similar to the concept of interpretation in hermeneutics. The translation of a text never reduces the text to a mere intermediary, a mere expression of the intentions of the author or the reader. The text, or the artefact, has its own horizon of meaning, its own semiotic autonomy. The autonomy of the text makes it an active participant in the meaning of translation. Hermeneutics therefore also adheres to a kind of symmetry in its treatment of author, text, and reader. ANT extends this hermeneutical principle beyond the realm of texts into relations between objects.[34] In the case of the man with the gun, their relation is symmetrical in that neither is able to use the other as mere intermediary, that is, as a passive instrument subject to deterministic causality. Through mediation both are "translated" into something that neither were alone and independent of each other.

"You are different with the gun in hand; the gun is different with you holding it. You are another subject because you hold the gun; the gun is another object because it has entered into a relationship with you. The gun is no longer the gun-in-the-armory or the gun-in-the-drawer or the gun-in-the-pocket, but the gun-in-your-hand, aimed at someone who is screaming. What is true of the subject, of the gunman, is as true of the object, of the gun that is held. A good citizen becomes a criminal, a good guy becomes a worse guy; a silent gun becomes a fired gun, a new gun becomes a used gun, a sporting gun becomes a weapon." (Latour 1994: 33)

The principle of methodological symmetry allows the observer to describe a process of mutual mediation which avoids the usual, indeed almost compelling, distinction between intentionality on the side of human agents

---

34 | "For a long time it has been agreed that the relationship between one text and another is always a matter for interpretation. Why not accept that this is also true between so-called texts and so-called objects, and even between so-called objects themselves?" (Latour 1988: 166)

and pure functionality on the side of technological artefacts. For ANT both intentionality and functionality are programs of action. When actors translate each other into hybrid networks new hybrid actors with new programs of action arise. John Law summarized this point succinctly when he stated:

"If you took away my computer, my colleagues, my office, my books, my desk, my telephone I wouldn't be a sociologist writing papers, delivering lectures, and producing 'knowledge'. I'd be something quite other—and the same is true for all of us. So the analytical question is this. Is an agent an agent primarily because he or she inhabits a body that carries knowledges, skills, values, and all the rest? Or is an agent an agent because he or she inhabits a set of elements (including, of course, a body) that stretches out into the network of materials, somatic and otherwise, that surrounds each body?" (1992: 382)

Networks are built up out of translations that mediate or associate actors into hybrid composites with distributed competencies that become new actors transforming thereby the programs of action that actors pursue in relation to each other. Methodological symmetry allows the observer to see these hybrid actors in a state before they have been subsumed under the categories of subject and object, human intentionality and technical functionality. It thereby brings something to the fore that usually is not allowed to appear in sociology, namely, actor-networks.

Let us recall the significance of the concept of translation within the hermeneutic tradition. The well-known Italian saying *traduttore traditore*, "to translate is to betray," sums up well the ambiguous result of interpretation. Interpreting a text, a work of art, an artefact, as we saw in Part 1, means to construct a new meaning and not hopelessly attempt to slavishly repeat an already given meaning. In the hermeneutic tradition translators are mediators. They move between linguistic worlds building bridges, making associations and creating meanings that are new and unexpected. Interpretation is performance. And performance is always in some way creative. It is for this reason that one can listen to a Mozart symphony again and again without becoming bored as one inevitably does, when one attempts to read the same newspaper a second time. In much the same way, actors construct networks by means of translation.

The methodological imperative to follow the actors means to empirically and meticulously describe how they translate each other into new and unforeseen associations. Methodological symmetry serves the purpose of allowing this description to be independent of the assumptions of modern epistemology and ontology. We are not dealing from the outset with active subjects on the one side and passive objects on the other. What the observer sees are neither subjects nor objects, but what Latour (2010) calls "factishes." The term is a neologism made up of "fact" and "fetish." A fact in the typically modern sense is a state of affairs given in the world patiently awaiting discovery by science, whereas a fetish is a construction by believers who then supposedly mistake what they have themselves constructed for an autonomous force, a spirit or a demon with a will of its own. What one discovers when following the actors is not a world divided either into facts or illusions, objects or subjects, but factishes. According to Latour, the concept

"[...] authorizes us not to take too seriously the ways in which subjects and objects are conventionally conjoined: that which sets into action never has the power of causation, whether it be a master subject or a causal object. That which is set into action never fails to transform the action, giving rise neither to the objectified tool nor to the reified subject." (2010: 56)

Observing an actor network resembles much more the hermeneutical practice of translation than the attempt to describe regularities, functions, and operations of a system or objectively given states of affairs in the natural world. ANT is methodologically closer to hermeneutics than to traditional social science. It is well known that Latour bases his understanding of translation on the work of Michel Serres. It is surely no accident that Serres introduces the term translation in a text entitled Hermes (1974). It would surely be interesting to attempt to trace the links between Serres and philosophical hermeneutics, but this would lead away from the present concern, which is to locate the kind of network science that ANT represents in relation to systems theory on the one side and hermeneutics on the other.

Ethnology of the Moderns

Latour sees himself as an ethnologist and ANT as a kind of ethnology of the "moderns," whereby "moderns" is to be understood in much the same way as, for example, the English anthropologist E. E. Evans-Pritchard speaks of the Azande in his famous monograph, *Witchcraft, Oracles and Magic among the Azande* (1937).[35] The "moderns" are to be studied just like any other ethnic group without presupposition and prejudice, as far as possible, and their practices, including those practices they call "science," are to be described such that the ways in which the "moderns" produce social order and meaning become understandable.

Latour follows Garfinkel's "Ethnomethodology" which is rooted, among other sources, in phenomenological philosophy, Heidegger, and Wittgenstein.[36] A key notion of Ethnomethodology is to derive concepts of order from the activities of members of a society that produce order, or as Garfinkel (2002: 72) puts it: "Phenomena of order are identical with [the] procedures for their endogenous production and accountability." The methodological principle of generalized symmetry is intended to allow sociological categories to emerge from the empirical practices and self-descriptions of the actors. The ethnologist describes the everyday practices of members of a society and their knowledge of these practices.[37] There is nothing going on behind the backs of the actors. If there are such things as Durkheim's *faits sociaux*, then they cannot be taken as given, but must be traced to those practices that produce them. The actors know very well what they are doing and the task of the ethnologist is to document these practices and their indigenous descriptions. This is not to say that the ethnologist may not discover "hidden" meanings, implications, and associations that the actors themselves are not at any particular time aware of. But it does imply that this knowledge must be measured against the self-understanding and acceptance of the actors themselves. The hermeneutical rule that no interpretation is valid unless it could be accepted by those who are being interpreted—otherwise there would be no mediation, no translation, no "fusion" of horizons, but simply an new horizon without integration into the old one—implies that social science cannot occupy a "critical position" free of "prejudice," free of the constraints of history and

---

35 | The reference to Evans-Pritchard is not accidental since Peter Winch in *Understanding a Primitive Society* used this text in order to initiate one of the most important discussions on the methodological foundations of the social sciences in the last 50 years. See the discussion of this controversy in Krieger (2006).

36 | For the development of Ethnomethodology see Garfinkel 2002.

37 | As Latour (2005: 23) put it: "The task of defining and ordering the social should be left to the actors themselves, not taken up by the analyst."

society, somehow over and above the self-understanding of the people being studied.

Garfinkel's Ethnomethodology supports ANT's critique of the modern self-understanding of science as value-free, objective knowledge. ANT claims that the work of the scientist inevitably becomes part of the network being described. If there is no critical position outside the actors and what they are doing, then critique must take the form of participation in the network being studied. Science as interpretation does not merely describe the world, it changes the world. This idea, which constitutes the traditional basis for critical theory from Marx to Habermas and postmodernism, receives a new foundation on the basis of actor-network theory. Unlike systems with their clear boundaries and their necessary exclusion of an environment, networks have no boundaries. They cannot exclude anything, and if so, then only more or less successfully and only for a short time. This means that science cannot be contained within a separate domain, a closed system that codes communicative actions into questions of truth or falsity and excludes everything else. The interpretive work of the ethnologist of the "moderns" cannot take place within a closed system whose operations do not flow over into politics, economics, art, education, and religion. Not only does the trajectory of Latour's writings from empirical studies of scientists in laboratory settings to political theory illustrate this "translation" of science into other domains, but empirical reality allows us to draw no other conclusion.[38]

Returning to the question of methodology in Luhmann's systems theory and in ANT, observation in both the systems approach and ANT can be said to "construct" its object, but "construction" means something entirely different in ANT. When the object of knowledge is not a system, but an actor-network, construction implies participation, at least in principle, in the network that is being observed. Observation is itself a process of "translation," of mediation, and finally, as the discussion of ANT in relation to philosophical hermeneutics shows, of interpretation. As Latour (2005: 33) puts it, "[...] any study of any group by any social scientist is

---

38 | See Latour's programmatic essay on The Impact of Science Studies on Political Philosophy (1991) for a discussion of ANT in relation to political thought. Interestingly, it is again ecological issues "happily conflating technical, scientific, ethical, and political issues, ranging from the rain forest to the ozone layer hole [...]" (5) that illustrate the futileness of attempting to separate science and politics.

part and parcel of what makes the group exist, last, decay, or disappear." Whereas for traditional sociology observers and actors are on different levels, for ANT they are "in the same boat all along and play the same role, namely group formation" (34).The significance of this self-understanding of the scientific enterprise deserves attention. Much of postmodern critique is concerned with the reflexivity of science. Social theory is "social" not merely because society is the object of study, but because science is social action. Indeed, critical theory has always claimed that any knowledge worth the name either serves emancipatory goals or it is mere ideology supporting the injustice of the status quo. This view of knowledge can be traced at least back to Marx, who made labor the condition of knowledge and envisioned science as servant of the class struggle. If science is not value-free, objective, apolitically, and socially as well as culturally neutral, then what is it? And if it is not value-free, objective apolitically as well as socially neutral, then whose cause does it defend? By what right can this cause claim to posses more (scientific) truth than any other? As noted in the discussion of philosophical hermeneutics, we are left with the conflict of interpretations and no stable, neutral, "critical" ground to stand on.

Circulating Reference and Immutable Mobiles

One answer to the question about the role of science in society, a role which has significantly influenced critical theory and the program of a critical sociology, is to look at science not as a finished product or as an ideal, but as it is actually done; not finished science, but science as a process, science in the making. Latour's ethnology of the moderns investigates science in action. It goes into the laboratories, the research centers, the coffee rooms, and offices and meeting rooms of scientists, research assistants, post-docs, administrators and staff, and attempts to document what they do and what they say they are doing. This research has had profound impact upon what is known as "Science and Technology Studies" (STS) or "Science Studies."[39] What the ethnologist, who has adopted a generalized symmetry with regard to the description of humans, artifacts, organizations, and also his or her own work, sees is people using instruments to do so-called experiments in order to inscribe information, which inscriptions take on many forms, such as hand-written notes, diagrams,

---

39 | See http://en.wikipedia.org/wiki/Science,_technology_and_society

images, models, data bases, etc. Latour (1986, 1987) calls these inscriptions "immutable mobiles" and he describes how they are constructed and how they move into other contexts in which they become translated into other inscriptions such as presentations for conferences, publications in scientific journals, forming thereby the basis of further inscriptions on ever higher levels of abstraction.

This process can be described as "cycles of accumulation" (219ff.) which involve ever more information linked to ever more experiments, instruments, inscriptions, researchers, laboratories, institutions, and so on. Such cycles of accumulation can be found in any discipline, whether it be cartography, geography, biology, physics, sociology, chemistry, history, or astronomy. The inscriptions that scientists produce are handed on to colleagues, criticized, rejected, revised, and linked to other inscriptions. Such immutable mobiles land on the desks of funding institutions, product developers, high-tech companies, think tanks, ethics committees, magazine and newspaper editors, and political policy advisors. They are translated into budgets, prototypes, contracts, R&D programs, proofs for theories, models, and arguments and emotions in cultural, social, and political controversies. Ecological issues, as Latour tirelessly points out, are a case in point. In any discussion of ecological issues on whatever level, one finds political, economic, scientific, cultural, and religious factors mixed together. This mix forms an entangled cycle of accumulation leading to decisions, policies, resource allocations, and perhaps even social unrest and violent conflicts. This is what science is. Immutable mobiles are mediators and actors that flow into the educational system, regulatory agencies, the offices of venture capitalists, advisory boards in government and industry, university policies, and back into the laboratories, building along the way complex, extended networks of associations held together by translations and enrollments.

One of the many examples that can be culled from ANT literature is Latour's (1999: 24–79) description of an expedition into the Amazon area in order to study the relations of forest to savanna. This example of science in action illustrates not only how inscriptions are made, how they move into other contexts, and how they construct a cycle of accumulation, but it also shows how science consists of what Latour calls a "circular reference" in which neither pure nature, nor pure knowing can be found. Science presents itself in the form of a mix, a hybrid of signs, things, and actors linking together to form heterogeneous networks.[40] The expedition is interdisciplinary. Botany, pedology (soil science), and geography are represented. The question to be answered is how and to what extent the savanna is pushing back the rain-forest or the other way round, the forest is encroaching on the savanna. Out in the field the group of researchers does not confront an undifferentiated, pure nature, but a piece of land where forest and savanna meet which is already in some ways known. They are already equipped with a few aerial photographs and a rough map to serve as orientation. A previous botanic expedition marked some of the trees. Although the terrain is mostly unknown, one cannot speak of a pure nature, since the map, the photographs, and the marked trees have already drawn a rough net of coordinates over the area and integrated it into a system of signs, a semiotic world.

As philosophical hermeneutics would say, without these and many more presuppositions, this particular piece of land could not even come into awareness as problematic or as a subject of investigation. Even out in the wilderness far away from universities, libraries, and laboratories, the researchers do not find some kind of "thing in itself" or "pure nature," but a pre-given interpretation, no matter how rough and undifferentiated it may be. As philosophical hermeneutics pointed out, there is no understanding without pre-understanding. *Dasein* is always already thrown into a world of possibilities. Even for natural science, the world is always already in some way interpreted and made meaningful. Bateson (2000: 459) asked what made the map different from the territory and came to the conclusion that is was information, that is, differences. Latour turns the question around and asks what makes it possible that the map can represent the territory and comes to the same conclusion. Differences are introduced into differences. Scientific facts arise within a circle of references and not in a mythical confrontation with a supposed pure nature.

The first action the researchers take is to lay an abstract quadratic topology over the area with the help of steaks driven into the ground, thread, and a compass. The next step is to take samples of soil at regular intervals between savanna on the one side and the forest on the other within the measured areas. The samples are textually documented in detail with

---

40 | "I want to show that there is neither correspondence, nor gaps, nor even two distinct ontological domains, but an entirely different phenomenon: circulating reference." (Latour 1999: 24)

regard to time, place, depth, color, and consistency. The samples are carefully placed in a quadratic device made of wood and cardboard called a "pedocomparator," which serves not only to preserve the samples as they were taken from the ground for later analysis in a laboratory, but also to preserve the on a reduced scale the spatial relation they had to each other in the field. The pedocomparator can be closed like a suitcase and transported with the samples it contains back to the laboratory in the city. Because it is a fixed and stable thing, the pedocomparator can be considered immutable. Because it can be transported unchanged back to the laboratory in the city it is mobile. It is both matter and form. It serves as a kind of concrete sign, a material graphic illustration, something between reality and sign that can be said to represent the land under investigation. The samples of soil placed in relation to one another according to the coordinates of the marked out land are a translation of the land into a new form that nonetheless serves as a "representation" of the land. The representation can be transported to any laboratory anywhere in the world, compared to other such representations, and be further translated into a graph, or a table of numeric values, which in turn can be translated into a text, a report, or a recommendation to the ministry whose responsibility it is to protect natural resources. Each inscription is at once matter and form. It is form for the inscription that precedes it and matter for the inscription which translates it into a different form. Following this network of associations among immutable mobiles shows that science never leaves the world of meaning in order to somehow confront a pure nature. Nonetheless what is constructed in this process are so-called scientific facts. Facts are not given. They are fabricated or constructed within an activity that moves from translation to translation joining more and more hybrid actors together into a network of circulating reference. This process ends in most cases, as it did with the expedition into the Amazon, with a typical final report.

"The prose of the final report speaks of a diagram, which summarizes the form displayed by the layout of the pedocomparator, which extracts, classifies, and codes the soil, which, in the end, is marked, ruled, and designated through the criss-crossing of coordinates. Notice that, at every stage, each element belongs to matter by its origin and to form by its destination; it is abstracted from a too-concrete domain before it becomes, at the next stage, too concrete again. We never detect the rupture between things and signs, and we never face the imposition of arbitrary and discrete signs on shapeless and continuous matter. We see only an unbroken series of well-nested elements, each of which plays the role of sign for the previous one and of thing for the succeeding one." (Latour 1999: 56)

The ethnologist of science finds inscriptions that let the facts speak for themselves by fabricating them, translating them in a certain way. Inscriptions maintain an unchangeable connection to that which they inscribe and at the same time can be transported far away from the place and time of the inscription. These immutable mobiles are translated into each other, enrolled into programs of action, and inscribed into networks. They refer not to something outside the network, but to the network itself. A so-called scientific fact is a circulating reference of immutable mobiles. Looking closely at science in action reveals a science that gains its validity, its persuasiveness, its solidity and credibility not from nature itself, whatever that might be, but from the complexity, variety, number, and adhesiveness of the immutable mobiles that are constantly being translated and enrolled into networks.

Immutable mobiles are not mere passive instruments in the hands of the researcher, but active participants in the construction of what they transport and the associations they enter into. If the land itself, the constitution of the soil, the distances between the samples, etc. did not influence the pedocomparator and the way it translated the soil, the inscription would be mere fiction instead of fact. Inscriptions such as a measurement, a photo, or a diagram, a report are science because they are not constructed by researchers alone. The design and use of the pedocomparator challenges the soil to speak for itself while at the same time forcing it into the abstract constraints of a measurable representation. Were this not the case, then scientific inscriptions would be indistinguishable from the productions of literature or art. What is inscribed is a hybrid association in which the researcher and, for example, the soil, the trees, or the savanna play active roles. Just as the man with the gun is different from the man without the gun, or the gun in the drawer, so is the pedocomparator with samples different from the unsampled soil or the wooden construction lying empty on the floor of the stockroom of the laboratory. Together they constitute a new hybrid actor that enters into the circulating reference of the scientific research, is able to translate other actors, such as diagrams or graphic representations, which in turn can enroll other actors, such as colleagues, environmental agencies, and so on. Both soil and pedocomparator are actors and together with many other actors they make the circulating reference that constitutes scientific knowledge as an actor-network.

The circulating reference of immutable mobiles may be compared to the hermeneutic circle. Hermeneutics moves from part to whole and from whole to part without being able to somehow break out of the circulating references of interpretation and come face-to-face with something like meaning-in-itself, or the final truth. The enclosure of interpretation within meaning has always been a thorn in the flesh of critical theory. Habermas, for example, claims that science can only legitimate its claim to truth if it is able to break out of the hermeneutical circle of meaning. For Habermas literary texts differ from scientific texts precisely because the reader of a scientific text breaks out of the text, goes through it, so to speak, directly to the world itself. Scientific "[...] criticism does not refer to the text and the operation of world disclosing that it carries out, as aesthetic criticism does; rather, it refers to what is said in the text about something in the world" (Habermas 1992: 224). It must be possible to break out of the circle of references if science is to be science, if the claims of the text are to be verified or falsified by confrontation with "facts." Were it not possible to confront the text with reality itself, then scientists would be no different from theologians and philosophers; they would be doing nothing but making translations of translations. This is, however, precisely what ANT proposes. So-called "scientific facts" are constructed by means of cycles of accumulation of immutable mobiles. What signs refer to are actor-networks and not something somehow beyond semiotic coding.

The critical theory of society that Habermas proposes presents us with a divided world. One world is filled with brute facts and ruled by deterministic causality, whereas another world is filled with intentional subjects prone to fantasy and illusion. There is still another world of signs and symbols attempting to somehow reach over to the world of facts and be "adequate" to and thus "verified" by them. And finally there is a social science that attempts to explain why these attempts so often fail. For Latour this typically "asymmetrical" world view of modernity fails to take account of the actors themselves, who do not fit into any of these different worlds. He rhetorically challenges Habermas and the moderns:

"Instead of giving ourselves (1) cause-objects filling every possible gap in the external world, (2) source-subjects endowed with interiority and crammed with fantasies and affects, (3) more or less arbitrary representations groping about, more or less successfully, in an effort to establish a fragile tie between the illusions of the ego and harsh reality as known by the sciences alone, (4) new causal determinations to explain the arbitrary origins of these representations, why should we not abandon the double notion of knowledge/belief, and populate the world with the tangled entities that emerge from the mouths of the 'actors themselves'." (2010: 41-2)

Social Space is Flat

There is a further consequence of methodological symmetry that is equally at odds with traditional sociological theories. According to ANT the topology of social space is flat. Order is not necessarily hierarchical. This runs counter to the very foundations of sociology as a scientific discipline in its own right. At least since Durkheim sociology has legitimated itself as a science by postulating the existence of "social facts" (*faits sociaux*), that is, so-called "macro" social structures that condition and constrain individual actors. Norms, social roles, functions, classes, economic infrastructures, groups, institutions, organizations, morality, religion, and entire social systems are examples of social structures that go beyond individual actors and influence, if not, determine, their behavior. According to traditional sociology at least since Durkheim it is these structures that make up the proper object of the social sciences and distinguish sociology from psychology, history, economics, biology, and other related sciences. Indeed, it is these macro-structures that constitute the social as such. They are what society is made of. A number of dissociated individuals, no matter how large, do not make a society. Psychological individuals go through a process of "socialization" by which they are more or less forced to become "members of society."

Social reality is therefore always in some way hierarchical with individual actors at the bottom of the scale, families, clans, groups, associations, organizations etc. at the "meso" level and large structures such as religion, political institutions, forces of production, norms, and cultural standards at the top. Generally, the higher up one goes in the hierarchy, the more durable, stable, powerful, and oppressive the structures become. According to traditional sociology, the topology of social space is vertical and is defined by a gap between the micro and the macro. On the micro level there is individual data and on the macro level there are structures, regularities, mechanisms of integration, long lasting institutions and forms of organization. Individual social actors are considered mere informants that yield data from which the macro-structures can be derived. It is these structures that influence, if not determine and therefore explain the meaning of the individual data. This generates the question of how macro structures constrain micro actors and how micro actors through their supposedly free and intentional actions give rise to macro structures. It also grounds the claim of critical theory that it is possible, even necessary, to apply scientific methods in order to discover what is going on behind the backs of individual actors, discover the mechanisms of power and oppression, unmask the ideologies hiding these mechanisms from the actors, and thus enable emancipatory action.

ANT stands in the tradition of the sociology of Gabriel Tarde instead of Durkheim.[41] Latour rejects the micro/macro dichotomy entirely and assumes that if one follows the actors closely one never leaves the one common ground of actors and their "attributes," that is, their ties with other actors. ANT proposes a sociology of associations which does not assume at the outset that society consists of certain social facts and then proceeds to demonstrate how these macro-structures influence individual behavior. The result of sociological explanation is not the description of macro structures, of determining mechanisms behind the backs of individuals, but an ever more detailed and individualized description of actors and the associations that arise from their activities of translating and enrolling.[42] The more data is taken account of, the more the individual actors in their uniqueness and particularity come into view and the more the supposed macro structures disappear. That which appears in their place is more or less large and more or less durable networks. As Latour (2005: 64) puts it,

---

41 | See the discussion of the influence of Tarde's work on Latour in Wieser (2012: 220ff.).

42 | "What is a collective phenomenon once you deploy all the information you have about individual associations? It is certainly not something superior to the web they form by sharing their profiles. What is it then? Probably something inferior, something smaller than the parts. This is what Tarde always objected to with Durkheim: the whole is necessarily less complex than the individual who makes it possible, provided, that is, you accept not to reduce individuals to self-contained atomic entities but let them deploy the full range of their associates—which means of course that you need to have a lot of information about their profiles." (Latour 2010b: 13)

the social "doesn't designate a domain of reality or some particular item, but rather is the name of a movement, a displacement, a transformation, a translation, an enrollment." There are no social facts, fixed and given structures making up society. Instead, the social "is a name of a type of momentary association, which is characterized by the way it gathers together into new shapes" (65).

Networks are therefore not to be conceptualized as macro structures like systems that emerge irreducibly from the interactions of individual actors. Unlike systems, networks are the activities of the actors participating in them and nothing more. Grading a student's paper in a seminar on Kant is not the instantiation of institutional constraints, but a concrete network wherein the various actors can be followed in all directions almost indefinitely with the effect that the actors become more and more individualized, particular, unique, rather than disappearing into the macro structures of the university, the intellectual class, the educational system, and so on. Contrary to most sociological theories, and explicitly in opposition to main tenets of the systems model, ANT claims that the whole is always less than the sum of the parts.[43]

A further important concept on the methodological level is the idea of a "setting" or "setup" (French *dispositif*). Since everything is somehow connected with everything else the question arises of how something in particular can become an "object" of scientific investigation. For ANT it is clear that whatever can become an object of inquiry is not some kind of social atom, an individual entity originally lacking attributes that must then be found in the structures in which the individual is embedded, but a network of associations, a collection of human and non-human actors with distributed competencies and "performances," that is, activities, effects, influences, and "affordances" (Gibson 1977). This collective, which is always individualized and concrete, becomes a "setting" or a "setup" the moment a "crisis" (Latour 1994: 36) disturbs the smooth and taken for granted functioning of a network. In order to overcome the crisis and return to business as usual, actors step forward and begin to repair, transform, strengthen, or dismantle the network by means of translations, inscriptions, enrollments, and programs of action. It is these network building activities that can be observed and described by the social sci-

---

43 | See the programmatic essay by Latour et al. (2012) "The Whole is Always Smaller Than Its Parts. A Digital Test of Gabriel Tarde's Monads."

entist. An observable actor-network appears because it is dysfunctional. This reminds one of Heidegger's description of "equipment" (*Zeug*). A hammer, for example only appears as such the moment it is broken or no longer works properly and thus falls out of its embeddedness in a network of other things and activities. The broken hammer suddenly falls out of its relations with other tools, materials, and practices and appears as an individual entity. This calls for action in order to repair, replace, or exchange it for another tool so that one can get on with the work at hand.[44] Disfunction and breakdown, however, are not the only ways that the social appears. A crisis can arise by the appearance of the new, whether as intended innovation or as unexpected discovery. Historical, geographical, or cultural distance, as hermeneutics well knows, also disturbs the self-understanding of the interpreter and calls for interpretation, translation, and networking. Finally, imagination and creativity appearing in surprising, unexpected events in all areas break open black boxes and lead to networking activities that can be observed and traced.

Translation

That which appears within a setting is activities of translation. The concept of translation by and large replaces the traditional sociological concept of "action." In the place of intentional action by human agents ANT finds many different forms of agency, influence, and causality that can be ascribed to all kinds of entities, both human and non-human. Agency in ANT describes the communicative processes by which the interests, goals, identities, influences, and activities of actors are associated and brought together in order to construct heterogeneous networks. It is the activities of networking that constitutes "reality" in the epistemological and ontological sense of the term, since reality appears as "resistance" to "trials" (Latour 1988: 158). The constructivist, relational ontology of ANT is based on the communicative actions described by concepts such as translation and mediation. Where philosophical hermeneutics speaks of "understanding" and "interpretation," ANT speaks of translation, mediation, and enrollment. Through translation the various programs of both human and non-human actors are adapted to each other in such a way that a common

---

44 | See Being and Time §§ 14–24 and the discussion of the hermeneutical "as" above.

program with common goals emerges and with it stabilized role-definitions, functions, and identities. Just as the autonomy of a text grounds the possibility of new meaning emerging from the process of interpretation, so are all artifacts, objects, and entities original sources of influence upon all other artifacts, objects, and entities, including human individuals. Traditional sociology has overlooked these influences in that they use the term "social" to describe two entirely different phenomena, neither of which describes networking. On the one side the social designates "the local, face-to-face, naked, unequipped, and dynamic interactions; and on the other is a sort of specific force that is supposed to explain why those same temporary face-to-face interactions could become far-reaching and durable" (Latour 2005: 65). Networking, however, is neither intentional human agency alone not is it the force of macro social structures manipulating individuals behind their backs.

For ANT all carriers of meaning are considered "actors." A theoretical innovation of ANT is to declare the process of interpretation, that is, of building networks, a matter of translating the autonomous programs of action of all involved entities. If long-lasting, organized cooperative action is to be at all possible, then actors must be "enrolled" in identities and functions that are coordinated and mutually reinforcing. Agency is complex and not reducible to the intentionality of an individual consciousness. "Action is not done under the full control of consciousness; action should rather be felt as a node, a knot, and a conglomerate of many surprising sets of agencies that have to be slowly disentangled." (Latour 2005: 44) When ANT ascribes agency to non-humans this has at least two important implications. First of all, even traditional sociology has always recognized some form of super-individual agency. Social forces, social structures, social facts have always been influencing, if not determining, individuals to act in certain ways. Secondly, against the tradition ANT distances itself explicitly from the kind of agency that technology, things, objects usually have been granted, namely, determinate causality. Techno-determinism asserts that human actors are mere puppets in the hands of objective forces. In the example of the man with the gun discussed above, the techno-determinist would claim that the gun makes the man into criminal. The human actor is reduced to a mere intermediary carrying out the program of the weapon.

Following the actors in their networking shows what traditional sociology has overlooked. Mediation is complex and involves many different kinds of agency. Latour (2005: 72) points out that "there might exist many metaphysical shades between full causality, and sheer inexistence. In addition to 'determining' and serving as a 'backdrop for human action', things might authorize, allow, afford, encourage, permit, suggest, influence, block, render possible, forbid, and so on." What is innovative in this view is not merely that non-humans are ascribed agency instead of determinate causality, but that they play a decisive role in extending social ties beyond fleeting and unstable face-to-face interactions. Mediators are "delegates" in that they make action extend beyond transient speech into solid, durable networks. It is these networks that have assembled many different kinds of hybrid actors which then appear to traditional sociology as social facts, as structures, as macro social phenomena.

If all actors, without privileging the human subject, are allowed to play their part in networking, then the constellation of actors in which a common program has emerged can be called an "actor-network". Actors are not human beings struggling for identity, but can be anything at all: human beings, artifacts, institutions, technologies, rivers, microbes, subatomic particles, traffic lights; in short, *any thing* that does modify a state of affairs by making a difference" (Latour 2005: 71). Although this view sometimes appears as a new form of animism in which anything and everything suddenly takes on characteristics of agency and intentionality, terms like actor and agent are not used with the same meaning as in traditional sociology and psychology. ANT also does not simply do away with functionality, automatism, and mechanism. Once actors have been "inscribed" into a stabile network, they may appear as "black boxes," that is, functional elements that have been "delegated" fixed input/output roles within a closed system. But in fact they are themselves heterogeneous, hybrid constructions, whose functions represent inherently unstable agreements that at any time are subject to translation and enrolment into other actor-networks. From the point of view of hermeneutics, this is what grounds the openness to the emergence of new meaning and thus the possibility of "critique." Even when actors become "inscribed" into certain functions within a specific network, nothing can prevent them from being deconstructed and re-inscribed in other networks or in extensions and transformations of the present network. Black boxes can be opened up, become actors, make unexpected translations, and reconfigure a network. Networks, as will be discussed below in terms of the social operating system, can be said to be "flexible" in a way that systems are not.

As opposed to systems, which require strict functionality of elements, an actor-network is not constructed on the basis of a difference between system and environment and the exclusion of all that cannot be functionalized as an element within the system. Actor-networks, unlike self-organizing, complex systems, are not self-referential in the sense of operational and informational closure. In short: actors are not system elements. Actors, as opposed to elements within autopoietic systems, can be enrolled simultaneously in different networks and maintain multiple identities. Networks do not have clear boundaries and can include practically anything. This accounts for the typically blurred contours of networks, their scalability, flexibility, and multi-functionality. We will return to these typical characteristics of networks when discussion networking from the perspective of new media below.

From the ontological point of view, the world does not consist of things that somehow come into relations with each other. Instead, networking translates and enrolls actors into forms of social order that are durable, long-lasting, and thus have the appearance of social structures, macro-actors, or organizations. Networking is neither interaction nor organization. It is that form of communicative action whose function is the building and maintenance of all the various associations, both small and large, both material and immaterial, of which the world is made. Radical constructivism which is based upon cognitive science, psychology of perception and epistemological skepticism has always suffered from the contra-intuitive assertion that the world is somehow only in the mind.[45] Building constructivism on the foundation of networking can help solve this problem, since the starting point is communicative action, interpretation, translation, and association of humans and non-humans and not the individual human consciousness. The success of networking depends upon the continued "mobilization" and "delegation" of ever more actors, both human and non-human, in ever more complex and differentiated associations. In order to hold all the actors that have been mobilized in place they are connected by "intermediaries," such as names, salaries, uniforms, contracts, machines, offices, titles, badges, degrees, appointments, authorizations,

---

45 | See for example the concise statement by Alexander Riegler (2001: 5): "The Radical Constructivist Postulate says that the cognitive system (mind) is operationally closed. It interacts necessarily only with its own states."

documents, protocols, and much more. Through intermediaries actors are brought into relatively stable associations with each other.[46]

Intermediaries can be considered as "black boxes" who relay input to output without noise, distortion, transformation, and interpretation. In general, it can be said that the more intermediaries there are the larger the network becomes. The larger the network becomes the more stable and therefore the more *real* it appears. This appearance arises from the fact that a large network requires more effort to maintain itself and more effort to be transformed. This implies that the concept of "reality" may be understood not only as relational, but also as a function of the effort required to change relations, roles, identities, and programs. Object permanence, resistance to change, identity, continuity and other traditional attributes of the real may be reinterpreted to refer to the solidity, stability, durability, and scale of an actor-network. Reality is a function of the human and non-human resources that are constantly being mobilized to keep everything together. Returning to an example from cultural anthropology, for a society that constantly mobilizes enormous economic, social, cultural, religious, material, and personal resources in order to determine who is a witch, and counter the harmful influences of witchcraft, witches are real and magic is an effective way of dealing with them.[47]

It can be said that the larger the network, the more effort is constantly going on to mobilize, translate, and enroll actors, to create associations, and add intermediaries. Consequently, the more effort it takes to influence a network, to change its course, to question the validity of its goals, to redefine roles, procedures, habits, conventions, views, and practices, the more *real* it appears and the lesser the chances that attempts to subvert it will

---

46 | "Everything in the definition of macro social order is due to the enrolment of nonhumans—that is, to technical mediation. Even the simple effect of duration, of long-lasting social force, cannot be obtained without the durability of nonhumans to which human local interactions have been shifted. [...] Society is the outcome of local construction, but we are not alone at the construction site, since there we also mobilize the many nonhumans through which the order of space and time has been reshuffled. To be human requires sharing with nonhumans." (Latour 1994: 51) See also Strum/Latour (1987) for a discussion of the difference between the social behavior of humans and baboons on the basis of delegation of action to things.
47 | See the discussion of Evans-Pritchard's study on witchcraft among the Azande in Winch (1964) and Krieger (2006).

arise, or if they do, will be successful. This is why grading a paper on Kant is important and why it is more than it seems. Even such a simple thing as acknowledging a student's interpretation of Kant to be "correct" or "appropriate" is an action that is influenced by and also responsible for the entire weight of a certain academic world. Grading a student's paper is an act that either maintains or deconstructs a complex actor-network including not only the primary text and secondary literature, but also and just as importantly, professorial authority, curricula, credit hours, institutions of higher education, pedagogical traditions, research projects, scientific disciplines, peer-reviewed publications, linguistic conventions, libraries, philosophical societies, opposing schools of thought and much more. As we know, butterfly effects can change everything. How would the network change if, for example, the professor accepts a modification of the Wikipedia article on Kant as fulfillment of the seminar requirement? What changes in roles would be set in motion if the seminar were conducted as a MOOC? What if learning assessment measured group activities, patterns and traces of communication throughout the Internet, instead of individual achievements on a standardized test? It is because the work of interpretation is networking that it becomes important for professors to make decisions about who passes the course on Kant and who does not in the specific way they do, regardless of what criteria they appeal to. Networking aligns a student, an idea, a specific constellation of sources, a linguistic convention, a possible research project, a technology, a publication, and so on with a program and a narrative. The professor attempts to mobilize all these actors and stabilize their associations by using intermediaries such as grades, praise, criticisms, recommendations, and external evaluators, to mention only a few.

In summary, actor-networks are at least one form of network phenomena that should neither be understood according to a systems model nor subsumed under the categories of traditional sociology. In an actor-network the whole is not more than the sum the parts. Furthermore, building an actor-network means making associations, connections, and links between as many heterogeneous elements as possible regardless of whether they are human or non-human, individual or collective, subjects or objects. The network is actually nothing more than the networking done by all these different actors. It is the sum of those activities that maintain it at any time. Networking involves ascribing agency, translating actors and enrolling them in programs of action they previously did not participate in, disfunctionalizing them in opposing networks and refunctionalizing them in one's own, inscribing them into grand narratives that assign each its place and its role, and extending influences through delegations and intermediaries as far as possible. Networking strives for continuity, works with fuzzy boundaries, and has nothing against infinite inclusion. Systems, on the other hand, depend on differences, on sharp, if not exclusive, binary oppositions. Systems require their own domains. The elements of the system are constructed by processes of selection, relationing, and steering. System elements are functions and nothing more. To a certain extent, mathematical models of social networks also attempt to reduce the complex, unforeseeable activities of networking to abstract regularities. A social network analysis of communication within an organization can indicate implicit forms of organization that are not reflected in official organigrams, but it cannot describe the heterogeneous actor-networks that make up the organization beyond its official self-understanding.

For networking, the more mediators there are and the less functional black boxes, the better the network. A network lives or dies in every unforeseeable decision of every actor at every point in the chain. What philosophical hermeneutics calls the conflict of interpretations Latour (2005: 254) refers to as *"the progressive composition of the one common world"* and he sees it not only as a more or less useful contribution to what could be called network science, but as "the way to redefine science and politics." Consider for example, not only what is at stake in a seminar on Kant, but what is at stake in terms of inclusion and exclusion and commitments to action in the decisions made by creationist teachers in Bible Belt schools in the USA, by Gurus in traditional Hindu Ashrams or by Imams in Koran Schools in Afghanistan. Interpretation understood as networking is serious business. It does not work merely with language or texts, but gets its hands dirty with politics, business, stones, metal, machines, weapons, Holy Scriptures, courts of law, age old traditions, and moral sanctions. It reaches deeply into social and material reality in order to construct a *world* that is hard, durable, immovable, and authoritative, if only for a moment.

3. New Media

Let us return to the seminar on Kant. Reading Kant we claimed is not merely an exercise in textual interpretation, but is far more complex and bound up with many other activities that are best described as networking. The seminar is not limited to being an interaction between professor, text, and students, but also includes, more or less explicitly, creating and maintaining associations with curricula, credit systems, colleagues, administrators, libraries, publishers, donors, alumni, faculties, and much more. When professors interpret Kant in a philosophy seminar, then they are involved in many forms of mediation, that is, networking on a major scale. One question that has not been raised so far is how the students themselves experience the networking that their professors are doing. One the one hand, they are themselves interpreters attempting to translate themselves, professors, university requirements and so on into an actor-network which moves them from studying to graduating and finally to getting a job. One the other hand, they are being interpreted, that is, translated into roles, functions, and identities that perhaps do not fit with their own programs. How do the programs of action fit together? The conflict of interpretations appears from this perspective to be synonymous with socialization. Whether socialization, and for that matter innovation, creativity, generational conflict, historical change, etc., can be considered a rational process or whether rationality only then becomes possible after socialization has created a consensus on fundamental criteria of meaning, truth, and value is a question that has become more important in a fast changing, multicultural world. The dream of modernity, that science and technological progress will bring about the *End of History* (Fukuyama 1992) understood as a succession of ideological, irrational, and religious worldviews has turned into the nightmare of a *Clash of Civilizations* (Huntington 1996). There is no reason to believe that this conflict can be settled with a program of "enlightenment," any more than one can hope there will be a final and universal consensus on the meaning of Kant and on the purpose of attending a university seminar. And, of course, even if one did find a reason to believe in enlightenment, it would still be one belief among others. Does a network society offer possibilities of conducting the conflict of interpretations in ways that deemphasize closure and exclusion and emphasize openness and variability? Does a paradigm shift away from closed systems toward open networks make the search for meaning that constitutes the primary goal of philosophical hermeneutics relevant again?

After Luhmann proclaimed that society does not consist of human beings, but of communications (1984: 346ff.) we know that communication is important. And recalling McLuhan's famous dictum "The medium is the message" (1964), we know that one important aspect of communication is media. For McLuhan media strongly influence, if not determine "the scale and form of human association" (1964: 9). Media revolutions are also social and cultural revolutions. It is surely no accident that much of the current discourse on networks coincides historically with the development and deployment of networked forms of media. Castells (1996), for example, derives his concept of the network society directly from the new communication and information technologies. If the advent of digital media brings with it a different kind of society, it is not wholly wrong to speak of a digital revolution in communication and of a network society based on these new forms of communication (Castells 1996, Benkler 2006, Shirky 2008, Tapscott 2008, Weinberger 2012). There is reason to believe that if networks and networking are changing under the impact of digital media, the nature and conditions of hermeneutics might also be changing. Understanding hermeneutics as networking opens up the perspective of extending and enriching philosophical hermeneutics as well as ANT with concepts derived from the discourse on "new media."[1] The attempt to link up philosophical hermeneutics, ANT, and new media studies should result in more than a mere juxtaposition. It should become at least plausible that the digital revolution in communication contributes to a new and different understanding of the meaning and importance of

---

1 | For an overview of what is meant by "new media," see the Wikipedia article of the same name.

networking as it has emerged from the discussion of actor-network theory and philosophical hermeneutics.

MEDIA STUDIES

Media became an important topic for the modern program of critical theory with the idea of the "culture industry" put forward by Max Hork-heimer and Theodore W. Adorno (2002 [1944]) of the Frankfurt School. Industrial society had created a mass market for standardized products and transformed the masses into consumers, who were integrated into a mass culture in which values, identities, and political behavior were dic-tated by the newly arisen mass media. Against this background Herbert Marcuse put forward his theory of the "one dimensional man" complete-ly subjected to the instrumental rationality of industrial and technical production and consumption. What appeared in the media as a demo-cratic, free, and egalitarian society was in reality controlled by industrial interests and the mass media. Horkheimer and Adorno understood the production of culture by the mass media similarly to the production of standardized consumer products by big industry. Movies, radio, books, magazines, newspapers, etc. represented the world in which participation in society amounted to nothing more than passive consumption of prod-ucts that capitalism and mass advertising declared that people needed. Consumers were not free citizens, but cogs in the industrial machine. Not only were these products that industry puts on the market unnecessary, but the mass media suppressed "true" culture, the intellectually more demanding high arts, and finally the media served an ideological func-tion by disguising the inequalities and injustice of the capitalist system. Consumerism, effectively realized through the mass media, was nothing more than a form of social control perpetuating the power of the few who controlled industry and media. The task of critical theory was to discover and lay bare the mechanisms of injustice operating behind the false image of the world projected by the media.

Continuing the tradition of critical theory, Roland Barthes (1972) brought semiotics into media studies. Media products are to be understood as signs that could be interpreted on different levels. A bottle of wine, for example, as it is presented in an advertising campaign is constructed by the media to suggest health, conviviality, and happiness, whereas in reality it can signify the opposite. The media construct "myths" and do not represent reality as does scientific knowledge. The structuralist critique of the media aims to replace mythology with science, illusion with scientific truth. Just as for the Frankfurt School, media studies pursue a liberating function and claim as their legitimation the same epistemological status as any science. It is this claim that was challenged by poststructuralism, postmodernism, and deconstruction.

Poststructuralism showed that there is nothing behind the image, except perhaps, another image. What the media portray is not disguising anything, for there is no "structure," no "truth" behind the signs, operating behind the backs of media consumers. Poststructuralism dissolved the "grand narrative" of *the truth* that traditional critical theory was based upon. Since there is nothing behind the image, nothing behind the representation of the world that the media produce, there is no difference between simulation and reality. In the wake of poststructuralism, Jean Baudrillard (1994) formulated his influential theory of the "simulacrum," the image that does not represent the real, but becomes the real. Baudrillard's simulacrum is neither a copy of the real, nor a disguise thereof, but instead a "hypereality" in which the distinction between reality and representation becomes meaningless. This bold thesis leads media studies to the same insight that guided philosophical hermeneutics half a century earlier. There is no place beyond language and all knowledge and experience is "mediated." A simulation is something that appears "as" something it might not "really" be. A simulacrum has no real and final meaning and can therefore not disguise or simulate anything. As philosophical hermeneutics pointed out, there is no "thing-in-itself," no one and true fixed meaning for anything. There is only the hermeneutical "as." This is the foundation of the autonomy of the text. When the text, or an artifact, becomes an actor its existence is not merely given, but shows itself in the trials that is withstands. It ceases to be a substance and becomes a mediator.

It was above all Paul Ricoeur who emphasized the mediating role of writing in establishing the autonomy of the text. If knowledge and experience are to be in any way fixed and made lasting, they must be inscribed in a text, a work, an artifact of some kind. The process of inscription, as discussed above in Part 1, transforms meaning into an autonomous work that calls for interpretation. Interpretation overcomes the distance of the work from the reader by mediating the horizons of both the work and the interpreter. Understanding is a "fusion of horizons" such that new meaning is created and with it a new horizon of further possible meaning. What philosophical hermeneutics conceives of as a fusion of horizons is for actor-network theory a process of "translation" and "enrollment" whereby new hybrid actors are integrated into networks. Understanding becomes networking. One of the important insights gained from the discussion of philosophical hermeneutics and actor-network theory is that "mediation" is a central concept for both. Media theory itself has come to the point of understanding media as the production of hyperreality, that is, a world of knowledge and action based on media production. The moment that media are generalized to include all forms of mediation, then media studies become a kind of epistemology of the social world and of communicable experience. The kind of mediation that media do is an integral part of any theory proposing to link the goals of philosophical hermeneutics with an understanding of the construction of meaning as networking.

WHAT ARE NEW MEDIA?

As controversial and as provocative as Baudrillard's thesis was in the 90's, the idea of hyperreality has become a commonplace since the Internet, the World-Wide-Web, and digital media have come to dominate media studies. To speak of media today means to speak of so-called "new media." What is new about new media? Are new media really media in the sense that old media used this term? There is no unified theory of new media and no consensus on appropriate methods and goals for research into what may be termed new media. Despite the lack of consensus on basic concepts and methods in new media studies almost everyone agrees on one thing, new media are "digital." Cubitt (2013: 16) defines new media in terms of a particular date, October 13, 1993, which is the date of the release of the Mosaic web browser. He concedes that one could just as well date new media to the deployment of the personal computer in the 1980's, but from the point of view of media studies the decisive event was mass access to the Internet which set in with the Mosaic browser. Mark Poster (1995) spoke of the "Second Media Age" in distinction to the age of broadcast mass media. In an introductory review of current literature in media studies, Hartley, Burgess, and Bruns (2013: 2) generalize this view and argue that what counts as new in the media world is anything that radically departs from the older broadcast mass media, whether print or electronic. They offer a definition of new media as "those media that are associated with the postbroadcast era of interactive or participatory communication using networked, digital, online affordances [...]" (3). Furthermore, they suggest that "media" be understood as "those applications that have achieved sufficient ubiquity across populations and territories to be usable by ordinary consumers [...]" (3).

Feldman (1997) offers a systematic analysis of new media from the point of view of digitalization. Media are often discussed in terms of the Shannon/Weaver model of messages encoded at a source and sent through a channel to be decoded by a receiver. Regard must be paid to reducing noise caused by the channel by creating redundancy. Upon this basis digital media are then distinguished from analogue media with regard to the technologies of encoding, decoding, and transmission. Digital media, according to Feldman (3) are characterized by encoding procedures that create manipulable, dense, compressible, and impartial information transmitted by network technologies. Encoding information into bits and bytes transforms the analogue world into a virtual world of numbers. Numbers, as mathematicians well know, can be almost endlessly manipulated. This means that digital media change the character of information into something malleable, and this at both ends of the chain of communication, at point of origin as well as the point of reception. In fact, the users of digital media usually have the ability to change the information and use it however they wish. This leads directly to what Feldman considers the major distinguishing characteristic of digital media, interactivity. The fact that media consumers can also become media producers is revolutionary with regard to media throughout human history and has major implications for all areas of society.

A further essential characteristic of digital media according to Feldman is that it is networkable, that is, information can be shared and exchanged by large numbers of people simultaneously. Instead of hierarchical top-down communication as the standard for large groups, digital media make it possible for large numbers of people to interact. Traditional sociology has often distinguished between interactions at the level of face-to-face communication among two or more people in small groups and the need for centralized, top-down communication as soon as a group becomes larger than a handful of people. It could be claimed that network technology has led to a "digital media revolution" by introducing the possibility of many-to-many communication. If the origin of social organizations lies in the need to structure communication top-down in large groups, with digital media and the possibility of interaction in large groups, the very basis of traditional forms of social organization becomes obsolete. We will return to this later in the discussion of the social operating system as a new form of social order arising from the possibility of many-to-many communication.

A further distinguishing characteristic of digital media is what Feldman calls "density." Since numbers are virtual, and transistors very small, great amounts of information can be squeezed into a very small physical space. This has implications for the amount of information digital media can make available. Entire libraries can be stored on a present day micro disk and the tendency is toward even greater storage capacities in smaller physical units. Density is related to the characteristic of "compressibility." What density is to data storage, compressibility is to data transfer. Bandwidth may be limited, but there appears to be no limit to how much data can be compressed in order to move more and more data through limited transmission channels. Density and compressibility make it possible to access and use information that in the days of analogue media could not even have been dreamt of. Finally, Feldman points out that digital media are "impartial" to content. This means that anything and everything can be digitalized and transformed into information. It makes no matter what the content is. Content is impartial to its source and to its perceptual specificity. It can be images, text, music, video, code, software, or any combination thereof. This leads to what has come to be called media convergence, that is, the integration of different forms of content that previously required different forms of encoding and transmission, into one single digital channel. Another popular term for convergence is multi-media, the combination of text, audio, video in one media product. Add to this interactivity and you have a digital media revolution that is changing not only the world of traditional mass media, but also business, politics, education, and every other area of life.

Another major theorist of new media is Lev Manovich, whose "Language of New Media" (2001) has greatly influenced new media studies. Manovich bases his description of new media more on the content than on the technologies of transmission. New media are above all characterized by the kind of objects they mediate. The *new media object*, according to Manovich (49ff.), is first of all digital in much the same sense as Feldman described the virtualizing effect of transforming information into binary code. Manovich speaks of "numerical representation" to express the fact that new media objects are numbers, code, products of algorithms, devoid of analogue materiality. Secondly, the new media object is "modular." Modularity refers to the fact that once digitalized, content can be broken down into independent elements that can be used for other purposes, recombined with other modules to create new content. This is not only true of content, but also of the programs that manipulate content. As the example of object oriented programming suggests, software can consist of functional modules that can be integrated into more complex applications. Images, for example, can be broken into layers, where one layer consists of a white background, another of a text, another of a particular color. The layers can be used in other images and combined at will. The typical cut and paste operations well known from word processing or other wide spread applications are examples of modularity.

The third principle of new media objects is what Manovich calls "automation." Automation is what algorithms do with digitalized data. When one wishes to change the font of text in a word processing document one click automatically transforms Times Roman into Helvetia throughout a five-hundred page book. Automation goes much farther than this into domains such as artificial intelligence. Automation makes it possible to create intelligent agents, robots, and cybernetic control systems. The fourth principle of new media objects is "variability," that is, the fact that digital, modular content can exist in infinite variations and combinations. There is no new media object that cannot be transformed into something else. It is hard to find a photograph today that has not been run through Photoshop and transformed into something other than what has come through the lens of the camera. It is a commonplace in the film industry to say that there is nothing that cannot be visualized. Other examples are personalization of media content and delivery on the basis of user data. New media objects can be almost infinitely personalized. This is exactly the opposite of the principle of standardized, one-size-for-all contents typical of mass media.

Finally, "the most substantial consequence of the computerization of media" Manovich (2001: 45) calls "transcoding." Transcoding is a technical term for the conversion of one data format into another. As a principle of new media it describes how "the logic of a computer can be expected to significantly influence the traditional cultural logic of media; that is, we may expect that the computer layer will affect the cultural layer." Transcoding stands for much of what is being discussed under media convergence and hyperreality. Transcoding refers to the fact that new media objects are actually not "media" objects at all; they are the only objects we have. The principles that constitute new media objects spill over into other domains of reality and, recalling McLuhan's dictum, the media is the message, they condition cultural and social life in general. Society and human life are being "transcoded" into new media objects that are numerically representable, modular, automated, and variable. Indeed, Manovich's claim is that "cultural categories or concepts are substituted, on the level of meaning and/or language, by new ones that derive from the computers ontology, epistemology, and pragmatics" (2001: 47).

The transcoding of society along the lines of digital media and computer networks can be considered "revolutionary." One of the important consequences of the digital media revolution is the transformation of age old communication structures. Human society has long been structured by either one-to-one interaction or, as soon as the number of people involved in interaction no longer permits everyone to speak to everyone, by one-to-many, that is, top-down, hierarchical communication. The digital communication revolution may be considered a revolution precisely because asymmetric, one-to-many communication and the hierarchical social structures which for centuries have been a precondition of cooperative action in larger groups is no longer the only means of constructing social order and in many areas is becoming increasingly inefficient (Tapscott 2006, Shirky 2008, Weinberger 2012). Above the level of face-to-face interaction, that is, on the levels of groups, organizations, institutions, and social systems, communication need no longer be hierarchical and one-to-many. The affordances (Gibson 1997) of digital media modify the spatial and temporal parameters of communication such that it has now become possible for communication to take place in the mode of *many-to-many*, whereby, as ANT has shown, not only human, but also non-human actors participate in communication. This means that social structures no longer must be built along vertical processes for producing, distributing, and controlling information.

Flattening out hierarchies in all forms changes the nature of knowledge from objective *facts* into disputable links and associations. As Weinberger (2012) points out, it changes the very structure of knowledge from a *pyramid* into a *cloud*. One-to-many, hierarchical communication fosters an

economy of scarcity in knowledge, with a small number of experts and authorities at the top of the pyramid and the masses at the bottom. Top-down
communication is characterized by limitation, exclusion, and restricted
access. Knowledge in the digital age is no longer a pyramid, but a cloud. It
is non-hierarchical, inclusive, connected, complex, and public. Instead of
a sequential, progressive, and deductively ordered and thus stable edifice
of facts, the digital revolution has created an unbounded, heterogeneous,
uncoordinated network of links. The digital media revolution is revolutionary because it has replaced the pyramid as the central icon of social
order with the cloud.

From the point of view of actor-network theory it can be claimed that
digital technologies have not only become influential actors in the network
society, but that mediation, translation, enrollment, and inscription into
networks is fundamentally conditioned by the non-hierarchical communication of new media. This is changing not only society, but also all the various actor-networks of which society, and the world for that matter, consist.
Networking understood as the construction of associations among actors
is now more and more dealing with new kinds of actors and new kinds of
associations. Networking is becoming revolutionary. The digital revolution
has moved beyond being an object of media studies and has entered into
areas of society that are not usually considered media at all. It has given
rise to many new concepts. Here are some of them: globalization, digital
infrastructure, ubiquitous connectivity, crowdsourcing, open innovation,
social media, co-creation, semantic web, collective intelligence, intelligent
agents, prosumers instead of consumers, conversational markets, learning organizations, informational overload, open educational resources,
flows, knowledge workers, identity management, distributed cognition,
connectivism, virtual organizations, the cloud, knowledge management,
decentralization, self-organization, viral communication, and much more.
These terms are not to be found only in media studies, but in every area
of society including education, health care, science, politics, art, law, etc.
If we decide not to dismiss these terms as superficial buzz or merely the
latest hype, then they can be understood to describe a fundamental shift
in the way that networking is done and also in the world that arises from it.
Concepts such as the above describe a different kind of world and a different kind of reality than that which was built on the foundations of analog,
hierarchical communication. This world and the kind of reality it consists
of we suggest calling "mixed reality."

MIXED REALITY

The impact of digital information and communication systems upon all aspects of life has raised the question of the relation of the physical world to so-called "virtual reality." Already such visionary thinkers as Norbert Wiener and J. C. L. Licklider had prophesized a human-computer symbiosis on the basis of automated information systems. Jean Baudrillard's "hyperreality" described a situation in which the distinction between the physical and virtual realities no longer made any sense. New media studies have pointed out that business, politics, education, health care etc. are becoming increasingly determined by processes, activities, and communication that occur via digital media, digital information processing, and intelligent automated information systems. Indeed, new media studies have shown that a process of "transcoding" (Manovich 2001) is reconfiguring the social along the lines of digital media, which amounts to admitting that new media are not media at all in the traditional sense, but general conditions of communicative action as such. Information is not a message, but condition of being, an ontological category. The reinterpretation of hermeneutics from the perspective of actor-network theory that we are proposing must acknowledge that access to and usage of digital information and communication is changing the conditions under which networking is done and what kinds of actors and associations are being made. Much as Kantian categories new media are becoming the conditions of the possibility of constructing viable actor-networks. If new media become general conditions of constructing social order, this has consequences for ontology and the understanding of the real.

New media are not confined to a purely virtual world of images, representations, and information. New media do not merely transport text, images, video, and audio. They do not "transport" at all, they "mediate" information into artefacts and action in all areas of life. As Norbert Wiener foresaw, all ordered actions are steered by information. Media in the broad sense of information systems are controlling, conditioning, shaping, and informing all aspects of social life. Digital media steer production processes in factories, the behavior of airplanes, ships, and automobiles, financial transactions, logistic systems, and much more. A computer connected to a 3D-printer can produce almost anything, from toys, to weapons, and even organic tissues. Computer models and simulations are replacing directly observable physical, biological, or social systems as the object of research.

Offices, laboratories, classrooms, transportation hubs, and public buildings are being redesigned into interfaces that integrate the physical and the virtual in order to accommodate flows of information, interaction, and communication. Not only computer screens and smart phones, but also walls, windows, floors, columns, roads, landscapes, indeed everything, is becoming an "interface" allowing interaction with "intelligent" non-human actors as well as access to digital information and virtual communication. Digital media are being transcoded, as Manovich would say, into social process, cooperative action, and the objects and spaces with which and in which these occur.

Connectivity is an expected and normal part of everyday life, available not only at the workplace, but also at home, in shopping centers, restaurants, schools, public buildings of all kinds, on the road, and all over the world. The "hardware" of the network society is not merely the computer, the laptop, the tablet, or smart phone, but also houses, automobiles, schools, offices, hospitals, clothing (wearable computing), animals, plants, indeed, every "thing" that the world is made of, since there is no limit to what can be outfitted with sensors, connected to networks, and integrated into information and communication systems. Intelligent agents are not only gathering, storing, transporting, and evaluating data of all kinds in enormous quantities, but processing it in order to assist human actors or even make decisions themselves faster and better than human actors can do. Alongside the actors we have hitherto known and accepted as members of society, the digital revolution is creating a world that is populated with "virtual" beings that are playing an ever more important role in constructing the network society and thus in transforming what the very concepts of knowledge, action, and reality mean.

The integration of the real and the virtual worlds has many different names. Experts speak of virtual reality, augmented reality, augmented virtuality, mediated reality, diminished reality, amplified reality, and virtualized reality (Schnabel et al. 2009). Castells (2001) speaks of a culture of real virtuality that is characteristic of the global network society, a culture that is "virtual because it is constructed primarily through electronically based, virtual processes of communication. It is real (and not imaginary) because it is our fundamental reality, the material basis on which we live our existence, construct our systems of representation, practice our work, link up with other people, retrieve information, form our opinions, act in politics, and nurture our dreams. This virtuality is our reality (203)." The term "mixed reality" has gained a certain acceptance as a common term for the integration of the real and the virtual. There are various forms in which this integration takes place. On the one end of the scale, reality is re-presented within an immersive simulation, for example, the popular immersive virtual world "Second Life." On the other end, digital information is imposed onto the non-digital world, as for example in smart glasses (see Google Glass). Mixed reality defines spaces that are both physical and virtual. The concept is useful to define a reality that is more like an interface than a substance, more like a communicative process than a structure. Interfaces allow access to both worlds simultaneously and contiguously.

The digital media revolution is transforming reality into an *interface*. Interfaces have traditionally been understood as computer monitors, the screens of mobile devices such as tablet computers or smart phones, but they can also be sensors or cameras built into anything whatever; beds, floors, furniture, clothing, automobiles, tools, machines, devices monitoring blood pressure, pulse, movement, etc. The sensors can be connected to each other via the Internet to create an "ambient intelligence" or an "internet of things." *The interface is the ensemble of things and information. The interface is the space of mediation, irreducibility (Latour), association, translation, interpretation, and networking.* We are proposing the interface as model of the real, that is, when the real is considered as mixed reality. Technically, the interface establishes the connection between the physical and the virtual. The interface allows interaction. The interface coordinates physical-virtual networking. It serves much the same purpose as the "horizon" in philosophical hermeneutics, insofar as it permits or restricts the flow of all kinds of information in all directions and to all actors. It defines a hybrid space that is neither real nor virtual, but a mixture of both. Recalling the hermeneutical circle that constructs meaning in the movement from part to whole and from whole to part, the interface allows movement from physical to virtual and from virtual to physical, such that meaning and reality become an indistinguishable mixture of both.

For hermeneutics the part is in the whole, but the whole is only accessible through the part. The concept of horizon blocks any attempt to mistake the part for the whole, that is, to attain closure, totality, and thus stop the ongoing task of interpretation. The horizon distinguishes and unites the part and the whole, but it does this in such a way, that both part and whole are transformed into the interpretation and no longer independently accessible or even analytically distinguishable. In a similar way, the interface distinguishes and unites the physical and the virtual, but it does this in such a way that both are no longer independently accessible or analytically distinguishable. If we can no longer speak of the real and the virtual, of things and signs, of the same or the different, how is mixed reality to be described? What can be distinguished after reality has become an interface is no longer a physical world and a virtual world, but a world made up of *layers* and *filters*. Mixed reality is not made up of physical parts and virtual parts, like gin and tonic in a mixed cocktail. The digital media revolution has transformed reality into a mixture of filters and layers.

LAYERS AND FILTERS

In the wake of the digital revolution networking breaks out of traditional spatial and temporal limitations on access to information and cooperative action such that new and unforeseen possibilities emerge. Communication and the interpretive work of translating and enrolling actors into networks have traditionally been conditioned by spatial, temporal, and physical or bodily parameters. What could be perceived, known, and communicated and the conditions of action were determined largely by the physical "context," the place and time where an actor was bodily present. Someone standing on a street corner in Lower Manhattan experiences a different world, has access to different information, and has different possibilities of action, then someone herding goats in the Pyrenees. The information available to these persons and the opportunities of action open to them is of course also determined by their education, the location of the nearest library, the available means of transportation, and the time, effort, and cost required to contact someone in order to get an answer to a question, initiate a financial transaction, coordinate cooperative action and so on. In the network society these spatial, temporal, and physical conditions are no longer the primary parameters of knowing and acting. Instead reality presents itself as a play of *layers* and *filters*.

Mixed reality does not privilege spatio-temporal and physical parameters. After the digital revolution knowing and acting are no longer primarily conditioned by spatio-temporal and bodily contexts as they have been throughout history. Mixed reality dislocates the perspective of the embodied subject (Karppi 2012) by superimposing virtual information upon physical space. In order to describe this new basis for knowledge and action, it can be said that mixed reality consists not of places, times, and bodies, but of layers and filters. The concept of layer in digital technology usually refers to functional levels within a system of protocols or elements of digital images, which can be superimposed upon one another. A filter is usually defined as an algorithm that automatically changes digital information processing in a specific ways. A search query in Google can be considered a filter, whereas the results of the application of the filter make up a layer. Traditionally the notion of a filter refers to a selection process. Certain elements are allowed to pass through a filter, and certain are held back. A coffee filter, for example, holds back the coffee grounds and lets the coffee through. With regard to information, filters have often been associated with censoring information. Only that information which the authorities and experts standing at the top of the pyramid decide to be appropriate is allowed to pass down through the filter. Filtering doesn't have to be negatively connotated. Under the conditions of one-to-many communication and an economy of scarcity of knowledge, parents, teachers, experts, religious authorities and so on have long been responsible in society for performing filtering duties.

Leaders have always had access to information that the masses did not have access to. Information producers and the media have always made decisions about what and how to publish, and what not. To a certain extent, as Weinberger (2012) has pointed out, these decisions were necessitated by the economy of scarcity that print media and the regime of one-to-many communication were based upon. Not everything that could be known and communicated could be printed. Only a small part of the vast amount of information in the world could be put into the form of print. Heavy and costly books could not be made available to everyone everywhere. The production, distribution, and use of knowledge were limited by the constraints of print media. This economy of scarcity created a hierarchical form of knowledge in which experts and authorities played important roles in the production, distribution and use of information and in which filtering information was necessary. In addition to this, the filtering function of the mass media has long been a topic in media studies, political science, and sociology. Filtering not only brings with it the negative connotations of censorship, but also the positive connotations of selecting appropriate information and protecting those not in the position to make decisions about using information. It is within this context that issues such as "sensitive" data, privacy, and data security have arisen. Many of the important and still unresolved ethical, political, and legal issues raised by the digital communication revolution have to do with filtering in one form or the other. No one, however, denies that some kind of filtering is necessary.

In the age of the cloud and of information overload filters no longer derive their function from an economy of scarcity. They are no longer necessarily associated with hierarchy and privilege. They have become a general condition of the possibility of knowing and acting and may be considered presuppositions for accessing and using information in any way whatever (Leaver/Willson/Balnaves 2012). The concept of filter we are proposing here should be understood on a general level as a defining characteristic of mixed reality. Furthermore, the concept of filter we wish to introduce is intended to describe what hermeneutics has termed the fore-structures of knowing and what actor-network theory understands by a program of action. Just as the fore-structures of knowing condition the way in which anything appears within a question and as a task for understanding, so does a program of action condition what actors are translated and enrolled into which network. Interpreters are guided by their pre-understandings, just as actors are guided in their networking activities by programs of action. From the point of view of an ontology of mixed reality and an epistemology based on digital media, filters are general conditions of knowledge and action. Filters are a condition of the possibility of knowing and acting in the network society. Whatever options for knowledge and action that are available for any actor are a result of filters and filtering. Out of the endless amount of information in the cloud, filters select a finite set of data. Networking amounts to applying filters. That which results from the application of filters can be called "layers."

The information processed by a filter is a layer. As a defining characteristic of mixed reality, the concept of layer refers to the sum of relevant information and possibilities of action delimited and made accessible by a filter. Layers are domains of knowledge and action. The ontology of modernity also recognizes domains. Domains are, for example, nature, society, the mind, and the transcendental. One of the important theoretical innovations of actor-network theory is to call these domains of reality into question. Latour proposes dropping such distinctions altogether and simply speaking of the collective. The collective consists not of a domain of material entities under the regime of deterministic causality distinguished from a domain of the social or a domain of the mind. What the moderns distinguished, Latour proposes to mix into one collective composed of networks. Interpreting ANT from the point of view of new media studies allows us to reintroduce the concept of domains in the sense of layers. Whereas for ANT networks are opposed to domains, we propose defining domains as layers, whereby layers can be understood as a translation of ANT's concept of networks from the point of view of new media. If the construction of meaning that hermeneutics places at the center of being is understood as networking in the sense described by ANT, then from the point of view of digital media networking is the construction of layers. A filter is a set of parameters linking information on the basis of relevance criteria. A filter is a rule for selecting, relating, and processing information. A query and a search algorithm, for example, filter the almost infinite amount of data available on the World Wide Web so as to extract and present a limited and therefore usable set of information. In systems theory, it is the operation of selection, relationing, and steering that creates a system. In digital networking it is the application of filters that selects, relates, and presents a domain, a network, a layer.

Traditionally it was place, time, and physicality that functioned as primary filters. On the basis of this spatio-temporal filter, physical reality as it appeared within the perceptual capabilities of the located and embodied subject made up the primary layer. We called this the "real world." Depending on where someone was, when they were there, and who they were, information was available or not, opportunities for action were available or not, other actors were available or not. Under the regime of mixed reality, place, time, and physicality are no longer the primary filters and therefore the "real world" is no longer the privileged layer. If the person herding goats in the Pyrenees has a smartphone, internet access, and the right Apps, they could know and do much the same things that the person standing on the street corner in Lower Manhattan could do. The shepherd in the Pyrenees could initiate stock trading on Wall Street, buy a new suit at Bernie's, chat with friends living on 5th Ave., and arrange a trip to Las Vegas including hotel and show tickets. The person in New York on the other hand could see photos of Saint-Lizier in the Pyrenees, or even zoom in live over a webcam, identify the goats of the region, order the local cheese, etc. In addition to this, the person in New York could overlay what they are presently seeing and hearing on the corner of Worth and Hogan with information (images, documents, etc.) from the history of the city going back to the time of the "five points," when the area was a slum full of disease and crime. They would see Lower Manhattan the way it looked in 1827 or in 1930. They could see where historical personages lived and even read their private correspondence. Indeed the entire world of information on all topics such as architecture, art, politics, business, science, culture etc. can be filtered and presented according to different parameters as a particular layer. The opportunities of knowledge and action created by these layers may be more significant and more "real" in their effects than anything known or done under the conditions of space, time, and embodiment alone.

Mixed reality is perhaps best visualized as the cloud. It is characterized by the fact that there is no primary layer and no privileged filter. What is usually termed the "real world," that is, physical reality with its time-space parameters as opposed to what is called virtual reality does not constitute a privileged filter. The information anyone on the basis of physical presence can perceive, remember, or otherwise access including activities based on this information does not constitute a privileged layer. On the contrary, being limited to the filter of physical presence can be a disadvantage when everyone else has access to digital information. Those living and working in mixed reality know more and can do more with the information than the person who does not have access to the network. Thinkers sensitive to the significance of the transition to mixed reality have raised the problem of the so-.called "digital divide." The network society draws the line of exclusion in terms of connectivity. Connectivity, as will be discussed below, is a network norm and one of the constituting principles of the social operating system.

As the name suggests, layers can be stacked, added to each other one on top of the other, and reduced or subtracted from each other. A layer of "gourmet restaurants within a radius of two hundred yards," for example, could be added to what can be seen from the corner of Worth and Hogan. Filters open up or disclose layers. They add or reduce layers. Filters are questions, they are "matters of concern" (Latour). The search query in Google for gourmet restaurants on the basis of GPS location is a filter. Any question is a filter, whether it be the question of where the nearest gas station is, or Heidegger's "question of being." From the point of view of actor-network theory, it may be said that filters are the "programs" of actor-networks, the selectors of information, the codes that relate and steer flows in networks, and guide the processes of translation and enrollment that construct the network. Applying a filter entails all the communicative actions that translate, enroll, and inscribe actors into a particular network. Layers can be seen as the actor-networks that result from the application of filters. In terms of Harrison White's (1992) relational sociology, actors "switch" between layers and construct their identity by means of the stories that connect these switches together in an ongoing struggle for identity and control. Applying a filter is, of course, not the same thing as starting a search query in Google. This might be a part of what is happening in applying filters and constructing layers, but it is only a part. Applying a filter entails all those activities that ANT describes as translating, enrolling, and inscribing actors into networks. In short: filtering is networking.

Wittgenstein equated the limits of the world with the limits of language. From the perspective of a hermeneutics for the digital age, it could be claimed that the world is the sum of all possible layers. My world is at any time a function of the filters that are being applied in those networks which constitute my identities, personal, social, cultural, and ontological. In terms of sociological theories, basic concepts such as communication (Luhmann), translation (Latour), or transaction (White) can be re-defined as the application of filters. Social actors apply filters and construct layers of information with accompanying opportunities for action. The communicative actions and the interactions that apply filters and construct layers can be seen as the hermeneutics of the digital age. They are the construction of meaning, the networking, the ways in which networks are built, and the ways in which identities are constructed, maintained, and transformed under the conditions of mixed reality.

On the basis of mixed reality, new possibilities for actors and their associations fundamentally alter what hermeneutics as networking is all about and how it is done. Applying filters and constructing layers is not as easy as clicking on an App. There is more to navigating successfully through mixed reality, as we shall see below in the discussion of the social operating system, than being technically savvy. Networking is more than use. Actors are not just "users." Networking, the application of filters and the construction of layers is guided, indeed made possible, by a complex set of norms that structure and characterize a network society. In the following we attempt to describe what hermeneutics as networking after the digital revolution is and how it operates.

THE SOCIAL OPERATING SYSTEM

Mixed reality describes a form of social and cultural evolution that merges digital technology with all aspects of life such that houses, workplaces, offices, schools, universities, libraries, public buildings, hospitals, indeed, entire cities including the complex systems of transportation, energy, logistics, and communication they depend upon become interfaces, that is, one great complex, automated information and communication system. Building the associations, enrolling the actors, translating their programs, navigating, managing, coordinating, and making use of this heterogeneous, hybrid network of humans and non-humans is the job of what may be called the *social operating system*. An operating system, such as Windows, iOS, or Linux is the key software of a computer. It enables and controls input and output devices, coordinates functions, guides processes, and monitors the operation of all elements of the complex hardware and the various applications that run on it. It holds the entire system together. The idea of a social operating system was made popular with the rise of Web 2.0 and what is called "social media" (Spivack 2007). It refers to the increasing dependence of almost all activities on digital information and communication and to the integration of technological systems into work, play, learning, health care, etc.

As opposed to systemic and cybernetic approaches that are oriented toward prediction and control, the idea of the social operating system emphasizes the interdependence of automated systems and human participation and decision making. Above all, it refers to the emergence of a social order that is fundamentally bottom up, participatory, and self-organizing as opposed to a hierarchical, top down model, with closed feedback loops directed to maximizing efficiency and functionality. What is social in the social operating system is that it operates in such a way that functionalized intermediaries and black boxes are transformed into actors and mediators. The concept of a social operating system is based on hermeneutics to the extent that it assumes the "autonomy" of the object as a carrier of meaning beyond the intentions of either authors or interpreters. It is based on actor-network theory to the extent that it assumes the irreduciblity of entities and the primacy of mediation over functionalism. It can be claimed that the directives, the guiding principles of the social operating system are the structuring principles of the network society, in so far that is, as the network society is not reduced to the dystopian vision of the perfectly functioning cybernetic machine in which freedom, contingency, serendipity, and the unexpected are sacrificed for functionality, efficiency, and security.

NETWORK PRAGMATICS

Just as the industrial society before it, the network society has its own structures and dynamic, its own principles and norms. On the basis of an empirical long-term study, Tapscott (2008) identified typical "norms" or "distinctive attitudinal and behavioral characteristics" (74) of the so-called "Net-Generation." Tapscott's approach to understanding new media is based on investigating what the actors do with digital media and how the uses of new media influence what rules they follow in constructing their identities within the networks in which they live. In the following we will follow Tapscott's lead in attempting to identify the rules of the game of networking, that is, those forms of communicative action that construct, maintain, and transform networks. In keeping with the basic insights of philosophical hermeneutics and actor-network theory, we will extend the idea of norm to include not only human intentional actors. The result may be understood as structural principles or norms of a network society. In short, these can be listed as connectivity and flow, communication, transparency, participation, authenticity, and flexibility.

This list of network norms or principles differs from the usual attempts of new media thinkers, for example, Feldman or Manovich, who attempt to list the distinguishing characteristics of digital media proceeding from either computer network technology or digital content. Networking, we will claim, is not adequately to be understood in terms of such characteristics as numerical representation, density, compressibility, modularity, and variability, although these concepts are indisputably important for a theory of digital media. Indeed, networking is not adequately to be understood on the basis of a description of new media alone, but on the basis of philosophical hermeneutics and actor-network theory as well. Networking is not merely using and being influenced by digital media. *Networking is constructing meaning by constructing actor-networks under the conditions of digital media.* In much the same way as language can be seen from different points of view, syntax with regard to structure, semantics with regard to contents, and pragmatics with regard to usage, the theoretical status of the network norms we propose below is that of a *general pragmatics of networking*. We propose considering network norms much the same as Habermas has proposed a general pragmatics of communicative action. Network norms function as normative guidelines for the construction of meaning and identity. They are meant to describe what it means to be "rational" in a network society. It may seem odd to define rationality as something normative. Nonetheless, it must be admitted that rationality has never been a necessary condition of human existence or of reality. Neither actors nor the world have to be rational. The construction of meaning need not be successful, no more than there is any necessity that there be Being instead of Nothingness. Playing the language-game of networking is, as it were, contingent and voluntary. There will be many networks that are not constructed properly, that is, according to the norms and principles described below. Perhaps these networks will become large, durable, and powerful. Perhaps they will fill the front pages of newspapers and prime time broadcasts. They will even cause much suffering and cost many lives. But they will not, at least this is our hope, be able to compete in the long run with those networks that are constructed according to the norms discussed below.

We would like to emphasize that our list of network norms claims neither to be exhaustive nor exclusive. The fundamental characteristics of what has come to be described as a network society are very much in dispute and a matter of ongoing discussion. It would be premature and contra-productive to attempt to close this discussion or limit it in any way. In addition to this, we do not claim that the network norms and principles we have identified apply to networks as such, any and all networks, but specifically to networks in the sense of actor-network theory interpreted on the basis of philosophical hermeneutics. When speaking of networks and the norms that regulate their construction, we are referring to actor-networks and to the socio-technical forms of constructing meaning that can be understood as disclosing a world in the sense described by philosophical hermeneutics.

Connectivity

Connectivity refers to the quantitative and qualitative degree of relations, connections, and ties between nodes in a network. Much of what new media studies have identified as essential characteristics of digital media such as numerical representation, density, compressibility, automation, variability, and modularity are descriptions of the connectivity characteristic of digital networks. Generally, it can be said that connectivity stands in reverse proportion to the quantity of time and space that a network requires in order to operate. An example is the comparison between an older, fixed installation, desktop telephone and a new mobile telephone. The old telephone is located on the desk in someone's office. Depending on where a person is and what they are doing when the phone rings it takes a certain amount of time and space in order for a connection to be established. If the person happens to be in another room or at the other end of the office, it could take so much time to reach the phone that the caller might have already hung up before the receiver is picked up. If, however, the person is carrying a smartphone with them, then it takes much less time and space, all other things being equal, to make the connection. With the smartphone, the temporal and spatial conditions of connectivity tend toward zero, which means that connectivity has increased.

Of course it is not enough simply to carry a smartphone in one's pocket all the time, one must know how to use it and also want to. One must know what such a thing is good for and be socialized into a culture that uses this technology in many ways. This means that connectivity, considered as network norm, is not a merely technical concept, a name for the infrastructure of a telecommunications or data network, or certain kinds of devices. Connectivity in the sense we propose defining the term refers to an entire social and technical assembly including human and non-human actors. The human and non-human components are not mere cogs in a machine. They are actors in the specific sense that ANT uses the term. Actors are not black boxes with fixed input/output functions. They are "mediators" that contribute constructively and unexpectedly to the operations of the network. For this reason, the term connectivity could be replaced by the term "connectability," that is, the ability to resist and transform functionality, to influence other actors in unexpected ways, to translate, enroll, and inscribe other actors into a network. Connectivity (and connectability) are practically synonyms for the "social," that is, insofar as society is taken not to be a kind of substance, but "a trail of associations between heterogeneous elements [...] a type of connection [...]" (Latour 2005: 5).[2] For ANT

---

2 | Similarly for Luhmann society is an autopoietic, self-referential system of communications. Since the operations of an autopoietic system must refer to

the smart phone is an actor who makes a difference in the behavior of human users. This is also true of the technical network infrastructure, the mainframes, the routers, the software, and even the algorithms. If these actors are black-boxed into systemic functions and invisible forces determining social behavior, they lose their voice as actors, mediators, and as participants in the collective. In this case, connectivity is no longer a norm, but a technical requirement and nothing more. In fact this is usually how the term is understood in network science. Connectivity in the purely technical sense becomes a mere automatism, a mechanism foreign to the social and thus capable of "colonizing the life world" as Habermas would say.

Defining connectivity as the effort of connecting, of linking the actors to each other in an always contingent series of trials of strength transforms mechanism into negotiability and opens up the network to the social. For Latour (1988) "everything is translated" (167) and "everything is negotiable" (163). This is what accounts for the "social" side of the idea of a socio-technical network. As a network principle in the sense we wish to use the term here, connectivity is to be understood as a socio-technical concept. Connectivity is therefore not merely a matter of glass fiber cables, routers, antennas, protocols, packet switching, smart phones, computers, and so on. It is also not the internal connectability of one communication to another in an autopoietic system of communications, which Luhmann emphasizes, as when greeted by someone in the street we are obliged to respond. All these things undeniably make up part of what connectivity involves. But they do not define connectivity as a network norm. Connectivity on the level of networking refers to the ability to mediate, to translate, to do unexpected things and influence others. From the point of view of new media studies connectivity includes not only technical infrastructure, but also individual knowledge and motivation, organizations, regulations, laws, and many other things that under the conditions of being networked together have the effect of increasing or reducing the spatial and temporal

---

other operations within the system, communications must connect to further communications if the autopoiesis of the system is to continue. Within the systems model, communication is therefore also defined by connectability, although Luhmann does not use this term. The dynamic of the social system is the connectability of communications. In opposition to ANT, for Luhmann it is unclear whether non-humans can communicate.

conditions of communication. In this regard, connectivity, like the other network norms and principles, is a socio-technical concept specifically designed to describe the structure, operations, and guiding norms of the network society. Connectivity and the other network principles and norms discussed below refer at once to technical, social, institutional, political, economic, and other factors, insofar as all these are associated together to form heterogeneous actor-networks.

Defining connectivity in terms of reducing spatial and temporal limitations on networking is a quantitative definition. Connectivity, however, is not merely a matter of quantity, but also of the quality of communication. If the telephone call mentioned above was about the new architectural blueprints for a housing project and some accompanying design changes, then the person in question would also have to walk into the next room where the fax machine is installed or even wait a few days for the plans to come by post. With the smartphone, communication is not limited to voice, but brings with it also images, videos, hyperlinks, documents, and much more. New media connectivity is not only quantitatively, but also qualitatively condensed, multidimensional, and more complex than the connectivity that was possible before the digital revolution. This is not only the case for telecommunication networks, but for all kinds of networks. The fact that we can enjoy fresh strawberries in New York in the middle of January speaks for the connectivity of global transportation networks.

Connectivity (and connectability) as a network norm has bearing upon the much discussed issue of a digital divide. Connectivity as a network norm undermines any attempts to restrict access to the technical infrastructure and social competencies of networks. It undermines any attempt to make actors into mere intermediaries or black boxes and to eliminate the unexpected. The very discussion of a digital divide makes this clear. The structural dynamic of a network society operates to increase connectivity in all directions and finds no advantages in erecting "digital divides" or basing mechanisms of exclusion/inclusion on access to network infrastructure or network usage. We are not claiming that a network society knows no exclusion and marginalizes no one. We are claiming that exclusion and marginalization are not primarily matters of access to networks, that is, to the means of communication, as is often assumed in discussions of inequality and injustice under the rubric of the "digital divide." Models of oppression based on possession of the means of production typical of industrial society, critique of capitalism, and modern critical sociology cannot be taken over into the network society. This is not to say that the digital revolution has eliminated power and privilege. It has changed the terrain upon which inequality must operate and the conditions under which economic and political action takes place. Hierarchy is no longer an inevitable given of social order. Contests of power and trials of strength need not be modelled within a hierarchy, where those on top attempt to stay there and those on bottom attempt to get on top. Social change, emancipation, even revolution need not be a matter of moving up or down any kind of hierarchical ladder. After the digital revolution, top-down is not the only way communication under the conditions of scale and complexity can function. With the fall of the pyramid and the rise of the cloud the conditions under which power and privilege can be gained and maintained have changed. Connectivity is that network norm that dismantles hierarchies and creates the cloud.

Flow

Once a network has attained a certain level of connectivity, the "flows" of whatever moves between the nodes also detach themselves from the limiting conditions of time and space. There arises a "space of flows," a "timeless time" (Castells 1996: 407ff, 460ff.), which leads to deep structural changes in society. As we have seen above, connectivity means being connected via digital media with other people and with various sources of information. It means having access to the World Wide Web via many different channels and by means of different devices and carrying out different personal and social activities over automated information and communication systems. Flow follows from connectivity. On one level it refers to the movements of contents through the various connections within the network. Flow in this sense refers to the fact that everything is moving through networks in one form or another, goods, services, money, people, information, etc. On another level flow refers to unpredictable activities and influences of all actors within a network. Where there is connectivity, there is movement of actors making associations. And where actors are busy making associations, there are unexpected and unpredictable events. As Latour (2005: 132) puts it, a network is nothing more than the "trace left behind by some moving agent." Networks should not be seen as stable social structures, but as "flows of translations" (132). Flow is closely related to what we term "flexibility," which will be discussed below. The specific characteristic of flow as opposed to flexibility arises from the fact that connectivity has become so complex that flows are increasingly difficult to predict, to control, and to steer.

In complex, non-linear network interactions and transactions flows are not subsumable under hierarchical forms of organization and management. This makes it difficult to model networks as systems, for systemic order necessarily depends on selection, relationing, and steering. This is also the reason why the concept of filtering information has lost many of the negative connotations it had when to filter meant to censor information on its way up or down the hierarchy. Under the regime of the pyramid every form of filtering was also a form of exclusion and therefore censorship, a problem which was solved by attempting to legitimate in various ways the instances controlling information. Experts, authorities, leaders, bosses, and similar positions were established within the hierarchy by means of certification, mandate, majority vote, birth right, etc. Within the cloud, filtering takes on an entirely different function and can neither be explained nor legitimated by traditional political theory or by systemic imperatives of predication and control.

Self-organization and emergent forms of order, as well as those characteristics of new media objects that Manovich referred to as modularity and variability, can be said to be based on flow. Flow is an anti-hierarchical principle that makes it difficult to set up effective channels and barriers in networks and enforce unidirectional movement. Flow opens up black boxes and transforms purely functional intermediaries into actors, participants, and mediators. When interactions among large numbers of actors become the rule and knowledge reconfigures itself into a cloud in which, as Weinberger (2012) puts it, every fact has an equal and opposite fact, this is a consequence of flow. Many of the more sensational phenomena of digital media which have received much attention both pro and contra, such as viral communication, shit storms, flash mobs, Facebook parties, the loss of privacy, and to a certain extent whistle blowing and the rise of social capital, can be traced back to connectivity and flow. When long established democratic governments such as the United Kingdom react to social unrest by attempting to shut down Facebook or Twitter, this indicates that flow has become a structuring principle of society that cannot be accounted for within the modern understanding of democracy. When entire industries that are based on proprietary control of information—

the music industry is a case in point—lose most of their income within a few years, this indicates how flow is transforming not only politics, but also basic economic models and the conditions of doing business in a network society.[3]

Communication

Communication as a network norm refers to all practices, techniques, activities, influences, and negotiations that contribute to integrating nodes into a network and connecting them to each other. In short, communication means networking, constructing networks of all kinds, and therefore building social order. As a network norm, communication does not refer to what has traditionally been understood by the term. Communication is neither merely something that human beings do, nor does it appear in a binary opposition of either face-to-face or one-to-many. Ever since the beginning of history there seem to be only two forms of communication, egalitarian face-to-face interaction among small groups, and hierarchical one-to-many communication for large groups. The path leading from the one to the many is not only stony and steep; it is a journey that requires a kind of magic in order to perform the task of social integration, that is, to make the many individuals into the one society. Social theory relegates one-to-one communication to a supposed "micro" dimension of society, whereas one-to-many communication takes place in a "macro" dimension characterized by social systems, organizational structures, norms, and social forces constraining the freedom and arbitrariness of individuals. Communication, in the sense we wish to give the term as a network norm, means interpreting, translating, and networking, which takes place neither in micro interactions nor on the abstract plane of macro structures. Connectivity and flow presuppose a new form of communication in all areas of society; in business, politics, science, law, education, and health care; a form of communication not bound by the gap between micro interactions and macro structures and not subject to the constraints of functional differentiation and systemic closure.

The concept of communication as a network norm and as a principle of the social operating system orients itself on the problems addressed by

---

3 | See Anderson (2006) and Tapscott (2006) for a discussion of the impact of new media on business and economics.

the prominent place held by the concept of communication in present day social theory. For both Habermas and Luhmann it can be said that society consists of communication, or at least, is based on communication. It is communication that bridges the gap between the individual and the group. Communication makes cooperative action possible. It is through communication that cooperative action is structured into functional sub-systems such as business, law, politics, science, education, and art. Communication somehow jumps from the level of concrete one-to-one interaction up to the level of abstract and structured one-to-many communication in such a way that it grounds cooperative action and makes social order possible. For this reason, discovering and describing the conditions and forms of communication has become the major concern of contemporary social theory.

For Habermas, communication is grounded in a universal pragmatics. As "critical theory," Habermas's approach distinguishes itself from Luhmann's systems theory by assuming a "crisis" of legitimation (Habermas 1976) in society. The problem of legitimating macro structures on the basis of micro interactions can be solved by understanding how communicative action can be based on the discursive rationality that Habermas finds in interaction. Argumentative discourse can reconquer a life-world that has been colonized by functional forms of order. Under functional rationality Habermas understands prediction, control, efficiency, and calculability, that is, the typical characteristics of cybernetic systems. For Habermas, it is apparent that the functional imperatives and principles of systemic order are dominating what he refers to as the "societal community," or in another formulation that we will discuss at length below, "the public sphere" (1962 [1989]). This amounts to what Habermas refers to as the "colonization of the life-world" (1987). The idea of colonization refers to the domination of a people by a foreign power. The foreign power which in this case is said to be "colonizing" society is, according to Habermas, systemic rationality as it manifests itself in Fordism, formal and bureaucratic procedures, capitalism, and technocracy.

For Luhmann the point of departure for theorizing the social is very different. Society does not consist of human beings, but of communications. In words echoing Heidegger's remark that language speaks, Luhmann says that communication communicates. Luhmann sees the social system exclusively as a self-referential, operationally and informationally closed, autopoietic system of communications, wherein it can be said that it is communication that communicates and not individual psychic systems. Indeed, individual human beings are not participants in society at all, but are excluded from the social system, which consists solely of communications referring to further communications. It is not *what* is said that matters, and not even who says it, but what *can be said* about what is said. This doesn't mean that speakers are unimportant. On the contrary, one of the important things that can, indeed, must be said about communication is ascription and accountability, that is, who is talking and whether they are doing it correctly. But this information is only important because it enables communication to connect to further communication. The purpose of communication is nothing other than communication. In this way, society refers its operations to itself and guarantees its autopoiesis. Communication communicates only for the sake of communication, and nothing else.

One of the interesting and important consequences of Luhmann's theory of society is the status that speakers have within a system of communications. If the operations of the social system are communications, then actors are only relevant to the system insofar as they communicate. Actors, it may be said, are constructed for the sake of communication. They are functional elements like the tops and legs of tables. The table system needs tops and legs, but it doesn't care what serves as tops or legs. It could be wood, metal, glass, whatever. Generally, it can be said that it doesn't matter what the elements of a system are, as long as they serve their function. As long as communication takes place and this in such a way that other communications can follow, then the requirements of the social system are fulfilled and its autopoiesis guaranteed. In contrast to Habermas, it is therefore possible within the general framework of Luhmann's theory that not only human beings may play the role of actors. Any source of communication may be considered a social actor, although Luhmann reserved this role for humans in the form of socially constructed "persons." It is nonetheless interesting to note that both for Luhmann and ANT, anything that communicates can be considered a social actor. In this respect the theory of social systems and ANT see eye to eye. For ANT networks are constructed by translating, mediating, enrolling, and inscribing actors into certain roles. This activity is not the prerogative of humans alone. The gun in the hand can play a role in making someone into a criminal. The samples in the pedocomparator can represent the dynamic interaction of forest and savanah. Scientific facts "speak" for themselves. A social actor for ANT is a mediator, a translator, a networker. Even though there is a certain similarity in the way social actors are conceptualized in ANT and Luhmann's systems theory, they vary significantly on what communication means.[4]

The systems model is not bound to a theory of action in the traditional sense of limiting agency to intentional human actors. From the point of view of systems theory communication must only be self-referential. All that is required in order to construct a systemic actor is self-reference, that is, on the level of meaning, an identity. Groups have identities, companies have identities, institutions have identities, entire nations, supernatural beings, abstract concepts like "justice" (which "speaks" in every legal decision) and so on; all may have identities, all may be actors. Human beings, in other words, do not invent signs and use them to exchange information, as Habermas following traditional views would say. Instead, meaning systems construct actors (and not merely humans as every religion will testify) and use them to relate and steer communicative operations. When a world of meaning emerges out of chaos there emerges with it a myriad of actors, of self-references and sub-self-references, "who" carry and organize the communicative operations of the system. Generally, it can be claimed that a semiotic system constructs identity upon various levels: ontologically, for the system as a whole, culturally, for a group sharing a relatively wide spectrum of frames of action, socially, for various social roles, and finally personally, for individual actors human and non-human.[5] The internal differentiation of the system, that is, the "self-organization" of functionally differentiated subsystems such as politics, law, business, education, religion, art, and so on does the work of integrating the many into the one and transforms relatively unstructured interactions into semi-autonomous subsystems within society. For Luhmann, social integration is not fundamentally a problem of legitimation, as it is for Habermas.

Luhmann's theory of the central significance of communication for society is of course not derived from a theory of networks, but from the

---

4 | ANT has a much broader concept of communication as translation, mediation, and networking which is not bound to the standard model of interaction, namely, someone says something to someone which is reflected in Luhmann's communication theory as selections of information, utterance, and understanding.

5 | See Krieger (2009) for a discussion of the internal differentiation of meaning systems.

principles of autopoietic, self-referential, informationally and operationally closed systems. Functional sub-systems make up the macro-structures
into which communication "autocatalytically" emerges and which constrain the free and undetermined interactions of individuals. Out of the
"noise" of the egalitarian one-to-one interactions among individuals there
"emerges" hierarchical systemic order. The theory of social systems is not
a theory of a network society as are the theories of Castells, Latour, and
White. Nonetheless, these thinkers share Luhmann's radical definition of
communication as something that is not a product of individual speakers, who themselves are much rather constructs of communication. Social
actors cannot be thought of in terms of the modern view of the autonomous, rational subject as the foundation of a social contract. For Latour
communication is understood as a set of activities based on translation,
enrollment, and inscription. For Harrison White social actors are not human beings, but "persons" produced by "transactions" (1995) or practices
of "switching," and telling "stories" (2008). Introducing the concept of
communication as a network norm intentionally docks on to these new developments in social theory while maintaining a critical distance to both
Habermas and Luhmann.

From the perspective of new media studies, communication can be
said to refer to the use of the digital communication and information
technologies. Digital communication for its part is significant because of
the new forms of social networks that have arisen from it. Indeed, from
the point of view of new media studies, communication via digital media
is paradigmatic for communication in all its forms. For the first time in
human history, thanks to the digital media revolution, a completely new
form of communication has become possible; *many-to-many interaction*.
Traditional sociology is based upon only two forms of communication;
face-to-face, or one-to-one, co-present interaction on the one side and formalized, hierarchical one-to-many communication on the other. There is
nothing in between. Microsociology is concerned with interactions. Mac-
rosociology is concerned with large numbers of people in organizations.
This results in a social order consisting of two fundamentally different
dimensions, interactions on one side and formal organizations on the
other. It also results in the classic problem of social theory, namely, how to
bridge the gap between these two incompatible dimensions, that is, how
to integrate the many different individuals, who as Rousseau points out

were born free, into the one social order in which they find themselves in chains.

The division of the social into micro and macro dimensions is not without reason. It is very difficult, if not impossible, to exchange information and coordinate action in a large group of people on the basis of face-to-face interaction when everybody is trying to talk to everybody at once. Turn-taking alone does not solve the problem. If one tries to bring order into chaos by insisting that everybody politely take turns, one never comes to an end. On account of the temporal and spatial limitations imposed on face-to-face communication, interaction must be restricted to small, informal, co-present groups. Quick turn taking in a conversation between two or three people allows for an efficient reduction of double contingency and the achievement of consensus with the result that people either agree to cooperate or move on. There is a good reason, however, why this kind of communication is known as "small talk." As soon as the group gets larger and the issues more complex, "big talk" requires a different form of communication.

It could be claimed that modern social theory is based on the problems created by the temporal and spatial limitations of communication. When only a few people are involved in communication, face-to-face turn-taking allows everyone to have their say. But when more than a few people are involved it takes much more time and effort for everyone to speak until it becomes almost impossible for everybody to have their say, correct misunderstandings, clarify their different points of view, and somehow make a collectively binding decision. As Martin Buber pointed out, "dialogue" is a matter for I and Thou. The larger the group, the more inefficient face-to-face interaction becomes. Effective cooperation among large groups on complex tasks depends upon making binding decisions in the face of uncertainties. In large groups this requires that communication switch from one-to-one to one-to-many. One-to-many communication is necessarily hierarchical. In the midst of the jabbering many, someone hast to stand up above and stand over the others. Someone has to take the lead, be appointed, inherit authority by birthright, or be chosen by God to speak to all the others. In face-to-face interaction among a few people no one is giving orders. Everyone is on the same level. Suddenly, there is a jump to an entirely different mode of communication in which someone is giving the orders and everyone else is following them. Social order under the constraints of time and place necessarily becomes a pyramid with the many at the bottom and one at the top. There is probably no organogram of any social institution, association, organization, or group that does not somewhere take the form of a pyramid. This radical shift in modes of communication and accompanying structures of social order is caused by the spatial and temporal limitations imposed upon face-to-face interaction. Small groups are in small spaces and conversation moves quickly between participants. Large groups need larges spaces and much more time to coordinate communicative actions. It can be claimed that throughout human history building society in space and time means building pyramids.

With the rise of digital media and the replacement of the face with the interface, time and space become increasingly irrelevant as conditions for communication. Many-to-many communication becomes possible for the first time in history. It becomes possible to build large, non-hierarchical groups which can efficiently reach consensus and initiate cooperative action, largely independent of spatial and temporal limitations. Another name for large, non-hierarchical groups is networks. And perhaps the best visualization of network order is a cloud instead of a pyramid. Castells locates the rise of network society at that point in history, when the internet became the dominant information and communication technology. And it is for this reason that Latour prefers to speak of a collective instead of society. The collective is a space of networks that does not resemble traditional society, which is a space structured by the mutually exclusive opposition of either one-to-one or one-to-many communication and all of the accompanying theoretical and practical problems of somehow bridging the gap between interaction and organization, of the turning the few into the many and the many into the one.

At this point it could be objected that since communication is constitutive for the social as such the idea of communication as a network norm is at least questionable if not impossible. How can communication be a norm if one has no choice but to communicate? One cannot not communicate, as Watzlawick would say, any more than the *cogito* could *non-cogito*. What sense does it make to speak of communication as a norm that could be broken, but should be followed? One answer to this question is to change the "what" question into a "how" question. The issue is not to decide between communication and non-communication, which is impossible, but between network communication and communication that does not support networking. Our question becomes: What is network communication and how does it replace traditional concepts of communi-

cation at the center of social theory, and what consequences does this have
for understanding society?

Private and Public

Before the digital media revolution, communication articulated itself into
two domains, interaction and organization. If one understands society
from the perspective of the theory of communication, this distinction can
be considered the foundation for the important distinction between *private* and *public*. The one-to-one communication of interaction produced
a private domain in opposition to a public domain of cooperative action
that was structured by hierarchical, one-to-many communication. Private
and public are dependent upon each other. Even when publically binding, formal communication sometimes appears in the form of interaction
among few people, for example, verbal contracts, legal judgments in the
court room, marriage vows before the alter, etc. interaction is primarily
a private matter, confidential, not necessarily open to public view. This
is the basis of trust in such relationships as doctor to patient, advocate
to client, friendship, and love. In the newly arising bourgeois society of
Western modernity it also became the basis for economic activities freed
from religious or political constraints.

The one-to-one communication of interaction characterized by freedom of expression and egalitarian turn-taking in which everyone has a
chance to express their opinion became the basis for economic activities
in a liberal capitalistic society. In the liberal view, business takes place in
a realm not directly under government control. From Luhmann's perspective this marks the differentiation of the functional sub-system of business in distinction to the political system. From Habermas' point of view,
the realm of free and unrestricted interaction became the basis, at least in
theory, for legitimating political power. It was supposed that if anyone was
to take on the role of speaking to the many, then this had to arise from out
of and in continuity with one-to-one communication in which everyone
had a chance to speak freely. Interaction, although only possible for small
groups, came in modern bourgeois society to mediate a "public sphere" in
which, as Habermas (1989) has pointed out, large numbers of individuals could openly and freely discuss not only their business plans, but also
criticize government policies and power. In modern democratic societies
the legitimation of government power and policy, as well as hierarchy of

any kind, is based upon communication in what has come to be known as the public sphere.

The continuity between one-to-one interactions and the public sphere, which of course consisted of very many people, was fragile and uncertain. The constraints on communication in large groups tended to force interaction into a dimension that was foreign to small group communication. What became of interaction when the small group turned into a large public? One possible answer is to say that it was forced out of the public sphere. But if there was no room in the public sphere for interaction, where did it go? What became of the social status and function of interaction? These questions arise from the contradictory and paradoxical character of the public sphere. The public sphere was a public space for private individuals. What is left for individuals and small groups to talk about, when all important matters such as business and politics required the participation of many people and therefore could not be settled in face-to-face interactions? These tensions led to the emergence of what has come to be known as "privacy." Beneath the public sphere there arose a deeper form of privacy in which those matters were communicated that had no place in the public, those matters that one wished to hide from public scrutiny as well as from government sanction. There arose a specifically Western form of individuality coupled with the concept of privacy. Privacy can be considered a byproduct of the contradictions implicit in the idea of a public sphere.

The public sphere of bourgeois modernity was presumably based on interaction—"private people came together as a public" (Habermas 1962: 27). This required that there be private individuals who somehow existed apart from being part of the public. The public needed private individuals. What does privacy mean? Privacy was constituted as a purely personal identity and as a privileged space not accessible to public discourse. The model of privacy was the dialogue of the soul with itself (Plato), a "back stage" (Goffman 1959) where the social actor could take off the mask, where the rules and sanctions of social performance did not apply.[6] Pri-

---

6 | Note that even for Goffman the "backstage" was not without performance. It is a part of the dramaturgical structure of communication and therefore not a real place in which naked actors could exist. Actors backstage are not absolutely alone, encapsulated in an impossibly asocial subjectivity. Privacy is therefore relative.

vacy is like a secret room with all doors closed and the drapes drawn, a room no one can look into, free from the scrutiny and sanctions of others. Coupled with the idea of the autonomous, rational subject, it became that place where reason could form its own judgments on the basis of its own laws and not on the basis of the external influences of tradition, authorities, priests, and kings. Reason saved the private individual from irrational idiosyncrasy and a-social barbarism by transforming individuality into universality. The Hobbesian war of all against all was ended by the unifying power of reason and the social contract. Idiosyncratic, irrational, emotional, and even perverse or barbarous individuals formed a body politic. The Leviathan that Hobbes so eloquently described was conceived of reason. When the Leviathan arose private individuals were transported out of interaction into hierarchical, one-to-many communication. But the Leviathan wasn't satisfied with being merely public. In opposition to both the exclusively private and a-social space of individuality and the paradoxical private/public sphere, there arose the domain of politics. In the political domain, government, administration, the so-called public services, organizations, and institutions communication was indisputably hierarchical and took place in the mode of one-to-many.

Habermas (1987: 181) admits that attempts to coordinate action among large numbers of people "'overburden' the communicative resources of the population and so some form of 'relief mechanism' must be found." The mechanisms that relieved one-to-one communication of the burden of the many in the public sphere took the form of mass media communication and the development of symbolic generalized media. For Luhmann symbolic generalized media are codes structuring communicative action within the different functional sub-systems of society. Political communication is selected, related, and steered by the binary code of power/non-power. The economic system is structured by the code of buying/non-buying. The legal system is structured by the binary code of legal/illegal. The educational system is structured by the code of certification/non-certification. The science system is structured by the binary code of truth/falsity. Each functional sub-system of society excludes all communications that cannot be selected, related, and steered by its unique code. These "relief mechanisms" are problematic. Neither the mass media nor symbolic generalized media such as money or power could bridge the gap between unconstrained one-to-one communication among free individuals and hierarchical one-to-many communication that inevitably took over as soon as the social group became large. Luhmann solved the problem by banning psychological systems into the environment of the social system. Individuals were simply no longer a part of society. Habermas warned that free and unrestricted communication in the public sphere is in danger and spoke of a "colonization of the life-world"[7] by functional rationality. It seems that modern social theory offers only two solutions: the free individual somehow searching for order or the autopoietic social system that constructs individuals as functional elements for its own sake.

Mass Media and Representation

It is within the context of this problematic situation that media theory has become important. The public sphere is supposed to be the domain in which everyone can speak freely to everyone in order to reach consensus and on that basis coordinate cooperative action. The inherent contradiction in this concept is that the spatial and temporal conditions of interaction make it impossible for everybody to speak to everybody. Within the parameters of modernity this contradiction could not be resolved. The media, at first print media in the form of leaflets, newsletters, and newspapers, and then electronic broadcast media came to be the forms of communication structuring the public sphere.[8] When private individuals came together to form a public, they lost their privacy and individuality and were transformed into anonymous masses. The defining characteristic of mass media is "that no interaction among those co-present can take place" (Luhmann 2000: 2). The private individuals of the public became the masses of the silent majority, who had restricted access to information

---

7 | With the concept of "colonization of the life-world" Habermas locates the structural problem of the public sphere in the dominance of instrumental action and functional reason and not in the covert transformation of one-to-one into one-to-many communication as we do. We argue that it is because the public sphere cannot resolve its internal contradiction between one-to-one and one-to-many that cybernetic solutions present themselves as unavoidable.

8 | "What we know about our society, or indeed about the world in which we live, we know through the mass media." (Luhmann 2000: 1) For Luhmann it was the invention of "technologies of dissemination which not only circumvent interaction among those co-present, but effectively render such interaction impossible for the mass media's own communications" (15) that lead to the emergence of the modern media system.

and could therefore be manipulated by those in control of the media. Co-operative action was in reality not the outcome of one-to-one deliberation, but of one-to-many, hierarchical communication. No modern politician, businessperson, or scientist denies the power of the media, and no one who does not use the media effectively will gain and maintain political power, successfully market their products, or even get research grants. Modernity attempted to solve this problem by means of the concept of representation. Representation explains how democracy is possible under the conditions of the dichotomy between interaction and organization. Democratic process and the counting of votes became the mechanism of transforming one-to-one into one-to-many. Under the regime of the pyramid, however, representatives could only *speak for* the people in the mode of *speaking to* the people.

Coupled with the idea of political representation, the mass media created a public sphere in which the representative *spoke to* the many, but with the claim to *speak for* the many. Political representation is a concept that only makes sense within a public sphere that pretends to be based on interaction, but is in fact a media-based one-to-many communication in which representation takes the form of *speaking to* in the guise of *speaking for*. On the basis of the concept of representation and the reality of mass media, the public sphere turned out not to be a commons of private individuals, but much rather to be a placeholder for the masses and the silent majority. Communication became either a purely private matter or a matter of media representation, whose inherent contradictions laid the ground for eliminating it altogether by integrating communicative action into the functionalism of cybernetic machines. The algorithm doesn't represent anyone. It doesn't communicate in any mode. It operates. In situations characterized by over-complexity it is dangerous and irresponsible to communicate, it is much more efficient to operate. The tendency of present day society to react to the problems of complexity by transforming social processes into cybernetic systems can be said to arise from the inadequacies of traditional modes of communication. Modernity is based upon a public sphere defined by the task of somehow mediated between the one and the many, without having an appropriate form of communication to achieve this goal. The impossibility of turning the one into the many and the many into the one generates forms of complexity that push society more and more into that which Habermas termed a "colonization of the life-world" and Luhmann clearly modelled as the reduction of complexity through the emergence of self-organizing complex systems. The "society" whose "self-observation" (Luhmann 2000: 97) occurs via mass media is no one in particular, an anonymous mass.[9] If we wish to avoid this consequence we must revise traditional assumptions about privacy, as well as the public sphere, and relocate the question of how large groups coordinate their activities onto the terrain of networking and new media.

The dichotomy between one-to-one and one-to-many communication has emerged in modernity as the dichotomy between a private sphere and a public sphere. Modern subjectivity is schizophrenically divided into these two domains. The modern subject consists of a personal self on the one side, absolutely autonomous and beyond the reach of any social, cultural, and national conditions, and on the other side there is a social self, who in order to legitimate the sovereignty claims of democratic citizenship had to bridge the gap between the one and the many by means of reason. Rationality took on the task of making the barbarous egos of Hobbes' "state of nature" capable and obliged to communicate with each other and enter into the public sphere in such a way as to consensually form public opinion and thus legitimate government policy and also to participate in hierarchical organizations of all kinds. The public sphere therefore not only depends upon the specifically modern concept of reason, but just as much upon some form of technology that carries the individual voice beyond the immediate spatial and temporal limitations of the face-to-face encounter. Within the parameters of traditional print media and electronic mass media, the public space was structured in such a way that representation instrumentalized the masses into the intermediary of a silent majority. Since the masses were silent, it was necessary to speak for them by speaking to them. But since they were the majority, they had to accept what was said to them as their own will and therefore do what they were told to do. This situation, at least in principle, changes radically with the advent of digital media.

---

9 | For Luhmann the public is precisely that domain which is beyond the specific coding of any of the functional subsystems of society. The public "always describes the other, inaccessible side of the boundaries of all systems [...]" (2000: 105). This leaves the public without any coding whatsoever; a chaotic realm in which anything goes, since every communication can with equal probability lead to any other communication or to none at all.

The Socio-Sphere

The digital media revolution has largely made both the private sphere and the public sphere obsolete, or at least, questionable, and has created a domain that is neither private nor public, a domain in which traditional forms of association, including politics, are being called into question.[10] Latour chooses not to use the terminology of modern social theory at all and speaks of the "collective," a space of networks instead of a public sphere bound on the one side by a radically individualized privacy and on the other by hierarchical and oppressive social structures. Following Latour we propose dropping the categories of private and public and exchanging them for a new term, the *socio-sphere*.[11] The socio-sphere is neither private nor public, but is based upon the new form of communication made possible by digital media, namely, "many-to-many" communication. The age old limitations on communication forcing it into either a one-to-one mode or into a one-to-many mode created a public sphere that was inherently contradictory. One-to-many communication disguised itself by means of the concept of representation and pretended to be one-to-one communication, that is, a form of communication in which all co-participate equally. The affordances of digital media create an entirely new form of communication capable of overcoming the limitations imposed upon

---

10 | See Castells on new social movements in the network society. Van de Donk et al. (2005) also point to the significance of network-based social movements. In the same volume, Bennett (128) concludes his study of networked global activism with the remark: "The rise of distributed electronic public spheres may ultimately become the model for public information in many areas of politics, whether establishment or oppositional."

11 | Albrow (1996: 161) used the concept of sociosphere within the context of a discussion of the global age as end of modernity. Characteristic of the global age as opposed to modernity is the diminished importance of the nation state as control instance for identity and economic and political activity, the central role of the consumer as opposed to producers, transnational associations and the growing influence of bottom up social movements. In contrast, Fuchs (2008) follows a systems oriented discourse popular in the 60's in using the term sociosphere in the sense of a domain independent from technology (technosphere) and nature (biosphere). We follow Albrow and use the term to interpret Latour's concept of the collective from the point of view of new media studies. This difference is marked by the hyphenated spelling: socio-sphere.

communication since the beginnings of human history. This is what the technology does. The possibility of many-to-many communication brings with it the hope of resolving the contradiction of representation created by traditional media, namely, that one *speaks for* the many by means of *speaking to* the many.[12] In the wake of the digital media revolution the public sphere, and with it, the private subject of modernity, vanish into the socio-sphere. There is no longer anything like privacy and there is no longer a specifically public space.

The concept of communication can serve as a network norm in that it refers to all practices, techniques, activities, influences, and negotiations that are neither private nor public, but take place in a different domain than either of these traditional social spaces. Regardless of whether we speak of a socio-sphere, a space of networks, or the collective, once the public sphere has been transformed by new media, attempts to communicate in traditional ways result in contradictions and conflicts. Critics of new media often lament the loss of privacy, while simultaneously decrying the vanishing of authoritative, representative one-to-many communication. A typical reaction to the digital revolution has been accusations of exhibitionism on the one side and the dethroning of authorities on the other. Within the egalitarian, non-exclusive, non-hierarchical cloud everybody is exposed, everybody participates, and nobody can control the flow of information. The critics are right to point out that privacy is no longer possible, but they often forget to mention that it no longer serves any social purpose. What good does it do to attempt to hide an email address or a mobile telephone number, when personal and professional advantages depend upon many people knowing this information? What good does a Swiss numbered bank account do, when bank data are automatically transferred internationally? What good is there in refusing to participate in social networks, when most hiring, and even school admissions and

---

12 | See Bohman (2004: 135) "At the very least, computer-mediated communication offers a potentially new solution to the problem of the extension of communicative interactions across space and time and thus, perhaps, signals the emergence of a public sphere that is not subject to the specific linguistic, cultural and spatial limitations of the bounded national public spheres that have up to now supported representative democratic institutions." Although we do not follow him in all points, Bohman (151) forcefully argues for "rethinking both democracy and the public sphere outside the limits of its previous historical forms."

finding a spouse are being done via LinkedIn, Xing, Facebook, Google, etc.? What gain is there in turning off GPS tracking, when I miss my bus or can't find my way through the city? Why does one need to hide, when there is no advantage to it?

On the other hand, digital media allow personal presence and participation in global social movements without the anonymity that centralized mass media require. Individuals must no longer accept anonymity as the price for public communication. Critics are therefore right lament the loss of authority in the public sphere. They sense that without privacy traditional public communication in the sense of identification with opinion leaders, representatives, political parties, associations, and so on makes no sense. What need does society have of representatives, of preselection of topics and information, when everybody can communicate with everybody about anything directly? If everyone can speak out to the world, no one needs to speak for anyone and no one can or need control what is being talked about. Why should one rely on experts, when the solutions coming from the "wisdom of the crowd" (Surowiecki 2004) are better, cheaper, and faster? Opinion making is no longer the prerogative of experts, authorities, or those who control mass media. No one needs to speak for anyone else, since everyone has access to the means of communication and many-to-many communication has for the first time in human history become possible.

The crisis of representation and the possibility of many-to-many communication as the basis for establishing a socio-sphere in the place of the incompatible and antagonistic domains of the private and the public should not lead to a simplistic and unrealistic hope in direct democracy or participatory politics. These terms have their natural home in the political theory of modernity and serve primarily the purpose of at once uncovering as well as disguising the inherent contradictions of the public sphere by holding out the hope of a solution without overcoming the fundamental concepts of modernity. In this vein, it has often been noted that early hopes in the democratizing effects of the Internet have not been fulfilled. Present day controversies over "net neutrality" are a case in point.[13] Nonetheless, these hopes are not unjustified. The digital media revolution has indeed set the stage for reconceptualizing the social as well as the politi-

---

13 | See the discussion of net neutrality for example in Wikipedia http://en.wikipedia.org/wiki/Net_neutrality

cal. Not only has many-to-many communication become possible and the socio-sphere been opened up, but political theory is beginning to envision new forms of representation. The significance of communication as a network norm and as a principle of the social operating system rests not alone upon its function in constructing networks, but also in the kinds of networks that it builds. Latour (2003, 2004) has developed the consequences of actor-network theory for understanding social and political action. Not only has the modern division into a private sphere and a public sphere become obsolete and dangerous, but it has made it necessary to rethink the foundational concepts of communication, deliberation, and representation.

The Collective

One of the most important consequences of the emergence of the socio-sphere is that what had hitherto been considered the public is now dramatically enlarged and differentiated. If the opposition of private and public, as well as the opposition of society and nature typical of modernity are left behind and if it is assumed that "the social world is no more made up of subjects than nature is made up of objects" (Latour 2004: 51), communication is distributed throughout the collective and not reserved for privileged actors. For Latour "[...] speech is no longer a specifically human property, or at least humans are no longer its sole masters" (65). Indeed, the collective is a result of *distributed communication* in which all actors, both human and non-human, are allowed to speak. Despite the provocative statements that ANT has made about non-humans taking part in social processes, Latour (2004: 67) knows quite well that no one believes that "particles, fossils, economies, or black holes speak on their own, without intermediaries, without investigation, and without instruments [...]" This is the new role of science in the collective; to give non-humans a voice and thus a way to participate in bringing the collective together. To this end science invents *"speech prostheses that allow nonhumans to participate in the discussions of humans, when humans become perplexed about the participation of new entities in collective life"* (67).[14]

---

14 | Of course Latour is aware that science has always let the facts "speak for themselves." But within the parameters of modernity the voice of the "facts" came from beyond society, the realm of nature. Scientific facts were not part of political discourse, not negotiable; absolute truth puts an end to political discus-

For Latour "Democracy can only be conceived if it can freely traverse the now-dismantled border between science and politics, in order to add a series of new voices to the discussion [...]" (69). These new voices are those of the many non-humans whose role under the regime of modernity had been reduced to transforming social relations into systemic functionalities, automatisms, and black boxes. They are the foreign power that Habermas could only perceive as a mechanistic force colonizing the life-world. By giving non-humans a voice, they cease to be a foreign power. They become partners in society and participate in the socio-sphere. Communication for Latour, in opposition to both Habermas and Luhmann, can only be the foundation of the social if it allows *all* to participate in the collective. This requires that those who do not have a voice, whether human or non-human, be given a voice. This is the function of representation, of "speaking for" another in ANT.[15] The digital revolution has opened up the socio-sphere as the place of many-to-many communication. It is within the socio-sphere constituted by the social operating system that all actors can be taken account of and at the same time "be *composed* in order to *design one* common world" (Latour 2005: 259). In the socio-sphere "speaking for" is no longer distorted into the mode of one-to-many, that is, into the mode of "speaking to" characteristic of the mass media. This is the significance of communication in the general sense of a network norm.

Transparency

Connectivity and flow are based on network communication. From the point of view of a theory of communication for a network society, communication is synonymous with networking. Networking, however, is not any kind of communication. Not everything we say and do contributes to building, maintaining, and transforming the networks of which the collective, the socio-sphere consists. Networking demands a communi-

---

sion. Latour's intention is to renew political ecology by bringing science into the socio-sphere.

15 | For Latour science and politics should not be confused. There are two tasks in composing the collective. Science has the task "of taking into account" whereas politics is concerned with "putting into order" (2005: 257). We will return to this distinction later.

cation that is essentially characterized by *transparency*. Habermas (1984) has pointed out that something like transparency must be assumed to be a condition of the possibility of any meaningful communicative action. Habermas' universal pragmatics of communication asserts that meaning depends not only on claims to the truth of what is being said, the appropriateness of any particular communicative action within a social context, the understandability of what is said, but just as importantly, the "truthfulness," that is, the sincerity and integrity of the speaker's intentions. Regardless of whether the claims to truth, appropriateness, understandability, and truthfulness in any particular case are actually valid or not, every meaningful communicative action, according to Habermas, must at least make these claims to validity and be able to be held accountable to some criteria for validating them. That every communicative action, at least implicitly, must claim truthfulness implies that the possibility of self-concealment and lying is a precondition of communicative action.[16] Actually, what is to be expected in communication is the lie. Truthfulness can become a criterion of meaning only when communicators can be and often are liars. If one cannot lie, then it is superfluous to equip every statement with the claim that one means what one says. Claiming that one is telling the truth, however, is not the same as claiming that what one says is the truth. False information can be communicated truthfully, and in most cases is, since people are often mistaken about information. When validating truth claims, one simply looks at the facts. When validating claims to truthfulness or sincerity, one cannot look at facts. In the case of claims to truthfulness the facts are not facts at all, but interpretations of what can be taken as evidence either corroborating or not-corroborating the claims of the speaker about their inner intentions, which no one can see. Often the jury must decide if a witness is credible and which interpretation of the evidence to believe. And sometimes they are wrong.

Habermas (1992: 205ff.) argues that a criterion of truthfulness without the typically modern subjectivity of privacy makes no sense and he laments the fact that postmodernism, as well as philosophical hermeneutics, have thrown out the baby (the subject) with the bathwater (transcen-

---

16 | The same is true for Luhmann (1995). Communication is an autopoietic process of selecting, relating, and steering information, utterances, and connections to further information and utterances (understanding), whereby psychic systems, including their secret intentions, are excluded from the system.

dental subjectivity).[17] If there is no critical position and no subjectivity beyond mediation, beyond the disclosure of world in language, beyond the circle of references in which meaning, whether literary or scientific, is disclosed, then the claim to truthfulness could not be validated except by another claim, which would lead directly into an infinite regress of claims without ever reaching solid ground. It would be as if the jury wanted to verify the credibility of a witness by asking him again and again if he is telling the truth.

Digital mediation of subjectivity in the network society has changed this situation radically. Self-disclosure is no longer a strategic decision in the hands of private individuals, but a data set, information dispersed over a multitude of data bases, digital traces, discontinuous and distinct digital activities, from e-business, to e-learning, e-shopping, e-government, participation in online communities, blogs, wikis, social networks, and so on. Together these traces make up a digital profile that cannot, or at least not without great effort, be erased or undone, hidden, or manipulated. In the place of a strategic approach to revealing and concealing an essentially private subjectivity typical of the modern self, there appears "identity management" which is concerned with access, authorization, multiple profiles, and choices about filters and layers. Although experts often speak of identity management as a way of preserving privacy (Fischer-Hübner/ Pettersson 2011), the modern self, which was constituted by an immediate self-presence void of information, no longer exists. The digital self is neither private nor public. This does not imply that it is a mere assemblage of data. It is the construct of connectivity, flow, network communication, transparency, participation, authenticity, and flexibility, the principles making up the social operating system. The self of the socio-sphere is not caught in the tensions, contradictions, and Freudian pathologies of a dialectic of concealing and revealing. Concepts such as "voyeurism" or "exhibitionism," or even "anonymity" that are often cited in critical discussions of network communication and social media simply do not apply. The digital self does not fit into the psychological, sociological, and philo-

---

17 | See Habermas (1992: 210) "[...] this movement of thought has made transcendental subjectivity disappear without a trace, and indeed in such a way that one also loses sight of the system of world relations, speaker perspectives, and validity claims that is inherent in linguistic communication itself."

sophical categories characteristic of the modern discussion of identity, privacy, and subjectivity.

As a network norm *transparency* refers not only to a pragmatic condition of meaning, but to a pragmatic notion of truth as well as truthfulness. Networks are built on the basis of communicative actions that function as translations, enrollments, and inscriptions of actors into programs of action. No network can compete that is built on lies and deceit. If the norm of transparency is not respected and for the most part actually followed, it would not be possible to successfully translate, enroll, and inscribe actors into a network and hold them in place long enough to attain the goals of any serious program of action. It may be so that there is honor among thieves, but digital transparency does not stop at the robbers den. Complex connectivity, uncontrolled flows, and transformation of the public sphere into a socio-sphere in the network society make it risky business and almost always contra-productive to try to keep secrets.[18]

In this context one has come to speak of "naked conversations" (Scoble/Israel 2006). What is at stake is nothing less than the construction of identity under the conditions of neither privacy nor a specifically public sphere composed of the masses. The structure and dynamics of networks require a form of communication that is open, self-critical, respectful, and honest. It is for this reason that transparency can be listed under the foundational network norms. The complexity of networks and the unpredictability of flows within complex networks, contrary to traditional forms of social order, make it increasingly difficult, if not impossible, to successfully monitor, control, and filter information from any privileged point of access (Weinberger 2012). The hierarchy as foundational metaphor of order has been replaced by the cloud. The program of suspicion which lies at the heart of critical theory and the critique of ideology, and which was doubtlessly legitimate within industrial society, a society divided into private and public, must reorient itself and seek a new foundation and legitimation on the basis of the social operating system. As a network norm and thus a principle of the social operating system, transparency is based on the pragmatic condition of effective networking. From this point of view it can be claimed that transparency inherits much of what the traditional program of critical theory and the critique of ideology was concerned

---

18 | See Rawlins (2009) for a discussion of transparency indicators and effects for organizations in social media.

with. Established privileges with regard to the production, distribution, and control of information do not need to be revealed (German: *entlarven*) through the work of criticism, they are simply becoming inefficient, costly, and impracticable. In short, there is no great advantage in trying to keep secrets any more. What the critical theorists with great effort and immense cunning attempted to discover behind the backs of unwitting social actors and to disclose, debunk, and reveal to public view, is already there for everyone to see.

An organization, a private company, a political party, a government, but also individuals who do not openly and transparently communicate, must assume that they will sooner or later be exposed. Wikileaks, Off Shore Leaks, Dell Hell, Snowdon, whistelblowers, hackers, stolen bank data, and many other examples show that whoever is not transparent with regard to the sources and reliability of information and their intentions, competencies, knowledge, and interests is already suspect and will be subjected to scrutiny. As a network norm transparency means that every product, service, every public and commercial activity, and every claim will be publically commented upon, "rated," and systematically evaluated. Markets of all kinds and in every sector have become "conversations" (Levine/Locke/Searls/Weinberger 2000) in which the key to success lies not in the use of hidden persuaders and hype, but in building trust and community. Transparency is not only a structural norm in business networks, but also in social networks. Despite legitimate concerns for the security of personal information, the traditional assumptions about privacy and the protection of personal data are changing. In the network society "publicy" (Boyd 2010) is the default and not privacy. The experience and assumptions about what is public and what private are presently undergoing a widespread transformation. It is becoming increasingly difficult and even counter-productive to attempt to keep the private realm completely separated from the public realm or to attempt to manipulate, steer, and disguise information.

In the political domain "e-transparency" (Zinnbauer 2007) builds the basis for e-services as well as e-democracy. Apart from the impact of digital media on the transformation of the public sphere such that new social movements arise independent of traditional media, e-government is changing the way politics function. Whereas e-services advance democratic empowerment by streamlining bureaucracies, making public services accountable, more flexible and personalized, and limiting misuse of bureaucratic power by allowing citizens greater control of public service administration, e-democracy such as online-voting, polling, online deliberations, etc. eliminate intermediaries and involve stakeholders more efficiently and more directly in public policy decisions. Neither e-services nor e-democracy can function properly without transparency, that is, "comprehensive information disclosure by all branches of government" (1567). E-transparency is based on the recognition of connectivity, flow, and network communication not only between government and citizens, but also between different governmental agencies. This calls for new freedom of information laws and practices which run counter to centuries long convictions that political power can and must be based on strict control of information, if not censorship and secrecy. The old saying "knowledge is power" must be revised. More than a decade of research and practice in knowledge management has shown that it is indeed true that knowledge is power, but only if knowledge is shared, enriched, transformed, allowed to flow, and applied in unforeseen and uncontrolled ways throughout many different networks.

Transparency has many meanings. Open information and e-transparency in the political domain take on the forms of open educational resources (OER) in education, open research in science and medicine, and open source software in the IT industry to name but a few of the various forms in which transparency is becoming a norm of the network society. Creative commons has arisen to make information more accessible and allow the use of information beyond the restraints of proprietary claims. Indeed, many business models based upon proprietary rights are failing and traditional copyright laws as well as their philosophical and cultural foundations are being called into question. In the place of traditional attempts to control information within either private or public domains there has arisen a new imperative for producing and using information by all. This can be described by the concept of participation.

Participation

Complex connectivity, unpredictable flows, and transparent network communication lead to the norms of *participation* and *authenticity*. The structural dynamics of networks make it increasingly difficult, if not impossible, to control or steer not only flows, but also and just as significantly, processes of media production, publication, and distribution. Everyone who has access to the Internet also has access to simple and affordable tools to become a media producer and distributer, from their own home, no matter where they are in the world. The Internet could be termed a decentralized, interactive mass media. The foundation of the postmodern critique of mass media, namely, that a monopoly of the means of cultural production leads necessarily to manipulation of information, false consciousness, and systematically distorted communication (Frankfurt School, Cultural Studies, etc.), has all but disappeared. The rise of the Internet as dominant communication technology has led to the rise of what has come to be known as "participatory culture" (Jenkins et al. 2009). The dismantling of traditional privileges of mass media and government with regard to information control has opened the doors for the vacuum to be filled by everyone (Shirky 2008, Anderson 2006, Tapscott/Williams 2006).

Participatory culture assumes a fully new relation between the individual and society. Bloggers expose intimate details about their private lives, last night's party is already on YouTube for the entire world to view; "citizen journalists" (Allen/Thorsen 2009), that is, normal people who happen to find themselves in the midst of an event, make videos with smartphones and post them on the Internet, tweet what is happening live, and often provide important information to the public and to government authorities long before the professional investigators and news teams from CNN or Aljazeera arrive on the scene. Google Earth illuminates every dark corner of the world in high resolution and makes it possible for anyone to add comments, photos, and other information. Postings in Facebook document the entire lives of persons and families. According to Jenkins (2005) participation means that network society is based on almost universal access to media production, wide acceptance from society for those who share content on or through the Web, willingness to help and assist others to solve problems and find and use information, peer evaluation and quality assessment, and community building through sharing. Much of what has come to be called "Web 2.0" and "Social Media" are facilitators of participation. Experts also speak of a "sharing economy" or "collaborative economy."

Not too long ago, fears of Big Brother and omnipresent surveillance were much discussed topics, and many would have taken to the streets to protest against video cameras on every corner. Today the climate has changed and people are eager to establish their own media presence and publish personal information of all kinds in the Internet. The dangers surrounding issues of data security are nonetheless greater today than ever before. Data of all kinds, but above all, personal data is becoming a new source of wealth. A contemporary slogan claims: "Data is the new oil"! (Palmer 2006). The possibilities of generating value from big data are an uncontestable mega-trend in all areas of society, from business over education to health care and beyond. Currently data is being gathered not only from video surveillance, but also from internet user profiles, tele-communications, GPS tracking, contributions to online social networks, online shopping, e-commerce, e-banking, e-learning, e-government ser-vices, and so on. If one enters one's own name in Google and nothing comes up, then this is increasingly problematic and a cause for concern. Personalization of products and services in all areas is based on big data, transparency, communication, flow, and connectivity. Without access to big data and authorization to use it, automated information systems will not know enough about people to help them find what they are looking for, to get the education they need in the way they need it, optimize their health care, and save time and money in a myriad of ways.

Let us take advertising as an example: If you have a choice between dumb advertising that bombards you with useless, irrelevant, and thus aggressive and offensive information and smart advertizing that gives you what you need to know about products and services you are truly interested in, then who wouldn't choose smart advertizing? But if you check the box for smart advertising, the next step is to tell the system all about yourself and give the system access to your profiles, search and buying histories, medical records, educational transcripts, and much more. Without this information the system can't become intelligent, it can't help you, and you can't profit from the potential intelligence of the network. The more data the network has, the smarter it gets. The smarter it gets, the smarter you get. Cooperative action in hybrid-networks therefore depends on access to big data and the authorization to use it. The most important source of big data is user generated content. This includes Facebook or Google+ post-ings, tweets, blog posts, images uploaded into Flikr and Instagram, social book marks, YouTube or Vimeo videos, articles in Wikipedia, information on websites, social media profiles, search lists, and much much more.

Participation means not only that the "self-observation of society" (Luhmann's definition of the function of the media) is pluralistic and a game everyone can play, but it also means that the boundaries between real and so-called virtual forms of presence and action are becoming fuzzy and blurred. Fully independent of the technical possibilities for insuring data security and authorization with regard to access to and use of information, the ontology of the network society is a mixed reality in which the foundational distinctions of modern Western culture have become questionable. Participation means that individuals automatically appear within the socio-sphere and heretofore public activities such as labor, consumption, and politics become entwined with personal activities. Not only are the boundaries between personal and public blurred, but the traditional distinctions between functional subsystems such as politics, business, science, education, health-care, religions, art, etc. can no longer be upheld. It becomes misleading to speak of "domains" or "social systems" as if we were talking about entities, substances, macro-structures that are somehow different from the participatory activities of the many actors involved. Latour (2005: 238) claims that the social "[...] is not a place, a thing, a domain, or a kind of stuff but a provisional movement of new associations."

What then becomes of those macro-actors who seemingly inevitably appear on the stage of society such as politics, business, law, religion, art, etc.? They become ways of networking. "What does it mean to speak of legal, religious, scientific, technical, economical, and political 'ways' of associating'?" (Latour 2005: 239) If they are considered to be actor-networks, and actor-networks do not allow for clear and strict boundaries, then one must find another way of analyzing the collective. Latour (2005: 241) speaks of "regimes of existence" or "modes existence" (2013) in order to describe different ways of networking. From the perspective of new media we propose speaking of filters and layers. Science is a kind of filter that produces its specific layer, which, of course, is made up of many different layers stacked up upon one another. The same can be said of religion, or art, or politics. In the place of distinct social systems each constituted by exclusion of other systems, a network society can be described in terms of more or less encompassing actor-networks that operate by means of applying typical filters producing more or less closely associated layers. Participation as a network norm means that the socio-sphere is not bound by exclusive system boundaries and clearly demarcated domains. The socio-sphere allows, even encourages, participation in many different ways regardless of traditional boundaries.

It has become a commonplace of the network society to claim that sharing information and knowledge instead of hording it and limiting its use within closed organizational boundaries is what produces value. Whoever attempts not to participate in the mutual production, sharing, and use of information beyond boundaries becomes marginalized. The digital divide runs therefore not along technical lines, not even along organizational divisions, but along motivational preferences and media competency, and the ability to participate. It is not access to technology or to information that systematically marginalizes people in the network society, but unwillingness to participate in network building (Jenkins et al. 2006). Participation does mean that a private individual has moved into a public sphere in which information is dominated by mass media. Participation means becoming part of the "crowd."

The concept of "crowd" has often had negative connotations. Before the digital media revolution crowds were any large group of people who were relatively disordered. A crowd was what happens, when many people try to interact, when everybody tries to talk to everybody, and no one person, the boss, the leader, the police, the king, the president has the say. Crowds assemble on the streets or in open spaces large enough to accommodate them. They can quickly turn into mobs and become a problem for public safety and political order. Crowds were not the public. They were what happened when the public sphere failed to mediate communication such that one-to-many communication emerged effectively from the chaos of interaction. Much of the practical wisdom of governance in modernity has to do with managing crowds, steering them into desired pathways, or simply dispersing them.

With the rise of digital media and the transformation of the public sphere into a socio-sphere crowds have reemerged into social theory in a positive sense. It has become fashionable to speak of the "wisdom of the crowd" (Surowiecki 2004). Before the digital revolution wisdom was reserved for experts. Surowiecki argues that digital media have turned the tables and made it possible for everybody to be an expert, that is, with regard to the production and use of information. In the socio-sphere a group of people can produce better results than an individual expert. Of course not just any group can be expected to be wiser than an expert. The group must be heterogeneous and diverse, the members of the group must be independent and able to make their own judgments and form their own opinions. The group must be diverse and decentralized, that is, not coming from the same place, having the same background, etc. And finally, there must be some mechanism by which the different opinions of the group members can be aggregated, sorted out, compared and formed into a single opinion.

Given these conditions, all of which have been set into place by the digital revolution, it can be expected, as Surowiecki showed by citing many examples, that the results of the group are better than any single expert. Indeed, the principle that almost everyone has some specialized and valuable knowledge in some area and is therefore an expert has been strikingly verified by Wikipedia. Wikipedia showed that the crowd can produce an encyclopedia that is as equally reliable as an encyclopedia produced by experts. The wisdom of the crowd has taken on many forms in the network society. There is not only "crowd sourcing" (Howe 2006, 2008) for answers to questions and finding solutions to problems, there is crowd testing, crowd funding, crowd investing, crowd crafting, innovation markets, co-creation, and many more forms in which open and unrestricted participation in the creation, distribution, and use of information of all kinds has moved knowledge and decisions out of the hands of experts and beyond the closed doors of institutions and organization into global networks. Participation is a phenomenon that has come to be important in theories of collective intelligence, distributed cognition, connectivism, and similar attempts to describe and explain the effects of the weakening of hierarchical principles of order in the network society.

Authenticity

Effective participation is only possible when coupled with the norm of *authenticity*. Authenticity is a concept that is not only anchored in the modern philosophy of the subject, existentialism, and psychology, but also plays an important role in media studies. From the point of view of new media studies, many of the traditional ideas about how the self relates to itself in both philosophy and media theory are being revised. Authenticity has to do with transparency, but specifically with regard to self-presentation in the socio-sphere. Traditionally, authenticity has been discussed in terms of originality, credibility, genuineness, and realness as opposed to simulation. Within the tradition of modern philosophy of the subject, it refers to the relation of the self to itself. In the public sphere of modernity this task was taken over by the media. Luhmann defined the social function of the media system as the self-observation of society. Society relates to itself through the media. Communication observes communication in the form of mass media communication. As is well known there has been, and continues to be, much discussion about the "authenticity" of the media. To speak of authenticity as a network norm and a constitutive principle of the social operating systems requires clarifying what is meant by authenticity from the point of view of hermeneutics, actor-network theory, and new media.

A study carried out by the psychological faculty of the University of Texas (Gosling et al. 2011) showed that online social networks were not places where people flee from their real selves in order to present a fictional self. On the contrary, virtual self-presentation is an extension of the self and of the personal and social reality of the offline world. The online characteristics of a person correspond largely with who that person is in their offline existence. Studies on self-presentation in online social networks in the early days of the Internet, Web 1.0, almost unanimously reported tendencies to fictionalize the self behind the mask of anonymity which virtual communication made possible (Turkle 1995). Virtual communication and authenticity were almost opposites. With the advent of Web 2.0 and Social Media authenticity has become an important issue in networking and an important norm of the social operating system.[19]

The first experiments with virtual communication in the days of the forums and chat rooms of Web 1.0 did indeed use the anonymity made possible by the Internet for forms of self-representation and construction of identity that could be seen as simulation, disguise, misrepresentation, and play, if not downright fraud. Identity in the early Internet was often anything else but authentic. The postmodern arbitrariness of early Internet communication, the play with appearances, simulation, and difference, however, can no longer be sustained in Web 2.0. The Internet has become a network of communication and action in which nothing is forgotten, nothing can be concealed or kept secret, and no one can remain disguised for long. Every blog post, every tweet, every order from Amazon or eBay, every search query, every digital transaction, every "like" or "friending" in Facebook, every profile in social networking sites like LinkedIn or Xing, every Website visited, every online shopping transaction, online hotel booking or car rental, and every file that has been up- or downloaded is "caught" in the net, registered, and archived somewhere. Regardless of whether it is technically, or financially, feasible to delete ev-

---

19 | See Näser (2008) for a discussion of authenticity issues in social networks.

ery trace one leaves in the Internet, in most cases network communication and network building makes use of the sum of all virtual activities in order to construct a self, an identity, that can tolerate contradictions and tensions, while at the same time mediating a unitary self for purposes of ascription and accountability.

Successful networking depends on authenticity. It is no longer a question of hiding, erasing, eliminating information about the self, but of managing it. Networks are places in which identities are constructed and socially validated. Nodes in a social network are not the empty placeholders of the masses assembled into a public sphere created by mass media. The socio-sphere is not filled with the masses or a silent majority. In the socio-sphere there is no need to hang on to a self that is able to relate to itself and be authentic apart from information and before entering into the network. The private subject of modernity, who became the hero of existentialism, could be authentic to itself only apart from any external conditioning factors. The private self was a self that defined itself apart from information. Information belonged to the world of the object, the other, and therefore could only be an appearance in opposition to true being. Within the socio-sphere which is neither private nor public this situation changes radically. The network self is a construction of the network, whether the communicative activities that build networks be considered as switching and storytelling (White 1992) or as translation, enrollment, and inscription (ANT). The self is information and nothing else.[20] This means that authenticity can no longer be understood as an immediate relation of the self to itself in opposition to mediation and information.

Personal and social identities are constructed in networks by means of those principles and norms that make up what we call the social operating system, that is, the self appears within the parameters of a mixed reality. The ontological basis of the network society, which we propose to describe as mixed reality, would have perhaps allowed Manuel Castells to understand the relation between the self and network society less conflictually than he did. For Castells, virtual communication is above all disembodied and independent of temporal and spatial limitations. The self, however, remains for Castells something essentially different from

---

20 | For an example of the embodied self as information see the "quantified self" movement and the many techniques of "body tracking" interpreted as ritualized performance of networking in Belliger/Krieger (2014).

information. Castells (1996) therefore can only see a basic contradiction between the non-informational embodiment, materiality, and locality of human beings and the virtual existence as information within the "space of flows" or the "timeless time" of the network society. He speaks of a "structural schizophrenia" (3, 459), or a "bipolar opposition between the net and the self" (3), which leads him to claim that the search for the self in the network society "is a foundational source of the social construction of meaning" (3). As much as we would agree with this last statement, we disagree with the reasons Castells bases it upon. Instead of postulating a fundamental contradiction between the self and the net, we argue that the socio-sphere is the way in which the self relates to itself and achieves authenticity in the global network society. The self of the traditional public sphere is either absolute privacy, an indeterminate pure subjectivity, or an alienated social self, a self somehow caught and entrapped in the other. In either case it is a product of an ambiguous and contradictory "public" which on the one hand is neither within the functional subsystems of society nor entirely outside the social in a realm of non-communicative individuality.[21]

The "society" that observes itself through the mass media is in reality nobody at all. This is why authenticity is a peculiarly modern problem. How can "society" relate to itself at all? Who is society? What kind of self-relation is possible for the masses and the silent majority? How can the masses or the silent majority be authentic, and if they could, who would they be? On the other hand, how can a self that is void of any information-al determination relate to itself, except as an absolute will that chooses an absolute and empty freedom in opposition to choosing to be anything in particular? Our claim is that the social operating system positions identity within networks as a condition of the possibility of ascription and account-ability. Networking requires actors who can mediate, translate and enroll other actors in unexpected associations. This in turn requires authenticity. Authenticity is not an isolated self relating to itself alone, but a condition of effective networking. It is informational self-determination in the sense

---

21 | For Luhmann (2000: 104-105) the public "always describes the other, inaccessible side of the boundaries of all systems" and is therefore an undetermined disturbance for social systems. "If [...] the system reflects that it is being observed from outside, without it being established how and by whom, it conceives itself as observable in the medium of the public."

of determining oneself as information. It is only on the basis of authenticity that actors can be identified as such and held accountable for translations, enrollments, and inscriptions. This does not condemn the self to alienation. Authenticity still has something to do with freedom. It frees the self from being either hopelessly indeterminate or over-determined in the sense of a mere intermediary and permits it to become an actor and a mediator. Only an authentic self has something to say, something to contribute, can make a difference that makes a difference. To say that the self is information is to say that the self is a difference that makes a difference. Without authenticity no actor could be assigned roles or accept a role long enough to stabilize any form of social order whatever.

In order to understand what is at stake in introducing authenticity as a network norm, let us turn to the problem of authenticity as posed in the modern philosophy of the subject. Modern theories of subjectivity, from Descartes' *res cogitans* to Husserl's and Sartre's transcendental intentionality and absolute freedom are not very useful for networking. The modern self is fundamentally opposed to mediation and thus to information.[22] It is independent of any temporal, spatial, or bodily conditions, immediately aware of itself without the help of anything else. As soon as the self appears in public it becomes alienated, a function of an impersonal system, a puppet of unconscious drives, a pawn in the game of power and possession. As Luhmann (2002: 62) puts it, individuals "neither must nor can communicate their identity." To relate to oneself through another is a contradiction, or at least, a detour through the domain of otherness that contaminates the purity of self-immediacy. The immediacy of the "cogito" does not depend on thinking of anything particular at all. It is not dependent on mediation and therefore defines itself in opposition to information. To be anyone at all in the sense of having a social identity, a role to play in society, or personhood, is already to be mediated, that is, to be alienated from oneself and to exist in the mode of inauthenticity.

---

22 | It could be claimed that this opposition lives on in Luhmann's distinction between psychological systems and social systems. Psychological individuals are conscious and able to perceive the world, but the moment they communicate they enter the social system in which communication is subject to the codes of the functional subsystems. There are no individual, psychological selves in society and for this reason Luhmann can claim that authenticity is impossible.

The modern self is caught between the antagonistic and irreconcilable domains of freedom and determinism. The only way out seems to lie in embracing an impossible claim to autonomy and indeterminateness that denies all translation, mediation, interpretation, and connection. The problem of the relation of the self to the world, the subject to the object thus became one of the forces driving the development of modern thought. If the modern subject did not subject itself to reason, as in the rationalists, Kant, and the tradition of critical theory, then it was practically nothing other than an empty placeholder for the possibility of being otherwise, a possibility whose only expression is negation and whose only being is will to power. If you say who or what you are, then you can be certain that who or what you really are is nothing but the possibility of being other than what you just said.

The modern world is a trap of inauthenticity and alienation. The attempt to escape this trap and to occupy the empty space of not being anything in particular required for Kierkegaard a "leap of faith," whereas Sartre simply became ill (nausea) in the face of the oppressive opacity of the other. Authenticity in existentialism was a concept that located the self beyond and outside of any form of mediation and therefore in opposition to information. If there was one thing that the self was, it was not the other and no road through the other led back to the self, at least, not without compromises and sacrifices. In psychology, Freud and following him Lacan, saw the self as a weak and fragile attempt to reconcile the forces of chaos (libido) and order (super ego). The self fared no better in sociology. Social theory for its part pitted the individual against the social Leviathan, that is, macro social structures determining individual social actors behind their backs. Social life became a desperate and always unsuccessful struggle for freedom and self-realization against overwhelming external forces of alienation. When the self was not equated with transcendental reason, it was caught between a metaphysical will and an equally metaphysical other in a seesaw of compromises, resolutions, dialectics, alienations, repossessions, revolutionary promises, and tensions whose various formulations fill the libraries of modern thought.

It is within this context that authenticity also became a prominent topic for philosophical hermeneutics, above all, the early Heidegger. But it is important to note that the idea of authenticity in hermeneutics was developed in opposition to the dilemmas of the modern philosophy of the subject. *Dasein* had to choose between being lost to its own being in the inauthenticity of "*das Man*" or turning to that which was its own (*das Eigene*) in the mode of "ownness" (*Eigentlichkeit*). Philosophical hermeneutics did not, as did existentialism, refuse all mediation. Paul Ricoeur (1991, 1992) defined the self in much the same way as any bearer of meaning. The self is at once subject to meaning on account of historical facticity as well as the subject of the creation of new meaning. Subjects like objects are semiotically autonomous in that they both bear and transform meaning. Philosophical hermeneutics also did not attempt to solve the problem of self and other by a total and final mediation as in the Hegelian tradition, and to a certain extent, in structuralism. For Heidegger it was never a question to get out of the contingency of the hermeneutical circle, but to get into it in the right way. The right way is for *Dasein* to interpret itself in the mode of being of existence and not to mistake itself for something it is not. Authenticity is not a Kierkegaardian either/or, but an interpretive both/and, or as Ricoeur (1992: 104) put it, both "disjunctive" and "conjunctive." Overcoming the forgetfulness of being (*Seinsvergessenheit*) is the task of hermeneutics as fundamental ontology. This is an ontology of facticity. It acknowledges both the concretely given and the infinite possibility of meaning. It acknowledges that constructing meaning is application, action, making a difference that makes a difference. Authenticity in philosophical hermeneutics describes how *Dasein* relates to itself as understanding, as interpretation, that is, as translation, mediation, and the construction of world. The more authentic the self appears, the more mediated it becomes, the more differences, relations, and associations it gathers around itself.

This view is fully compatible with actor-network theory. For Latour the self should not be seen as a pure subjectivity condemned to seek for itself in a world of objective facts. The solution is to "make every single entity populating the former inside come from the outside not as a negative constraint 'limiting subjectivity', but as a positive *offer* of subjectivation" (2005: 212–213). For ANT, the self is an actor-network, a quasi-object or a "factish." In Latour's view "The subject learns from mediation. It comes from factishes. It would die without them." (2010: 62) Following Tarde, Latour (2012) sees the self is a "monad" whose associations with other actors make up its "attributes." Networking makes the self unique, concrete, and individual while at the same time articulating it into the collective. With regard to the possibilities of using the newly available resources of digital data in sociological studies, Latour claims that access to the myriad traces of the self in big data allows sociologists to finally see that "there is more complexity in the elements than in the aggregates" (2012). In contrast to modern social theory, ANT does not need to assume a contradiction between the inside and the outside, the one and the many. There is no problem of integrating the subject with the object, the many individuals into the one social body. Associations constitute not only the social, but also the individual. From the perspective of new media theory, it can be said that in the socio-sphere that is opened up by the social operating system there is no difference between self and society. The self relates to itself and achieves authenticity in networking.

To a certain extent, new media studies have taken over the discussion of authenticity from the way it was handled in traditional media studies (Lindner 1996, Näser 2008, Gilpin et al. 2010). Already within the parameters of traditional media it was clear that the authenticity of a media product could not be based on truth, that is, on a kind of *adequatio medium ad rem*. The representation of the world produced by the media could be authentic, independent of the question of whether it was true or not. These issues have been discussed in terms of concepts such as "originality" or "uniqueness" of a work in relation to media content. Walter Benjamin opened up this discussion with an analysis of the originality of the work of art in an age of automatic reproduction. The discussion was carried further with regard to news reporting, film, and above all documentary film. The outcome is that today it is generally acknowledged that media productions can be accepted as authentic apart from proof of their truth. The conditions under which a media product could be accepted by an audience as authentic are relative to topic, genre, time, place, medium, audience, and other factors. What one audience would consider authentic, another audience would find inauthentic. Authenticity is a kind of "contract" (Hattendorf 1994) reached between producers and audiences in which conditions of authenticity are negotiated in the face of different expectations. Authenticity, originality, and integrity not only of media content, but of the self as media content, are context dependent. From the point of view of identity management, authenticity is a problem of *contextual integrity*.

Within the parameters of digital media, that is, within a socio-sphere conditioned by connectivity, flow, communication, transparency, and participation the media have become a relation of the community to itself, a self-observation of society (Luhmann), but in a very different way than mass media had made this possible. It is no longer the anonymous masses that must somehow relate to themselves through a media they do not control and whose content they do not produce. The affordances of traditional mass media create an inherently contradictory public sphere. The affordances of digital media do not create a crisis of representation when those speaking for others are forced to do this in the mode of speaking to. Authentic participation in the socio-sphere means precisely that what is mediated is the self, since it is the self that produces media content within a situation of contextual integrity. Speaking for others is no longer necessary, since the self occupies both the position of the subject and the object. For Latour this constitutes the distinguishing characteristic of what can be called the political.

The relation of the self to itself as at once producer and consumer of information within a network of many-to-many communication corresponds to what Latour has characterized as the true nature of the political. The political is not a closed, self-referential, functional sub-system of society, the struggle for power and office in parties, parliaments, and public campaigning. The political is a form of communication in which those delegating the right to speak for others are themselves being delegated by the others such that all are mediators and no one is instrumentalized and forced into the role of being an intermediary. "When I talk, someone else makes me talk—I obey—and that someone else says only what I tell him/her to say—s/he represents me" (2003: 157). The self is at once producer and product and for this reason the product need no longer be the empty, anonymous self that filled the ranks of the masses. In the socio-sphere there is no silent majority to be manipulated by those who supposedly represent them and no representatives who must pretend to be mere mouthpieces of the people. The political is neither an ideal speech situation (Habermas) nor a particular way of organizing those communicative actions that are solely concerned with gaining and maintaining office, influence, and power (Luhmann). Instead, the political is all the efforts that compose the collective, whether they have anything to do with the official political system or not. In politics, as in good networking, there are only mediators and no intermediaries.

From the point of view of authenticity as a network norm it can be claimed that politics is the self-mediation of the socio-sphere. Authenticity in this sense has nothing to do with privacy or with the public, that is, with those modern spaces created by the mass media and the impossibility of reconciling one-to-one with one-to-many communication. Let us recall that for Heidegger the problem of interpretation was a matter of getting into the hermeneutical circle in the right way. This had something to do with authenticity, with the way the self relates to itself. For Latour the right way to be in this circle is that I am speaking what another has told that I have told them. Mediation and translation mean that I am being made to say something by another, but what I say, I have made the other say. In terms of the hermeneutical circle, the part expresses the whole that itself is an expression of the part. The important point in this process is that although everyone is speaking for everyone else, no one is saying the same thing. No one simply repeats, no one is made into a mere mouthpiece. Everything that is said is an intervention, an action, a mediation that is in some way new and different. Understanding interpretation as networking admits many into the circle who were previously excluded, whether as pure subjects or pure objects. But this does not turn society into a disordered crowd of so-called "quasi-subjects" and "quasi-objects" all clamoring to be heard.

The crowd, the cloud, or the collective may be good metaphors for the socio-sphere that has been opened up by networking and the social operating system, but they emphasize only one aspect of many-to-many communication, namely, the many. Communication implies more than mere plurality; it implies authenticity as self-mediation. The effect of the social operating system is to produce a self that is the information that networking produces. It cannot take up a position somehow outside all networks and find its authenticity in an impossible choice to resist information in all forms. The new transparency and participation that arise from the affordances of digital media do, as critics point out, make authenticity impossible. The solution, however, does not lie in attempting to recover what has been irretrievably lost, but in acquiring a new understanding of the term. In the transparent and participatory culture of the socio-sphere every individual who participates in communication is the message. The socio-sphere is therefore essentially constituted by expectations of truthfulness in representations.[23]

The attempt to present oneself in social networks other than one is makes no sense and runs not only against contextual expectations of media producers and consumers, who are identical, but is doomed to failure.

---

23 | See the discussion of authenticity and betrayal of trust in Youtube in Näser (2008) und Munker (2006).

Participatory culture reacts critically to media practices typical of a non-participatory culture. Overflows of mass media production practices into the socio-sphere are quickly discovered and sanctioned by the community (Munker 2006). Authenticity is not opposed to networking, but much rather a constitutive mode of constructing networks. The authentic self is connected, involved in flows, communicates, is transparent, and participates. Inauthenticity on the other hand cannot be equated with mediation, the alienation of the self in the other, the presentation of the self as information. Instead, inauthenticity means denying connectivity, blocking flows, attempting to communicate in modes that do not support networking, attempting to preserve a privacy that is somehow other than information, refusing to participate in the socio-sphere, the space of networks, the field of interpretation. It is in this sense of the word that authenticity may be considered a network norm and a principle of the social operating system. Network theorists who emphasize the wisdom of the crowd and the significance of new bottom-up, self-organizing social movements point to the new ways in which the many can be aggregated, ordered, and composed offered by networks. Despite fuzzy borders, scalability, and flexibility networking is not messy. It is a process of creating social order, of not merely collecting, but of bringing the collective together into a society. It may be that networking, as opposed to system building, works with less powerful tools for reducing complexity, drawing boundaries, indeed, organizing. On the other hand, the point of no return on the road to over-complexity has perhaps long been passed and it could well be that the forces of systemic closure, of prediction and control are fighting a losing battle anyway.

Flexibility

Without stability there can be no social order, no reduction of double contingency, no shared expectations, no interactions, no organizations, no institutions, and no social structures. These are generally accepted assumptions of social theory. On the other hand, without variation, innovation, transformation, indeed, revolution, there could be no history and society would collapse under the burden of a petrifying conservatism. The tension between order and transformation is a major theme of history and a major problem for social theory. The debate between hermeneutics and critical theory (associated with the names of Gadamer and Habermas) is only one recent version of an age old discussion. The present proposal to renew philosophical hermeneutics on the basis of actor-network theory and new media studies must, of course, attempt to formulate and answer the question of social and cultural transformation in its own way. The claim that network society is structured and guided by a social operating system consisting of network norms and principles attempts to address the issue of social and historical transformation in terms of the norm of *flexibility*.

Flexibility is a term often found in network science. Chemical, biological, and even social networks can be characterized by structural and functional rigidity/flexibility. This characteristic of networks refers almost always to the complexity of systems. Flexibility or rigidity is defined by the quantity of possible states of a system as well as by potential influences in the environment. The more complex a system is, the more flexible it is, since it has more adaptive operations at its disposal. The less complexity, the less internal states available for adaptive operations, the more rigid the system appears. Of course, pointing to complexity, open borders, heterogeneity, and scalability does not in itself answer the question of stability and change, but it points in the right direction. In order to move towards an answer to the problem of social transformation we propose to redefine the concept of flexibility as a principle of the social operating system. Flexibility interoperates with the norms of connectivity, flow, communication, transparency, participation, and authenticity and is a constitutive principle of the social operation system. What makes the social operating system different from non-social operating systems is perhaps most easily explicated in terms of flexibility, for it is within the socio-sphere that fixed relations, black boxes, functional imperatives are brought into the open, questioned, and made contingent. From the point of view of the social operating system, it is not complexity that makes a network flexible, but the kind of networking being done.

Traditional social theory has mapped the question of stability and change onto the macro and micro dimensions of society. The omnipresent micro/macro distinction not only lays the foundation for discussions of integration and legitimation, as discussed above under the network norm of communication. It also answers the question of stability and order. The question of how collective structures emerge from the transient, essentially instable activities of individuals and how these structures then turn on individuals restricting their freedom and solidifying relations is a major issue in modern social theory. On the side of stability there are large social structures, social actors, social facts, such as roles, classes, systems, cultures, etc., whereas on the side of change, instability, uncertainty, and contingency there are the fee and restless individuals. How can the gap be bridged between micro and macro actors, between the small individual and the large, long-lasting collective? How can phenomena such as institutions, organizations, nations, rules, roles, etc. arise from the instable, fleeting, conflicting, and contradictory interactions of individuals? And once such social facts have arisen, how can the freedom, spontaneity, and contingency of human action be sustained against the overwhelming forces of such macro social structures? Without being able to answer, or even meaningfully ask, questions such as these, there would be no such thing as sociology, since every social question would be a question that could be answered by appealing to conditions and constraints coming from some other domain of reality, for example, psychology, biology, or even physics. If society is not a phenomenon *sui generis*, then there is no need for social theory and nothing to be learned from the social sciences. And if society is a domain of reality in its own right, then what does it consist of? What are the *faits sociaux* (Durkheim) that make up the social realm and constitute the objects of social science?

Social theories based upon communication such as those of Habermas and Luhmann have reformulated the problem of structure in terms of the conditions of communication. The mechanisms that connect individuals and integrate them into social forms of order are communicative structures. Habermas understood Parson's generalized symbolic media, for example, money and power as macro forces "colonizing" a life-world modelled on face-to-face interaction among free individuals. Macro social phenomena were to be considered legitimate only to the extent that they could be directly generated from unrestrained communication, that is, the unrestricted ability to make claims to validity against commonly accepted criteria of truth, correctness, truthfulness, and understandability. For Luhmann, the functional subsystems of society, such as politics, law, economics, science, religion, art, and the media themselves coded communication in terms of binary opposites in their own generalized symbolic media. Psychic individuals become social persons the moment they opened their mouths entering thereby at once into communication and into society. They were forced to leave their psychological individuality and contingency outside the door before entering the social system. Outside, individuality became a source of perturbations in the environment of the social system. Whether within or without society, individuals are the source of contingency and change, whereas macro structures in the form of generalized symbolic media and their constructions such as organizations, institutions, etc. guarantee redundancy, regularity, stability, durability, and order.

Philosophical hermeneutics rejected the dichotomy of micro/macro and with it the assumed antagonism of freedom and order typical of modern social theory. Hermeneutics explicitly located human existence within the historical and social world of facticity, wherein, despite the importance of tradition, the task of constructing meaning originated from an infinitely open horizon of possibilities. Indeed, *Dasein* exists as projection of its own possibilities and with this, the disclosure of a world of meaning in which these possibilities can be realized. Hermeneutical understanding is therefore never a mere redundancy, a slavish copying of the past, but the "being of such potentiality-for-being" (Heidegger 2010). It is semiotic contingency, the openness to other interpretations that guaranteed the autonomy of the text and its freedom from becoming instrumentalized as a function within a fixed structure. For Gadamer and Ricoeur, the "autonomy," or "distance" of the text, the artifact, the object of interpretation guaranteed the independence of interpretation from finality, closure, and totality, while at the same time grounding the facticity of the subject. Author, text, and interpreter are neither subjects nor objects, but mediators of meaning. Even if any interpreter attempted to establish a final interpretation, an absolute and unchanging truth, this would be only one interpretation among other possible interpretations. Even if understanding does not break out of the hermeneutical circle, it constantly extends and diversifies it with new meaning. For philosophical hermeneutics, the construction of meaning is a historical process whose dynamic does not result from the antagonism of freedom and order, but from the participation of all carriers of meaning in continually deepening understanding.

Actor-network theory locates the construction of meaning in the dynamic of networking. What Latour calls the "collective" consists neither of subjects nor of objects. It is a realm of associations in the making. Networks are not social structures. They are not large macro actors that somehow contain individuals, making them into functionalized elements within a closed system.[24] Networks do not arise from out of the absolute freedom of autonomous, rational subjects and become somehow distorted into oppressive structures from which individuals must continually struggle to free themselves by means of critical theory and explanatory methods of a value free and objective science. ANT suggests that we do not follow traditional assumptions about what society is and what it is made of, but follow the actors and their own ways of describing what they are doing. What thereby comes to light is a conflict of different interpretations and actors, who "are always engaged in the business of mapping the 'social context' in which they are placed" (Latour 2005: 32).

Far from it being the role of sociologists to debunk what actors themselves believe and reveal the supposedly hidden mechanisms operating behind the backs of actors, "Actors do the sociology for the sociologists and sociologists learn from the actors what makes up their set of associations" (32). Within the parameters of modernity, however, actors are not allowed to speak for themselves, they are silenced and excluded from the social world. Potentially fluid, contingent, open, and transformable networks became petrified into macro social structures oppressing individuals. This is the reason why questions of power, inequality, and injustice have remained unresolvable within traditional social theories. For ANT, the strict division of reality into the mutually exclusive domains of subject and object, society and nature has robbed exactly those actors of their voice who contribute most to making networks durable, long lasting, and stable, namely, non-humans.

ANT proposes to enlarge the discussion on stability and order by including all those actors who modernity banned from society. Objects, technological artefacts, and nature are not to be seen as outside the domain of society, forming a realm of deterministic causality, structure and order that can only be understood as a kind of foreign power capable of "colonizing" (Habermas) the social realm. "By putting aside the practical means, that is the mediators, through which inertia, durability, asymmetry, extension, domination is produced and by conflating all those different means with the powerless power of social inertia, sociologists, when they are not careful in their use of social explanations, are the ones who

---

24 | "[...] things are not ordered by size as if they were boxes inside boxes. Rather they are ordered by connectedness as if they were nodes connected to other nodes." Latour (2011: 6)

hide the real causes of social inequalities." (Latour 2005: 85) By giving all actors, human and non-human, their voice within the collective black boxes can be reopened, fixed functional roles can be transformed, and the flexibility of networks be restored.

According to ANT, it is the many non-human actors that play the most important role in stabilizing social order and determining the flexibility of networks. What makes groups or associations durable, long-lasting, and scales them up to the dimensions of seemingly inflexible institutions, cultures, nations, and other macro structures is the work of translating and enrolling actors and establishing intermediaries.[25]

"Everything in the definition of macro social order is due to the enrolment of non-humans—that is, to technical mediation. Even the simple effect of duration, of long-lasting social force, cannot be obtained without the durability of nonhumans to which human local interactions have been shifted. [...] Society is the outcome of local construction, but we are not alone at the construction site, since there we also mobilize the many nonhumans through which the order of space and time has been reshuffled. To be human requires sharing with nonhumans." (Latour 1994: 51)

What appears to be structural rigidity are the many actors that have become intermediaries, who have been black boxed into functional roles. From the point of view of systems theory, selection, relationing, and steering constructs system elements as functional entities. An element of a system is a function and nothing more. The individuality of such an entity can only be seen as a "constraint" that must be overcome in order for it to fit into the function that the system requires. Not anything and everything can easily be used to make a table, but with the right tools and enough effort almost anything will do. Only by constructing elements as functions can the operations of the system be steered toward attaining specific goals, and the difference between system and environment be upheld. What elements are for systems theory, intermediaries are in ANT. In opposition to mediators, intermediaries are actors that have been reduced to

25 | For Hernes (2008: 128) "[...] organization is about attempts at some ordering, redirection or stabilization in a fluid world forever in a state of becoming, where nothing is ever accomplished in a final state." On the basis of Whitehead, Latour and others Hernes pleads for analyzing organizations "as the process of connecting entities in the making" (129).

black boxes, that is, input/output processes. They have lost their own voice and speak now only for those actors that deploy them.

Extended networks of intermediaries create the durability, stability, and apparent fixity of those social phenomena that have traditionally been described as macro actors, as relations of power, and as social structures. The more intermediaries in a network the more effort must constantly be invested in keeping the black boxes closed, making input/output processes reliable, and maintaining the network by enrolling new actors. Networks that are large and diversified cannot without great effort be deconstructed or transformed. They take on the appearance of hard, durable reality; indeed, they are the "reality" of the network society. Regardless of how large and influential a network may become, for example, a large company such as Nokia, it is nonetheless made up of actors and mediators that are essentially open to reconfiguration and redeployment in alternative or even conflicting networks, as Nokia experienced when Apple reinvented the telephone. ANT "pictures a world made of concatenations of mediators where each point can be said to fully act" (Latour 2005: 59). Any part of the network can unexpectedly become dysfunctional and begin to "act" in unforeseeable ways. Functionalized intermediaries or black boxes can at any time be opened up to become "mediators triggering other mediators" such that "new and unpredictable situations will ensue" (59). This makes the social into "a type of momentary association which is characterized by the way it gathers together into new shapes" (65). Traditional issues of stability and change along with their founding assumptions in the opposition of intrinsically fee individuals to intrinsically oppressive social structures disappear altogether and in their place arise conflictual processes of networking in which both human and non-human actors are involved as participants.

From the perspective of new media studies it can be claimed that the digital media revolution has given the collective of humans and non-humans a new possibility of expression. It did away with the private as well as the traditional public spheres and has merged them into a new field of communicative action that we have termed the socio-sphere. When the isolated subject of modern social theory merges with information and becomes a participant in the socio-sphere, so do the voiceless objects of nature. The socio-sphere, as ANT would say, consists neither of subjects nor of objects, but actors, mediators. The affordances of digital media make it increasingly difficult to deny any actor a voice in the collective. In the socio-sphere all intermediaries become potentially mediators. The imperatives of prediction, control, and functionality lose their unquestioned dominance. Both humans and non-humans regain the voice they lost when they were banned into the realm of functional black boxes and silent objects of nature under the regime of deterministic causality. Indisputable facts become disputable, negotiable, and thus political.

The socio-sphere is constituted by the network norms of connectivity, flow, communication, participation, authenticity, and flexibility. On the basis of what has been said above about constructing meaning in philosophical hermeneutics and networking in ANT, the concept of flexibility can be defined not only as the inevitable transiency of social ties, but more importantly, flexibility is the normative rule to accept heterogeneity of those participating in the socio-sphere by allowing all a voice and the power of mediation. In opposition to attempts to reduce complexity by means of functionalism and systemic closure, networking follows the norm of flexibility by striving to increase complexity, blur boundaries, flatten out hierarchical communication, and support diversity. Innovation becomes a major value with its corollary of acceptance of process, dynamics, and change, and suspicion with regard to attempts to enforce stability, durability, and structure. New media studies have shown that networks become "smart" when they are open, heterogeneous, and dynamic (Surowiecki 2004). When innovation, change, dynamic process become values in the place of stability, structure, and order than the age old antagonism between structure and process disappears and in its place there appears networking.

Flexibility also implies the acceptance of differences of scale. Not everything that is big is beautiful. Small associations can often innovate better and faster than large organizations. Flexibility refers not merely to size, but change of size. Networking that is open to adding new actors and mediators, to docking on to other networks, depending on goals and conditions, and to self-organizing in different ways are more viable in a global network society than monolithic organizations and institutions bound to hierarchical communication and clear boundaries, no matter how complex they may be. Flexibility cannot be understood only as a function of complexity. On the contrary, the more possible states a system has, the stronger control mechanisms have to become if the system is to maintain its organization. Systems operating on the edge of chaos can easily disintegrate and find themselves transformed in unforeseeable ways. Evolution is a case in point. Instead of explaining the emergence of order from noise, why not admit that noise is communication. There are only actors making associations. Flexibility insures that networking supports relatively autonomous actors, uncontrolled flows of resources, information, and decisions, cooperative action on the basis of decentralized many-to-many communication, and quick adaptation to changing conditions. New ideas and new options for action arise independently from each other, are quickly distributed throughout the network, and decentrally coordinated. Flexible networks tolerate more internal complexity, more options, more connectivity, flow, communication, participation, transparency, and authenticity than do less flexible networks. Flexibility is therefore an important norm within the social operating system. If algorithms might be considered the social structures and macro-actors of a society governed by imperatives of prediction, control, and security, then a society whose networks are constructed, maintained, and transformed by a social operating system consisting of the norms of connectivity, flow, communication, participation, transparency, authenticity, and flexibility offer an alternative to the imperatives of algorithmic order and foster a vision of the social that is willing and able to take risks.

Conclusion

Media are changing. Communication is changing. Society is changing. It would be naïve to suppose that these changes will not affect the perspectives, concepts, and methods of philosophy and the social sciences. Philosophical hermeneutics, actor-network theory, and new media studies can enter into a mutually fruitful dialogue in order to reboot the blocked discussion of grand narratives, intercultural communication, and a common vision for the global future. The purpose of attempting to link these three different discourses that are often seen to be mutually exclusive is not only orientation in a postmodern, multicultural world, but programmatic in the sense of making an argument for doing society and doing culture in a way that has some hope of success. If a new understanding of society in the aftermath of deconstruction and in the face of a clash of civilizations is to be built on adequate foundations, interpretation must accept the task of re-interpreting itself. This is a major task that will require taking risks, mixing discourses, and being willing to revise foundational concepts such as meaning, reality, and rationality. If one were looking for a broader definition of "rationality," a definition capable of expressing how consensus and cooperative action beyond differences in criteria, culture, and convictions are to be possible, then perhaps it could be found within the context of those communication practices that effectively build and maintain networks within a digital network society. Perhaps it would do philosophy good to ask if there isn't such a thing as a "Facebook pragmatics" instead of assuming a universal pragmatics of rational discourse such as Habermas has proposed. Of course this is not about Facebook, Twitter, YouTube, or any of the other presently dominant forms of new media. It's also not about the Web 2.0, 3.0, 4.0 or whatever future technological and social development brings. It is about establishing and participating in a socio-sphere, a community of humans and non-humans in a mixed reality that is constructing local and global actor-networks on the basis of a social operating system not bound by, but also with the help of, algorithms.

The social operating system is based at least upon the norms of connectivity, flow, communication, participation, transparency, authenticity, and flexibility. Interpretation from this point of view can be seen as networking. Networking is what the social operating system does. This is going on in all areas of society. eBusiness, eGovernment, eLearning, eHealth, etc. have become commonplaces, even when their historical and cultural significance have yet to enter into mainstream philosophical discourse. Regardless of whether utopian hopes of direct democracy or dystopian total surveillance scenarios are projected upon the digital network society, the construction of actor-networks in and between education, business, research, health care, and politics is going on in a different way than ever before, namely, in the mode of mixed reality. Social space has become an interface. As a consequence of this, reality has lost its traditional durability and resistance to change making virtual reality and real virtuality indistinguishable. In the digital age the social operating system could not only replace algorithms and imperatives of systemic order, but also a pragmatics of making claims to validity against commonly held criteria of meaning, truth, truthfulness, and correctness. Indeed, in today's multicultural society there are no commonly accepted criteria of this sort. Through connectivity, flow, communication, participation, transparency, authenticity, and flexibility communicative action creates, changes, and maintains criteria of meaning, value, and truth within an array of actor-networks which are open, flexible, multicultural, heterogeneous, scalable, and innovative. Perhaps the closed boundaries, functional imperatives, and blind autopoiesis of systemic order steered by algorithms that are directed toward predictability, control, and security will not be as *viable* in the long run as will open networks. Perhaps it can even be claimed that systems will be replaced by networks. Interpretation, the age old task of constructing meaning, could be seen from a new perspective, a perspective that interprets interpretation as networking under the conditions of digital media.

Bibliography

Ackoff, R. L. (1981): Creating the Corporate Future, New York: John Wiley & Sons.

Adorno, T./Horkheimer, M. (2002): Dialectic of Enlightenment, Trans. by E. Jephcott. Stanford: Stanford University Press.

Albrow, M. (1996): The Global Age: State and Society Beyond Modernity. Cambridge: Polity Press.

Anderson, Ch. (2006): The Long Tail: Why the Future of Business is Selling Less of More. New York: Hyperion.

Asbhy W. R. (1956): An Introduction to Cybernetics, London: Chapman & Hall.

Austin, J. L. (1962): How to do Things with Words, The William James Lectures delivered at Harvard University in 1955, J. O. Urmson and M. Sbisà (eds) Oxford: Clarendon Press.

Bak P. (1996): How Nature Works: The Science of Self-Organized Criticality, New York: Copernicus Books.

Barabási, A.-L. (2002): Linked: The New Science of Networks. Perseus, Cambridge: Cambridge University Press.

Barabási, A.-L. (2012): Network Science, http://barabasilab.com/network sciencebook

Barney, D. (2004): The Network Society, Cambridge UK: Polity Press.

Barthes, R. (1972): Mythologies, New York: Hill and Wang.

Bateson, G. (2000) Steps to an Ecology of Mind, Chicago: University of Chicago Press.

Baudrillard, J. (1994): Simulacra & Simulation. The Precession of Simularca. Ann Arbor: University of Michigan Press.

Belliger, A./Krieger, D. (2006): ANThology. Ein Einführendes Handbuch zur Akteur-Netzwerk-Theorie. Bielefeld: Transcript Verlag.

Belliger, A./Krieger, D. (2014): "Die Selbstquantifizierung als Ritual virtualisierter Körperlichkeit," in: R. Gugutzer, R. (ed) Körper, Rituale, Vergemeinschaftung, Frankfurt a.M.: Goethe-Universität.

Benkler, Y. (2006) The Wealth of Networks: How Social Production Transforms Markets and Freedom, New Haven, CT: Yale University Press.

Bohman, J. (2004): "Expanding dialogue: The Internet, the Public Sphere and Prospects for Transnational Democracy," in: N. Crossley and J. M. Roberts (eds) After Habermas. New Perspectives on the Public Sphere, Blackwell, 131–155.

Bolter, J. D/Grusin, R. (1999): Remediation: Understanding New Media. Cambridge, MA: MIT Press.

Boyd, S. (2010): Blog Post, http://stoweboyd.com/post/797752290/the-decade-of-publicy (accessed January 2014).

Brandes, U./Robins, G./McCranie, A./Wassermasn,S. (2013) : "What is Network Science ?," in: Network Science 1(1), 1–15.

Buchanan, M. (2002): Nexus: Small Worlds and the Groundbreaking Theory of Networks, New York: Norton & Company.

Callon, M. (1980): "Struggles and Negotiations to Define What is Problematic and What is Not: The Socio-Logic of Translation," in: K. D. Knorr/R. Krohn/R. D. Whitley (eds) The Social Process of Scientific Investigation: Sociology of the Sciences Yearbook, Dordrecht/Boston, MA.: Reidel,197–219.

Callon, M. (1986a): "The Sociology of an Actor-Network: The Case of the Electric Vehicle," in: M. Callon/J. Law/A. Rip (eds) Mapping the Dynamics of Science and Technology: Sociology of Science in the Real World, London: Macmillan, 19–34.

Callon, M. (1986b): "Some Elements of a Sociology of Translation: Domestication of the Scallops and Fishermen of St. Brieuc Bay," in: J. Law (ed) Power, Action and Belief: A new Sociology of Knowledge? London: Routledge, 196–233.

Callon, M. (1987): "Society in the Making: The Study of Technology as a Tool for Sociological Analysis," in: W. E. Bijker/T. P. Hughes/T. J. Pinch (eds) The Social Construction of Technical Systems: New Directions in the Sociology and History of Technology, London: MIT Press, 83–103.

Callon, M. (1991): "Techno-Economic Networks and Irreversibility," in: J. Law (ed) A Sociology of Monsters? Essays on Power, Technology and Domination, London/New York: Routledge, 132–161.

Callon, M./Latour, B. (1981): "Unscrewing the Big Leviathan: How Actors Macrostructure Reality and How Sociologists Help Them to Do So," in: K. Knorr-Cetina/A. V. Cicourel (eds) Advances in Social Theory and Methodology: Toward an Integration of Micro- and Macro-Sociologies, Boston, Mass: Routledge and Kegan Paul, 277–303.

Callon, M./Law, J. (1997): "After the Individual in Society: Lessons on Collectivity from Science, Technology and Society," in: Canadian Journal of Sociology 22(2), 165–182.

Castells, M. (1996): The Rise of the Network Society. The Information Age: Economy, Society and Culture Vol. I, 2nd ed. 2000, Oxford: Blackwell.

Castells, M. (1997a): The Power of Identity. The Information Age: Economy, Society and Culture Vol. II, 2nd ed. 2004, Oxford: Blackwell.

Castells, M. (1997b): An Introduction to the Information Age, in: City 7, 6–16.

Castells, M. (1998): End of Millennium. The Information Age: Economy, Society and Culture Vol. III. 2nd ed. 2000, Oxford: Blackwell.

Castells, M. (2001): The Internet Galaxy. Oxford: Oxford University Press.

Cubitt, S. (2013): "Media Studies and New Media Studies," in: J. Hartley/ J. Burgess/A. Bruns (eds) A Companion to New Media Dynamics. Blackwell, 15–32.

Dorogovtsev S. N./Mendes J. F. F. (2003): Evolution of Networks: From biological networks to the Internet and WWW, Oxford: Oxford University Press.

Evans-Pritchard, E. E. (1937): Witchcraft, Oracles and Magic Among the Azande. Oxford: Oxford University Press.

Feldman, T. (1997): Introduction to Digital Media. London: Routledge.

Fischer-Hübner, S./Pettersson, J. S. (2011): "Usable Privacy—Enhancing Identity Management: Challenges and Approaches," in: D. Haftor/A. Mirijamdotter (eds), Information and Communication Technologies, Society and Human Beings. Theory and Framework, Information Science Reference, New York.

Fuchs, S. (2001): Against Essentialism: A Theory of Culture and Society, Cambridge MA: Harvard University Press.

Fuchs, C. (2008): Internet and Society. Social Theory in the Information Age, New York: Taylor and Francis.

Fukuyama, F. (1992): The End of History and the Last Man, New York: Free Press.

Gadamer, H.-G. (2004): Truth and Method, 2nd rev. ed, J. Weinsheimer/D. G. Marshall (trans), New York: Crossroad.

Gadamer, H-G. (1976): Philosophical Hermeneutics, D. E. Linge (ed and trans), Berkeley: University of California Press.

Gadamer, H.-G.,(1976a): "On the scope and function of Hermeneutical Reflection," in: Philosophical Hermeneutics, D. E. Linge (trans.). Berkeley: University of California Press.

Gadamer, H.-G. (1976b): "The universality of the Hermeneutical Problem," in: Philosophical Hermeneutics, D. E. Linge (ed and trans.). Berkeley: University of California Press.

Gadamer, H.-G. (1981b): "Hermeneutics and the Critique of Ideology," in: Hermeneutics and the Human Sciences, J. B. Thompson (ed. and trans), Cambridge: Cambridge University Press, 63–100.

Gadamer, H.-G. (1985): "Rhetoric, Hermeneutic, and the Critique of Ideology. Metacritical Comments on Truth and Method," in: The Hermeneutics Reader, K. Mueller-Vollmer (ed), New York: Continuum.

Garfinkel, H. (2002): Ethnomethodology's Program: Working Out Durkheim's Aphorism. A. Rawls (ed), Oxford: Rowman & Littlefield Publishers.

Gibson, J. J. (1977): The Theory of Affordances, in: R. Shaw/J. Bransford (eds), Perceiving, Acting, and Knowing: Toward an Ecological Psychology, Hilsdale, NJ: Lawrence Erlbaum, 67–82.

Gilpin, D./Palazzolo, E./ Brody, N. (2010): "Socially Mediated Authenticity," in: Journal of Communication Management, 14(3), 258–278.

Gladwell, M. (2000): The Tipping Point: How Little Things Can Make a Big Difference, Boston: Little Brown.

Goffman, E. (1959): The Presentation of Self in Everyday Life, New York: Doubleday.

Gosling, S./Augustine, A./Vazire, S./Holtzman. N./Gaddis, S. (2011): "Manifestations of Personality in Online Social Networks: Self-Reported Facebook-Related Behaviors and Observable Profile Information," in: Cyberpsychology, Behaviour, and Social Networking, 14(9), 483–8.

Granovetter, M. (1973): "The Strength of Weak Ties," in: American Journal of Sociology 78, 1360–1380.

Greimas, A. J. (1983): Structural Semantics: An Attempt at a Method, D. McDowell/ R. Schleifer/A. Velie (trans), Lincoln, Nebraska: University of Nebraska Press.

Habermas, J. (1970): "On Systematically Distorted Communication," in P.Kivisto (ed) Social Theory, Los Angeles: Roxbury, 369–375.

Habermas, J. (1976): Legitimation Crisis, T. McCarthy (trans), Cambridge: Politiy Press.

Habermas, J. (1984): Theory of Communicative Action vol. 1: Resons and the Rationalization of Society, T. McCarthy (trans.), Cambridge: Polity Press.

Habermas, J. (1987): Theory of Communicative Action. vol. 2: Lifeworld and System: A Critique of Functionalist Reason, T. McCarthy (trans.), Cambridge: Polity Press.

Habermas, J. (1988): On the Logic of the Social Sciences. S. W. Nicholsen/ J. Stark. (trans), Cambridge: Polity Press.

Habermas, J. (1989): The Structural Transformation of the Public Sphere: An Inquiry into a Category of Bourgeois Society, Cambridge: Polity Press.

Habermas, J. (1992): Postmetaphyisical Thinking: Philosophical Essays, W. M. Hogengarten (trans), Cambridge, MA: MIT Press.

Habermas, J. et al. (eds) (1971) Hermeneutik und Ideologiekritik. Frankfurt a.M.: Suhrkamp.

Haken, H. (1983): Synergetics: An Introduction. Nonequilibrium Phase Transition and Self-Organization in Physics, Chemistry, and Biology, New York: Springer.

Hartley, J./Burgess, J./Bruns, A. (2013): A Companion to New Media Dynamics. Oxford: Blackwell.

Hattendorf, M. (1994): Dokumentarfilm und Authentizität. Ästhetik und Pragmatik einer Gattung, Konstanz: Universitätsverlag.

Heidegger, M. (1971): Poetry, Language and Thought, A. Hofstadter (trans), New York: HarperCollins.

Heidegger, M. (1999): Ontology: The Hermeneutics of Facticity, J. van Buren (trans), Bloomington: Indiana University Press.

Heidegger, M. (2002) "The Origin of the Work of Art," in: Off the Beaten Track, Cambridge: Cambridge University Press.

Heidegger, M. (2010): Being and Time, J. Stambaugh and D. J. Schmidt (trans), Albany: State University of New York Press.

Helbling, D. (2013): "Globally Networked Risks and How to Respond" in: Nature 497, 51–59.

Hernes, T. (2008): Understanding Organization as Process. Theory of a Tangled World, London and New York: Routledge.

Heylighen, F. (2001): The Science of Self-organization and Adaptivity http://pespmc1.vub.ac.be/papers/EOLSS-Self-Organiz.pdf (accessed January 2014)

Howe, J. (2006): "The Rise of Crowdsourcing," in: Wired 14(6), http://www.wired.com/wired/archive/14.06/crowds.html (retrieved January 2014)

Howe, J. (2008): Crowdsourcing. Why the Power of the Crowd is Driving the Future of Business, New York: Crown Business Publishing.

Huntington, S. P. (1996): The Clash of Civilizations and the Remaking of World Order. Simon & Schuster: New York.

Husserl, E. (1936/1970): The Crisis of the European Sciences, D. Carr (trans), Evanston: Northwestern University Press.

Internet of Things, in: Wikipedia: The Free Encyclopedia. Wikimedia Foundation Inc. from http://en.wikipedia.org/wiki/Internet_of_things (accessed January 2014)

Jenkins, H. (2008): Convergence Culture: Where Old and New Media Collide, rev. edn, New York: New York University Press: New York.

Jenkins, H. et al. (2005): Confronting the Challenges of Participatory Culture: Media Education for the 21st Century, http://www.newmedialiteracies.org/wp-content/uploads/pdfs/NMLWhitePaper.pdf (accessed January 2014)

Kaufmann, S. (1993): Origins of Order: Self-Organization and Selection in Evolution, Oxford: Oxford University Press.

Karppi, T. (2012): "Exploring Augmented Reality. On User and Rewiring the Senses," in: Ctrl-Z http://ctrl-z.net.au/journal

Knorr Cetina, K. (1981): The Manufacture of Knowledge—An Essay on the Constructivist and Contextual Nature of Science, Oxford: Pergamon Press.

Krieger, D. (1996): Einführung in die allgemeine Systemtheorie. Stuttgart: UTB.

Krieger, D. (2006): The New Universalism. Foundations for a Global Theology, Eugene OR: Wipf & Stock.

Krieger, D. (2009): "Religion and the System of Meaning," in: M. Locker (ed) Systems Theory and Theology, Eugene OR: Wipf & Stock.

Latour, B. (1986): Visualization and Cognition: Drawing Things Together in H. Kuklick (editor) Knowledge and Society Studies in the Sociology of Culture Past and Present, Jai Press vol. 6, pp. 1–40.

Latour, B. (1987) Science in Action: How to Follow Scientists and Engineers Through Society, Cabridge, MA: Harvard University Press.

Latour, B. (1988): The Pasteurization of France. Cambridge MA: Harvard University Press.

Latour, B. (1991): "The Impact of Science Studies on Political Philosophy," in: Science, Technology, & Human Values 16(1), Sage Publications.

Latour, B. (1993): We Have Never Been Modern. Cambridge MA: Harvard University Press.

Latour, B. (1994): "On technical mediation—philosophy, sociology, genealogy," in: Common Knowledge 3(2), 29–64.

Latour, B. (1999): Pandora's Hope: Essays on the Reality of Science Studies, Cambridge MA: Harvard University Press.

Latour, B. (2002): War of the Worlds: What About Peace?, Chicago: Prickly Paradigm Press.

Latour, B. (2003): "What if we *Talked* Politics a Little?," in: Contemporary Political Theory 2, 143–164.

Latour, B. (2004): Politics of Nature. How to Bring the Sciences into Democracy, Cambridge MA: Harvard University Press.

Latour, B. (2005): Reassembling the Social. An Introduction to Actor-Network-Theory, Oxford: Oxford University Press.

Latour, B. (2010a): The Modern Cult of the Factish Gods, Durham: Duke University Press.

Latour, B. (2010b): Networks, Societies, Spheres: Reflections of an Actor-network Theorist. Keynote speech for the International Seminar on Network Theory: Network Theory in the Digital Ages, 19th February 2010, Annenberg School for Communication and Journalism, Los Angeles http://www.bruno-latour.fr/sites/default/files/121-CASTELLS-GB.pdf. (accessed January 2014).

Latour, B. (2011): Waiting for Gaia. Composing the common world through arts and politics. A lecture at the French Institute, London, for the launching of SPEAP, http://www.bruno-latour.fr/sites/default/files/124-GAIA-LONDON-SPEAP_0.pdf (accessed January 2014).

Latour, B. (2012): "The Whole is Always Smaller Than Its Parts. A Digital Test of Gabriel Tarde's Monads," in: British Journal of Sociology 63(4) 591–615.

Latour, B. (2013a): An Enquiry into Modes of Existence. An Anthropology of the Moderns, Cambridge, MA: Harvard University Press.

Latour, B. (2013b): What Language shall we Speak with Gaia? Lecture prepared for the Holber Prize Symposium. From Economics to Ecology, Bergen http://www.bruno-latour.fr/sites/default/files/128-GAIA-HOLBERG.pdf (accessed January 2014).

Latour, B./Woolgar, S. (1979): Laboratory Life. The Construction of Scientific Facts, London: Sage Publications.

Law, J. (1992): "Notes on the Theory of the Actor-Network: Ordering, Strategy and Heterogeneity," in: Systems Practice 5, 379–393.

Law, J. (1999): "After ANT: Complexity, Naming, and Topology." in: J. Law/ J. Hassard (eds) Actor Network Theory and After, Oxford: Blackwell.

Laslo, A./Krippner, S. (1998): "Systems Theories: Their Origins, Foundations, and Development," in: J. S. Jordan (ed) Systems Theories and A Priori Aspects of Perception. Amsterdam: Eslevier Science.

Leaver, T./Willson, M./Balnaves, M. (2012): "Transparency and the Ubiquity of Information Filtration?," in: Ctrl-Z: New Media Philosophy 2, hppt://www.crtl-z.net.au/journal (accessed January 2014)

Levine, F./Locke, C./Searls, D./Weinberger, D. (2000): The Cluetrain Manifesto, New York: Basic Books.

Licklider, J. C. R. (1960): "Man-Computer Symbiosis," in: IRE Transactions on Human Factors in Electronics, HFE-1, 4–11.

Lindner, R. (1998): "Die Idee des Authentischen," in: Kuckuck 1, 58–61.

Luhmann, N. (1975): "Die Weltgesellschaft," in: Soziologische Aufklärung, Bd. 2. Frankfurt a.M.: Suhrkamp.

Luhmann, N. (1984): Soziale Systeme. Grundriss einer allgemeinen Theorie, Frankfurt a.M.: Suhrkamp.

Luhmann, N. (1989): Ecological Communication, Cambridge: Polity Press.

Luhmann, N. (1995): Social Systems, J. Bednarz/D. Becker (trans), Stanford: Stanford University Press.

Luhmann, N. (1995): "Die Form "Person," in: Soziologische Aufklärung. Bd. 6. Die Soziologie und der Mensch, Opladen: Westdeutscher Verlag, 142–154.

Luhmann, N. (2000): The Reality of the Mass Media, K. Cross (trans), Stanford: Stanford University Press.

Lyotard. J-F. (1984): The Postmodern Condition, Minneapolis: University of Minnesota Press.

Maturana, H./Varela, F. (1973): "Autopoiesis and Cognition: the Realization of the Living," in: R. S. Cohen/M. W. Wartofsky (eds), Boston Studies in the Philosophy of Science 42, Dordecht: D. Reidel Publishing Co.

Maturana, H./Varela, F. (1987): The Tree of Knowledge. Biological Roots of Human Understanding, Shambhala: Boston.

Manovich, L. (2001): The Language of New Media, Cambridge MA: MIT Press.

McLuhan, M. (1964): Understanding Media. The Extensions of Man, London: Sphere.

Morris, C. W. (1938): Foundations of the Theory of Signs, Vol. I, No. 2, International Encyclopedia of Unified Science, Chicago: Univ. of Chicago Press.

Munker, B (2006): Die Enttarnung von Lonelygirl15. Online-Publikation: http://www.stern.de/computer-technik/internet/570087.html?nv=cb (accessed 2013).

Näser, T. (2008): "Authentizität 2.0—Kulturanthropologische Überlegungen zur Suche nach 'Echtheit' im Videoportal YouTube," in: kommunikation@gesellschaft, 9(2), Online-Publikation http://www.soz.uni-frankfurt.de/K.G/B2_2008_Naeser.pdf

National Research Council (2006): Network Science. Committee on Network Science for Future Army Applications.

"Network Science," in: Wikipedia: The Free Encyclopedia. Wikimedia Foundation, Inc. http://en.wikipedia.org/wiki/Network_science (accessed January 2014).

"New Media," in: Wikipedia: The Free Encyclopedia. Wikimedia Foundation, Inc. Available from http://en.wikipedia.org/wiki/New_media (accessed January 2014).

Newman, M. E. J. (2003): The Structure and Function of Complex Networks, http://arxiv.org/pdf/condmat/0303516.pdf (accessed January 2014).

Palmer, M. (2006): Data is the New Oil, Blogpost http://ana.blogs.com/maestros/2006/11/data_is_the_new.html (accessed January 2014).

Poster, M. (1995): The Second Media Age, Cambridge: Polity Press.

Ramsey, F. P. (1931): "General Propositions and Causality," in: R. B. Braithwaite (ed) F. P. Ramsey: The Foundations of Mathematics, London: Routledge & Kegan Paul.

Rawlins, B. (2009): "Giving the Emperor a Mirror: Toward developing a Stakeholder Measurement of Organizational transparency," in: Journal of Public Relations Research, 21(1), 71–99.

Ricoeur, P. (1970): Freud and Philosophy: an essay on interpretation, D. Savage (trans), New Haven and London: Yale University Press.

Ricoeur, P. (1974): The Conflict of Interpretations: Essays in Hermeneutics, D. Ihde (ed), Evanston: Northwestern University Press.

Ricoeur, P. (1976): Interpretation Theory: Discourse and the Surplus of Meaning, Texas: Texas Christian University Press.

Ricoeur, P. (1981a): "Hermeneutics and the Critique of Ideology," in: Hermeneutics and the Human Sciences, J. B. Thompson (ed.), Cambridge: Cambridge University Press, 63–100

Ricoeur, P. (1981b): "Phenomenology and Hermeneutics," in: Hermeneutics and the Human Sciences, J. B. Thompson (ed), Cambridge: Cambridge University Press, 101–130.

Ricoeur, P. (1981c): "The Hermetical Function of Distanciation," in: Hermeneutics and the Human Sciences, J. B. Thompson (ed), Cambridge: Cambridge University Press, 131–144.

Ricoeur, P. (1981d): "What is a text? Explanation and understanding," in: Hermeneutics and the Human Sciences, J. B. Thompson (ed), Cambridge: Cambridge University Press, 145–164.

Ricoeur, P. (1986): Lectures on Ideology and Utopia, C. Taylor (ed), New York: Colombia University Press.

Ricoeur, P. (1984–1988): Time and Narrative, Volumes 1–3, K. Blamey/D. Pellauer (trans), Chicago: University of Chicago Press.

Ricoeur, P. (1991): From Text to Action, trans. K. Blamey/J. Thompson (trans), Evanston: Northwestern University Press.

Ricoeur, P, (1992): Oneself as Another, K. Blamey (trans), Chicago: University of Chicago Press.

Riegler, A. (2001): "Towards a Radical Constructivist Understanding of Science," in: Foundations of Science, special issue on "The Impact of Radical Constructivism on Science" 6(1), 1–30.

Saussure, Ferdinand de (1983): Course in General Linguistics (trans. Roy Harris). London: Duckworth.

Schnabel, M. A./Wang, X. (ed) (2009): Mixed Realities in Architecture, Design and Construction, Springer. ftp://82.210.149.5/AiDisk_a1/eBooki/Arch%20Ebok/Mixed%20reality.pdf

Serres, M. (1974): Hermes III—La traduction, Paris : Les Éditions de Minuit.

Shannon, C./Weaver, W. (1963): The Mathematical Theory of Communication. University of Illinois Press.

Shirky, C. (2008): Here Comes Everybody. How Change Happens When People Come Together, New York: Penguin Press.

Spencer-Brown, G. (1969): Laws of Form. London: Allen & Unwin.

Spivack, N. (2007): "The Rise of the Social Operating System," Blogpost http://www.novaspivack.com/technology/the-rise-of-the-social-oper ating-system (accessed January 2014).

Stegbauer, C. (ed) (2008): Netzwerkanalyse und Netzwerktheorie. Ein neues Paradigma in den Sozialwissenschaften, Wiesbaden: VS Verlag.

Strum, S. S./Latour, B. (1987): "Redefining the Social Link: From Baboons to Humans," in: Social Science In formation 26(4), 783–802.

Surowiecki, J. (2004): The Wisdom of Crowds: Why the Many Are Smart- er Than the Few and How Collective Wisdom Shapes Business, Econo- mies, Societies and Nations, New York: Randomhouse.

Tapscott, D. (2008): Grown Up Digital: How the Net Generation is Chang- ing Your World, NewYork: McGraw-Hill.

Tapscott, D./Williams, A. (2006): Wikinomics: How Mass Collaboration Changes Everything, New York: McGraw-Hill.

Taylor, M. C. (2001): The Moment of Complexity—Emerging Network Culture, Chicago: University of Chicago Press.

Turkle, S. (1984): The second self. New York: Simon & Schuster.

Turkle, S. (1995): Life on the Screen: Identity in the Age of the Internet. New York: Simon & Schuster.

Uggla, B. K. (2010): Ricoeur, Hermeneutics and Globalization, New York: Continuum

Urry, J. (2000): "Mobile Sociology," in: British Journal of Sociology 51(1), 185–203.

Van de Donk,W./Loader, B./Nixon, P./Rucht, D. (2005): Cyberprotest. New media, Citizens and Social Movements, London & New York: Rout- ledge.

Watts, D. J. (2003): Six Degrees: The Science of a Connected Age, New York: Norton.

Weinberger, D. (2012): Too Big to Know. Rethinking Knowledge Now That the Facts Aren't the Facts, Experts Are Everywhere, and the Smartest Person in the Room Is the Room, New York: Basic Books.

White, H. (1992): Identity and Control: A Structural Theory of Social Ac- tion, Princeton: Princeton University Press.

Wiener, N. (1950): The Human Use of Human Beings: Cybernetics and Society, Boston: Houghton Mifflin.

Winch, P. (1958): The Idea of a Social Science and its Relation to Philoso- phy, London: Routledge & Kegan Paul.

Winch, P. (1964): "Understanding a Primitive Society," in: Aristotelian Philosophical Quarterly, 1, 307–324.

Wittgenstein, L. (1958): Philosophical Investigations.3rd Ed. G. E. M. Anscombe (trans), New York: Macmillan.

Zinnbauer, D. (2007): "Transparency and Information Disclosure in E-Government," in: Encyclopedia of Digital-Government, A-V. Anttiroiko/M. Mälkiä (ed), Idea Group Reference: London, 1566–1571.